Freud's Art – Psychoanalysis Retold

In *Freud's Art – Psychoanalysis Retold* Janet Sayers provides a refreshing new introduction to psychoanalysis by retelling its story through art. She does this by bringing together experts from the fields of psychoanalysis, art history and art education to show how art and psychoanalysis illuminate each other.

Freud's Art begins with major founders of psychoanalysis Freud, Jung, Spielrein and Klein. It then details art-minded developments of their insights by Adrian Stokes, Jacques Lacan, Marion Milner, Anton Ehrenzweig, Donald Winnicott and Wilfred Bion before concluding with the recent theories of Jean Laplanche and Julia Kristeva. The result is a book which highlights the importance of psychoanalysis, together with painting and the visual arts, to understanding the centrality of visual imagery, fantasy, nightmares and dreams to all of us, artists and non-artists alike.

Illustrated throughout with fascinating case histories, examples of well known and amateur art, doodles, drawings and paintings by both analysts and their patients, *Freud's Art* provides a compelling account of psychoanalysis for all those studying, working in, or simply intrigued by psychology, mental health and creativity today.

Janet Sayers (née Toulson) qualified as a clinical psychologist and psychotherapist at the Tavistock Clinic and with the British Association of Psychotherapists. She teaches psychoanalysis at Kent University, Canterbury and also works as a psychotherapist both privately and for the NHS.

Freud's Art – Psychoanalysis Retold

Janet Sayers

 Routledge
Taylor & Francis Group

LONDON AND NEW YORK

First published 2007
by Routledge
27 Church Road, Hove, East Sussex BN3 2FA

Simultaneously published in the USA and Canada
by Routledge
270 Madison Ave, New York, NY 10016

Routledge is an imprint of the Taylor & Francis Group, an informa business

Typeset in Times by RefineCatch Limited, Bungay, Suffolk
Printed and bound in Great Britain by TJ International Ltd,
Padstow, Cornwall
Paperback cover design by Nick Sayers

This publication has been produced with paper manufactured to
strict environmental standards and with pulp derived from
sustainable forests.

British Library Cataloguing in Publication Data
A catalogue record for this book is available from the British Library

Library of Congress Cataloging-in-Publication Data
Sayers, Janet
 Freud's art : psychoanalysis retold / Janet Sayers.
  p. cm.
 Includes bibliographical references and index.
 ISBN-13: 978-0-415-41567-5 (hardback)
 ISBN-10: 0-415-41567-5 (hardback)
 ISBN-13: 978-0-415-41568-2 (pbk.)
 ISBN-10: 0-415-41568-3 (pbk.)
 1. Psychoanalysis and art.   I. Title.
 N72.P74S23 2007
 701'.15—dc22
                                          2006034910

ISBN: 978-0-415-41567-5 (hbk)
ISBN: 978-0-415-41568-2 (pbk)

For Sean Sayers and our artist and musician sons Nicholas and Daniel

Contents

Figures

Acknowledgements

Whether or not they agree with what I have written in this book, I am grateful to relatives, friends, psychotherapy patients, colleagues and students at the University of Kent for teaching me much of what it contains. My thanks particularly to Mary Evans and Stephen Frosh for reading and helping me with an early draft, and to Kate Hawes, Claire Lipscomb, Jane Harris, Imogen Burch and Christine Firth for their work in editing and copy-editing the resulting chapters. I am also grateful to the following for their advice and support regarding various summaries and versions: Roger Cardinal, Martin Golding, Linda Hopkins, Mary Jacobus, Oya Köymen, David Maclagan, Richard Read, and fellow researchers at the Five College Women's Studies Research Center at Mount Holyoke College in Massachusetts.

My thanks to Jake Wartenberg for permission to include reproductions of our squiggle drawings in Chapter 1, to the Melanie Klein Trust for permission to include Richard's drawings in Chapter 5, to Ann Angus for permission to include a reproduction of a painting by Adrian Stokes in Chapter 6, to Margaret Walters for permission to include reproductions of drawings and paintings by Marion Milner in Chapter 8, and to Francesca Bion for permission to include reproductions of drawings and paintings by Wilfred Bion in Chapter 11. Other permissions are credited in the figure captions of the illustrations to which they apply. I have done my best to trace all permission holders. My apologies if this has resulted in any oversights or omissions. I have also included as end-notes, and in a concluding appendix, URL addresses for all images referred to but not reproduced in the following pages.

Abbreviations

C	*Cogitations* by W.R. Bion. London: Karnac, 1992
CP	*Collected Papers* by D.W. Winnicott. London: Tavistock, 1958
E	*Ecrits: The First Complete Edition in English* by Jacques Lacan. New York: Norton, 2006
EG	*Envy and Gratitude* by M. Klein. London: Hogarth, 1975
EO	*Essays on Otherness* by J. Laplanche. London: Routledge, 1999
CW	*The Collected Works of C.G. Jung.* London: Routledge, 1953–79
CWAS	*The Critical Writings of Adrian Stokes.* London: Thames & Hudson, 1978
IJPA	*International Journal of Psycho-Analysis*
LGR	*Love, Guilt and Reparation* by M. Klein. London: Hogarth, 1975
SE	*Standard Edition of the Complete Psychological Works of Sigmund Freud.* London: Hogarth, 1966–74
SM	*The Suppressed Madness of Sane Men* by M. Milner. London: Routledge, 1987
ST	*Second Thoughts* by W.R. Bion. London: Heinemann, 1967

Chapter I

Introduction

It is now over a hundred years since Freud's first momentous meeting with Jung. 'He invited me to visit him, and our first meeting took place in Vienna in February 1907,' Jung later recalled. 'We met at one o'clock in the afternoon and talked virtually without a pause for thirteen hours.'[1] Three days later, on 2 March 1907, Freud gave a talk linking the obsessional actions of his Viennese patients with religious rituals.[2] This was followed, in July 1907, by Picasso linking what he had learnt about ritual African masks with developments in European art, including paintings of female nudes, such as Cézanne's *Les Grandes Baigneuses* (1900–5)[3] and Matisse's *Le Bonheur de vivre* (1906),[4] in completing his painting, *Les Demoiselles d'Avignon* (1907),[5] regarded by many as marking the beginning of modern art.

The histories of modern art and psychoanalysis have often coincided. But Freud contrasted the two activities, painting and psychoanalysis. 'Painting', he said, 'applies a substance – particles of colour – where there was nothing before, on the colourless canvas.' Psychoanalysis is more like carving, which, he argued, 'takes away from the block of stone all that hides the surface of the statue contained in it'. Painting is more like treatment by suggestion which, he went on, 'superimposes something – a suggestion – in the expectation that it will be strong enough to restrain the pathogenic idea from coming to expression'. Psychoanalysis proceeds differently. Freud contended:

> [It] does not seek to add or to introduce anything new, but to take away something, to bring out something, and to this end [it] concerns itself with the genesis of the morbid symptoms and the psychical context of the pathogenic idea which it seeks to remove.[6]

Psychoanalysis discovers the genesis of the analysand's ills by its free association method of encouraging analysands to say whatever comes to mind in association to bits and pieces of their memories and dreams. It does not construct, like painting. It deconstructs, like carving.

Jung's approach was less analytic. It involved less deconstruction, more construction. He encouraged patients to paint, draw, dance, sculpt, or write down their fantasies and dreams so as to reconnect these signs of the unconscious, as he understood them, with archetypal symbols, which he believed we each individually inherit from our ancestors. True to this philosophy, he praised the neurotic patient who, he said, 'produces pictures of a synthetic character, with a pervasive and unified feeling-tone'. Schizophrenics, by contrast, he maintained, 'communicate no unified, harmonious feeling-tone but, rather contradictory feelings or even a complete lack of feeling'. Whereas the neurotic seeks meaning and the corresponding feeling and seeks to communicate this to the beholder, the schizophrenic, and Picasso too, Jung continued, 'seems as though he had been overwhelmed and swallowed up by [meaning], and had been dissolved into all those elements which the neurotic at least tries to master'.[7]

Picasso's 'motif of the prostitute', and the 28,000 people who, according to Jung, attended a 460-piece Zurich exhibition of Picasso's paintings (including *Woman in a Chemise Sitting in an Armchair, The Dance* and *Woman with a Mandolin*, to which I will return later in this book),[8] were symptomatic of the fate of 'modern man', said Jung, 'veiling the bright world of day with the mists of Hades, infecting it with deadly decay, and finally, like an earthquake, dissolving it into fragments, fractures, discarded remnants, debris, shreds, and disorganized units'.[9]

Yet followers of Freud and Jung have likened their therapeutic methods to painting and the visual arts, both ancient and modern. Furthermore the seeds of this were sown by Jung, and even more so by Freud. This is particularly evident if we liken the results of Freud's free association method to the doodling or scribbling vagueness in which art sometimes begins. Leonardo da Vinci, according to one writer, 'recommended staring at marks on walls to find ideas for paintings'.[10] In the mid-1820s, Goya did something similar. In 2006 a curator of a New York exhibition of these miniatures reported:

> [Goya] covered a tiny ivory chip with carbon black, then applied a drop of water to create shapes, which he developed into figures with touches of watercolor, scratching lines into the surface with a sharp instrument. Perhaps an old procuress and her young charge would emerge, as in the exquisite *Maja and Celestina*,[11] or a man delousing himself [*Man Looking for Fleas in his Shirt*].[12] These marvelous little improvisations share the subject matter of Los Caprichos.[13]

These emerging figures involved Goya presumably completing the shapes produced by water on ivory in terms of images they suggested from the store of those familiar to him, not least from the language of portraiture of his time, to which he contributed and advanced. In more recent times Matisse praised doodling for its psychological revelations and for serving as a means of innovating into the stultifying effects of rules governing drawing and painting in his day. 'In a post office in Picardy I was waiting for a telephone connection. To pass the time I picked up a telegram form which was lying on the table and with my pen traced a woman's head,' he wrote, adding

> I was drawing without thinking, my pen moving as it chose, and I was surprised to recognise my mother's face in its subtlest detail. . . . At the time I was still an assiduous student of the old school of drawing, seeking to believe in its rules, those useless leavings of the masters who went before us, in a word the dead part of tradition, in which whatever was not observed from nature, whatever sprang from feeling and memory, was despised and called 'fake'. I was struck by what my pen revealed to me.[14]

Freud too noted unforeseen meanings that random marks of a pen can suggest. 'Here the pen fell out of the writer's hand and wrote this secret sign,' he wrote to his fiancée, Martha Bernays. 'Please forgive, and don't ask for an interpretation' (Figure 1.1.1).[15] He also doodled. Examples include doodles he probably did during an early 1920s meeting of the Vienna psychoanalytic society (Figure 1.1.2).[16]

As well as relating analysis to art via similarities between the vagueness of the analysand's free associations (in which the analyst's interpretations begin)

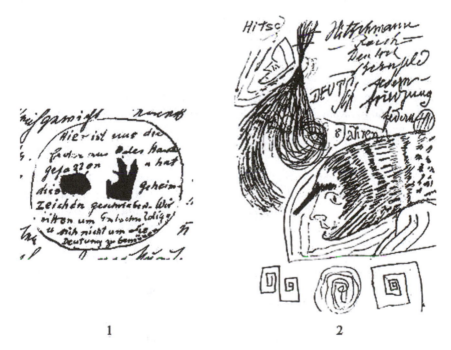

Figure 1.1 Freud: Inkblot and doodles

S. Freud (1882) Letter to Martha Bernays. In E. Freud, L. Freud and I. Grubrich-Simitis (eds) (1978) *Sigmund Freud: His Life in Pictures and Words*. London: Deutsch, pp. 95, 181.

and the vague doodling and scribbling (in which the artist's art begins), we can also relate analysis to art via the doodle or squiggle game. By this I mean the game in which players take turns completing each other's pencilled or painted doodle or squiggle into something in which both see meaning in terms of the languages of visual imagery of the society in which they play. The resulting drawings are akin to the cadenzas in a given key in classical music, and to call-and-answer improvisations on an initial theme in jazz. It is a two-handed version, in a sense, of the US Abstract Expressionist artist Jackson Pollock's one-man completion of blobs of paint on his canvas into his now well-known action paintings, such as his 1950 painting, *One: Number 31*.[17]

Similarities between the two-way dialogue, as it were, of painters with what they paint and the two-way dialogue of analysts with their analysands in turning the latter's free associations into interpretations, can be highlighted with illustrations from a squiggle game I played in western Massachusetts with an 11-year-old family friend, Jake, some months ago. The game began with my making a squiggle which Jake completed into a fish (Figure 1.2.1). He then made a squiggle which I turned into a face (Figure 1.2.2). Next he turned a squiggle of mine into another fish (Figure 1.2.3). We then created a succession of images (Figures 1.2.4–7), including one he called 'a hunched-over man' (Figure 1.2.6), and another which he described as 'a mangled, mutated, and damaged hand and dish' (Figure 1.2.7). The next and last image returned to the fish-theme with which our image-making began. He called it 'a fish on wheels' (Figure 1.2.8).

In thus repeating human, animal and fish-like images our jointly produced squiggle game images were akin to the 'nodal points' in which Freud's analysands' free associations converged, and on which he based his interpretations of the unconscious cause, as he understood it, of their ills. He described the analysand's associations to their symptoms:

> From a single scene two or more memories are reached at the same time, and from these again side-chains proceed whose individual links may once more be associatively connected with links belonging to the main chain.

Freud went on:

> Thus a particular symptom in, for instance, the chain of memories relating to the symptom of vomiting, calls up not only the earlier links in its own chain but also a memory from another chain, relating to another symptom, such as a headache. This experience accordingly belongs to both series, and in this way it constitutes a nodal point.[18]

Jake's and my squiggle game drawings also illustrate another aspect of psychoanalysis. For, just as psychoanalysis brings together two worlds of

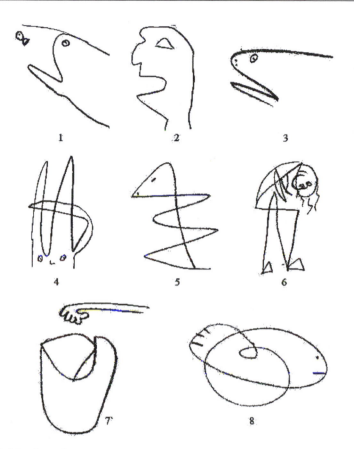

Figure 1.2 Jake: Squiggles

Reproduced by kind permission of Jake Wartenberg.

experience, that of the analysand and analyst, so too our drawings brought together two worlds of experience: Jake's experience of growing up mainly in western Massachusetts and my experience of living most of my life in South East England. Painting likewise brings together different worlds of experience. This is particularly evident in the use made by Picasso of the worlds of experience of European art and African religion in painting *Les Demoiselles d'Avignon*. 'Picasso's career shows that appropriating visual themes or devices from the work of others was repeatedly his way out of an impasse,' writes one art historian. Cézanne's paintings suggested one answer to the problem of large-scale figure painting. Matisse's 1906 painting, *Le Bonheur de vivre*, suggested another. *Les Demoiselles d'Avignon* drew on and went beyond both solutions in quoting, says this historian, 'African masks more or less directly'.[19]

Similarly, as I indicated at the beginning of this chapter, in the talk he gave to colleagues in Vienna three days after first meeting with Jung,[20] Freud brought together the worlds of experience of his obsessional neurotic patients in Vienna with what he knew of the experience of religious rituals. This led to his further developing his method of free association, initially forged to deconstruct the condensed images he believed constitute the symptoms of what was then diagnosed as hysteria. He went on to apply this method in deconstructing the repression and displacement of meaning from one object to another serving as its symbol, which he came to regard as the source not only of obsessional neurosis but also of schizophrenia.

Yet, despite the deconstruction constituting the essence of Freud's clinical method in seeking to discover what is thus repressed and displaced, his method also contained the precursors of the present-day alliance of psychoanalysis with constructive processes involved in painting and the visual arts. In telling the story of talking cure psychoanalysis, and the way it has been retold by Freud's followers, I begin, in Chapter 2, with similarities between psychoanalysis and art in so far as both make conscious what is otherwise unconscious. I focus mostly, however, in this, the longest chapter of *Freud's Art*, on detailing Freud's deconstruction method of free association and the problems it poses. In doing so I also note Freud's recommendation that, when the analysand's free associations prove insufficient or fail, analysts can usefully supplement them with knowledge of dream-symbols they evoke, just as, one could add, Picasso supplemented what paintings by Cézanne and Matisse evoked in him with what he knew of African ritual mask symbolism in painting *Les Demoiselles d'Avignon*.

Ironically, and despite his hostility to the art of Picasso, Jung adopted a similar approach. For, following Freud's recommendation that analysts supplement their analysands' free associations with what this evokes regarding their already acquired knowledge of dream-symbolism, Jung supplemented what his analysands drew and painted of their dreams and fantasies with what this suggested to him from his knowledge of Eastern and Western symbolism. I illustrate this in Chapter 3. In it I detail four of Jung's major analytical psychology methods – amplification, personification, individuation and active imagination – and their current development by art therapists.

Jung's analytical psychology methods all involve the analyst supplementing the analysand's images with what they know of culturally given symbols and what they mean. But what is to be done when the analysand uses these symbols to defend against their personal experience? Freud drew attention to this problem. So did Jung's first analysand, Sabina Spielrein, who became one of the first women psychoanalysts, and also one of the first analysts to relate psychoanalysis to art and to mothering, as I explain in Chapter 4.

Much more influential, however, on the history of psychoanalysis were the links made between psychoanalysis, art and mothering by Melanie Klein in her child analysis development of psychoanalysis. In recounting this, in Chapter 5, I also recount differences between her approach to child analysis and that of Freud's psychoanalyst daughter, Anna Freud, in initiating what has since become known as ego psychology. This version of psychoanalysis includes the analyst seeking to strengthen the analysand's ego or superego by encouraging their identification with the analyst. Klein, by contrast, emphasized the importance of deconstructing the fantasies involved. In doing so she developed an account of defences against what she called 'whole-object' and 'depressive position' recognition of ambivalence, of hating those we love, with the risk of harming or driving them away, by retreating into 'part-object' and 'paranoid-schizoid' fragmentation',[21] or into 'manic' omnipotence and control.[22]

In Chapter 6, I argue that Klein's account of manic defensiveness might have influenced the criticism by her analysand, the art historian, Adrian Stokes, of artists subjecting their material to omnipotent control. Most of all, however, I seek in this chapter to demonstrate ways in which Stokes' writings about the psychological impact of art and everyday scenery in making conscious what is otherwise unconscious illuminate ways in which psychoanalytic interpretations similarly operate, including inviting oneness with the 'object-otherness', to use Stokes' term,[23] of what they depict.

This brings me, in Chapter 7, to the surrealist-influenced work of the Paris-based psychoanalyst, Jacques Lacan. Like Klein and Stokes, he too exposed the defensiveness of the ego or superego as instrument of omnipotent control. In using and developing Klein's insights, however, he also went beyond them in highlighting ways in which we are seduced by others – by artists and analysts included – into identifying with the images they convey. In particular he noted our readiness in the male-dominated, patriarchal society in which we live to alienate ourselves from ourselves in identifying with whatever others desire as male, masculine and phallic.

Detailed instances of just such male-centred self-alienation can be found in the discoveries of the artist and analyst, Marion Milner, by analysing herself through doing free association writing and doodling. I use her findings in Chapter 8 to explain how they led her to develop an approach to psychoanalytic psychotherapy focusing on enabling the analysand to recover the female-centred oneness with otherness described by Freud as source of the 'oceanic' experience, or 'primary ego-feeling', which he attributed to persistence into adulthood of the infant's illusion of being one with the body of its mother in being fed by her.[24]

Recovery of this illusion might be less readily achieved by analysands than by analysts in practising the stance of 'evenly-suspended attention' recommended by Freud.[25] In developing this aspect of his theory and therapy, the artist and art education lecturer, Anton Ehrenzweig, as I detail in Chapter 9, argued that it is similar to the oneness of artists with their emerging artwork. He also argued that this oneness involves integrating two worlds of experience, unconscious and conscious. This brings me, in Chapter 10, to the development of psychoanalysis by the paediatrician and psychoanalyst, Donald Winnicott. Specifically I note ways in which he highlighted the bringing together, by psychoanalytic psychotherapy, of two different worlds of experience – that of the analysand and analyst – just as mothering brings together the two different worlds of experience of babies and their mothers.

The psychoanalyst and amateur artist, Wilfred Bion, further developed this aspect of psychoanalysis. In doing so he drew attention, albeit more implicitly than explicitly, to ways in which impressions made by the analysand evoke preconceptions from the world of experience of their analysts which they use in formulating their interpretations just as painters use what is evoked in them by their impressions of landscapes, for instance, in turning these impressions into paintings. In arguing this, however, as I also note in Chapter 11, Bion, like Klein before him, subordinated Freud's incest taboo and Oedipus complex theory of psychoanalysis to the pattern-making transformation of part- into whole-object, paranoid-schizoid and depressive position, disintegration and integration, detailed in Chapter 5.

This has been pointed out by the psychoanalyst, Jean Laplanche, together with his psychoanalytic colleague, Jean-Bertrand Pontalis. In doing so Laplanche returns to and extends Freud's account of ways in which unconscious fantasies and meanings originate in us developmentally through the 'enigmatic signifiers' first instilled in us, he says, by those who first look after us as babies.[26] This calls in analysis, he argues, as Freud and Lacan argued before him, and as I also detail in Chapter 12, for analysts to be as neutral as possible to maximize the analysand's free association projection onto them of these signifiers so they can be verbalized, deconstructed and dispelled.

What, though, is to be done when the analysand's free associations are blocked by melancholic depression or by phobic or obsessional neurosis? This leads me, in Chapter 13, to Julia Kristeva's development of psychoanalysis in terms of palpable signs as opposed to fully formed symbolic expression of unconscious fantasy. She illustrates this with early-fourteenth-century fresco paintings by Giotto and with paintings by later artists working variously in Europe and the United States. Kristeva's account of recent art installations, however, suggests that they may signal the end of the value of retelling Freudian and post-Freudian psychoanalysis not only in terms of, but also as analogous to painting and the visual arts, as I do in this book.

I nevertheless argue, in Chapter 14, that this twofold approach to retelling the story of psychoanalysis still has considerable and continuing value as means of highlighting the art-making images, fantasies, nightmares and dreams involved in the genesis of and recovery from the psychological ills which, just as they afflicted psychoanalysis's first patients, still afflict children and adults nowadays. Now, though, I will re-begin retelling the story of psychoanalysis, starting with Freud's book, *Studies on Hysteria*, written jointly with his teacher and colleague, Josef Breuer.

Chapter 2

Freud

An advantage of retelling Freudian and post-Freudian psychoanalysis not only in terms of, but also as analogous to painting and the visual arts is that, as I said at the end of Chapter 1, it helps to highlight the central role of imagery in the genesis of and recovery of children and adults from their psychological symptoms and ills. Imagery, specifically visual imagery, features centrally in Freud's and Breuer's 1895 book, *Studies on Hysteria*.

The book begins with Breuer recounting his treatment of a young German woman, Berthe Pappenheim, who later became a leading women's rights activist. Now known in the history of psychoanalysis as Anna O, and as inventor of the term 'talking cure',[1] Pappenheim's symptoms included hysterical paralysis of her arm. This symptom originated, it seems, in an image – a visual hallucination – in which, seated by the bedside of her dying father, she saw a black snake coming from the wall to bite him. Breuer added:

> She tried to keep the snake off, but it was as though she was paralysed. Her right arm, over the back of the chair, had gone to sleep and had become anaesthetic and paretic; and when she looked at it the fingers turned into little snakes with death's heads.[2]

Next day, retrieving a quoit she had been playing with from some bushes, she was reminded of the snake by a bent branch. At the same moment, her right arm became rigid again. Subsequently this hysterical paralysis of her arm occurred whenever she saw anything reminding her of her snake hallucination.

Freud called these bodily representations of hallucinatory experience 'mnemic images'.[3] The hysterical symptom – in Anna O's case, her hysterically paralysed and rigid arm – behaves in the same ways as a 'memory-picture', he said. Similar pictures recur, he noted, in patients pressed to recall scenes associated with the first occurrence of their symptoms. Pictures of these scenes, unlike the picture-imagery provided by the hysteric's symptoms – by Anna O's seemingly paralysed arm, for instance – occur involuntarily, he said. 'In fact, however, there is an uninterrupted series,' he argued, 'extending from the unmodified mnemic residues of affective experiences and acts of thought to the hysterical symptoms, which are the mnemic symbols of those experiences and thoughts'.[4]

This was first published in May 1895. Freud soon after wrote an essay, 'Project for a scientific psychology'. In it he developed the beginning of his revolutionary account of the unconscious not as a 'hypnoid' state of mind continuous with consciousness, as initially theorized with Breuer,[5] but as dynamically repressed from consciousness. Freud attributed this repression to current events evoking and giving traumatic meaning to experiences from the past, this causing them to be relegated to unconsciousness. He illustrated the point with the case of a patient, Emma Eckstein, whose symptoms included a phobia of going into shops alone. He attributed this phobia to an incident when she had gone into a shop and seen two shop assistants, one of whom appealed to her sexually, laughing at her clothes. At this she ran away, frightened. Why? Because, it transpired, what she then saw, heard and felt revived – with guilt-making sexual meaning on account of her now being sexually mature – a memory of herself aged 8 returning to a shop to buy sweets despite the shopkeeper having previously grabbed at her sexually through her clothes. The later incident awoke memory of this earlier event, now rendered traumatic due to its acquiring sexual meaning as a result of the sexual awakening of puberty, so that it acted, by 'deferred action', as a trauma from the past resulting in its repression into unconsciousness.[6]

Freud sent his essay, 'Project for a scientific psychology', in which he recounted this case, to his Berlin colleague and friend, Wilhelm Fliess, in October 1895. The next month an article by the art historian and novelist, Marcel Proust, was published in Paris. In it, and without any reference to Freud, whose work was then scarcely known outside Vienna, Proust drew attention to the power of art to awaken the past, by deferred action, as Freud might have termed it. Proust noted the power of art to give new and conscious meaning to what is otherwise unconscious, or subconscious, from the past. He wrote of Chardin's paintings in the Louvre:[7]

> You already experienced it subconsciously, this pleasure one gets from the sight of everyday scenes and inanimate objects, otherwise it would not have risen in your heart when Chardin summoned it in his ringing, commanding accents. Your consciousness was too sluggish to reach down to it. It had to wait for Chardin to come and lay hold on it and hoist it to the level of your conscious mind. Then you knew it.[8]

Proust wrote similarly that paintings by Monet, Vuillard and others enable us to experience consciously everyday objects of which we have previously only been unconsciously or subconsciously aware. Writing of the impact of paintings by a fictional character, Elstir, modelled on Impressionist and Post-Impressionist painters, Proust said:

I would now happily remain at the table while it was being cleared. Since I had seen such things depicted in water-colours by Elstir, I sought to find again in reality, I cherished as though for their poetic beauty, the broken gestures of the knives still lying across one another, the swollen convexity of a discarded napkin into which the sun introduced a patch of yellow velvet, the half-empty glass which thus showed to greater advantage the noble sweep of its curved sides and, in the heart of its translucent crystal, clear as frozen daylight, some dregs of wine, dark but glittering with reflected lights, the displacement of solid objects, the transmutation of liquids by the effect of light and shade, the shifting colours of the plums which passed from green to blue and from blue to golden yellow in the half-plundered dish, the chairs, like a group of old ladies, that came twice daily to take their places round the white cloth spread on the table as on an altar at which were celebrated the rites of the palate, and where in the hollows of the oyster-shells a few drops of lustral water had remained as in tiny holy water stoups of stone; I tried to find beauty there where I had never imagined before that it could exist, in the most ordinary things, in the profundities of 'still life'.[9]

Art can make us conscious of what was previously unconscious or subconscious. Proust later added:

This work of the artist, this struggle to discern beneath matter, beneath experience, beneath words, something that is different from them, is a process exacting the reverse of that which, in those everyday lives which we live with our gaze averts from ourself.[10]

Meanwhile Freud added to the case of Emma Eckstein, which he had reported in his 1895 essay, 'Project for a scientific psychology', other cases of patients in whom present experience revived and gave new meaning to the past. He described eighteen cases of hysteria and obsessional neurosis to his colleagues in Vienna. He argued that, in all instances, the analysand's symptoms resulted from an event occurring after the sexual awakening of puberty giving new and guilty sexual meaning to much earlier experiences in which the analysand had been seduced or abused as a 3- or 4-year-old child by an adult looking after them, or by another child who had been similarly seduced or abused.[11] Soon after announcing this, his so-called seduction theory of neurosis, however, Freud abandoned it in favour of the theory that, whether or not neurosis is due to childhood sexual seduction or abuse, we all experience amorous feelings for those looking after us when we are infants.

The visual and dramatic arts can revive and give new, traumatic sexual meaning to this experience. Hence, said Freud, the gripping power of seeing Sophocles' *Oedipus Rex* on stage. For it makes us see our childhood feelings for our parents as murderous and incestuous. 'Each member of the audience was once, in germ and in phantasy, just such an Oedipus,' Freud wrote, 'and each one recoils in horror from the dream-fulfilment here transplanted into reality.'[12]

Art can thus evoke past experience and, in doing so, give it traumatic meaning leading to its repression into unconsciousness. Another example from Freud's own experience was his seeing again in his mind's eye the portraits of the artists, Fra Angelico, and his successor, the painter of the fresco, *The Last Judgement*, in Orvieto Cathedral, included on the left of this fresco.[13] But Freud could not remember the name of the painter of this fresco. Other painters' names occurred to him, Botticelli and Boltraffio. So too did social issues in Bosnia and Herzegovenia where he was then travelling. Still unable to recall the painter's name, Freud was reminded of it – Signorelli – by an Italian he happened to meet. This reawakened a memory of learning, when he was visiting Trafoi, in the Tyrol, that one of his patients had committed suicide, 'on account of an incurable sexual complaint',[14] said Freud. Pursuing his associations to the various names and words involved, and the nodal points in which they converged, and which he included in a diagram (Figure 2.1),[15] Freud discovered, he said, the repressed and unconscious sexual meaning causing his neurotic forgetting of the painter's name.

In other instances art can lift repression. Proust suggested this in his essay about Chardin. Freud gave the fictional example described by Jensen in his 1903 novella, *Gradiva*, in which the sight of a statue (Figure 2.2.1)[16] in

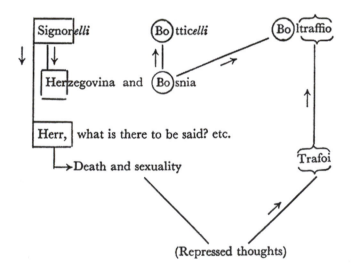

Figure 2.1 Signorelli: Diagram

Rome lifts from repression a German archaeologist's desire for a young girl in his home town of whom the statue reminds him. Another example is Michelangelo's statue, *Moses*,[17] also in Rome. Maintaining that the artist seeks 'to awaken in us the same emotional attitude, the same mental constellation as that which in him produced the impetus to create', Freud pursued his free associations to a detail of the statue, specifically to what he called, 'the attitude of his [Moses'] right hand, and the position of the two Tables of the Law'.[18] This led to images of the movements that might have preceded this detail, drawings of which Freud included in his article about the statue (Figure 2.2.2).[19] Together these associations resulted in his interpreting the statue as possibly impelled by an unconscious wish in Michelangelo to make, he said, 'the passage of a violent gust of passion visible in the signs left behind it in the ensuing calm'.[20]

But what is the origin in earliest infancy of such wishes? And how do they come into being in the form of images peopling our sleeping hallucinations

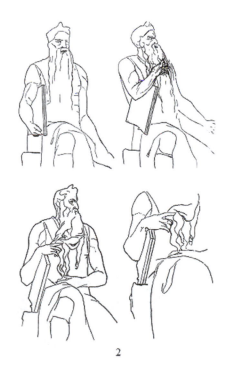

1   2

Figure 2.2 'Gradiva' and Moses drawings

S. Freud (1907) Delusions and dreams in Jensen's *Gradiva*. *SE9*: frontispiece. S. Freud (1914) The Moses of Michelangelo. *SE13*: 212, 222. Sigmund Freud, copyrights © The Institute of Psychoanalysis and The Hogarth Press, reprinted by permission of The Random House Group Ltd, and in the United States by permission of Basic Books, a member of Perseus Books, L.L.C.

which we recall as dreams? Findings in neuro-psychology suggest that these hallucinations result from inner or outer stimuli occurring while we sleep evoking what could be called squiggles of 'appetitive interest' of 'core consciousness' mediated by the frontal cortex of the sleeping brain.[21] This, in turn, triggers the junction of neuronal pathways from the brain's parietal, occipital and temporal lobes (Figure 2.3),[22] registering past somato-sensory, visual and auditory information. It is this that causes our sleeping hallucinations which we then revise in recalling them as dreams.

The preferred stimuli of our sleeping hallucinations are, said Freud, 'impressions from the immediately preceding days'.[23] He illustrated this with the example of his youngest child, Anna, when she was 19 months old. After being denied food because she had been sick, and after learning that her nurse attributed her sickness to her having eaten strawberries, she called out in her sleep, as though her wish for the forbidden food was there-and-then being realized, 'Anna Fweud, stwawbewwies, wild stwawbewwies, omblet, pudden!'[24]

Our sleeping hallucinations can be evoked not only by internal squiggles or twinges of appetite. They can also be evoked by external stimuli. Freud gave the example of one of his medical colleagues, Pepi H, who, hearing his landlady calling him to wake up, imagined, as he went on sleeping, that

> he was lying in bed in a room in the hospital, and that there was a card over the bed on which was written: 'Pepi H., medical student, age 22.' While he was dreaming, he said to himself 'As I'm already in the hospital, there's no need for me to go there' – and turned over and went on sleeping.[25]

Still active preoccupations from the previous day, as in the above-cited example of the infant Anna Freud, can also prompt wish-fulfilling sleeping

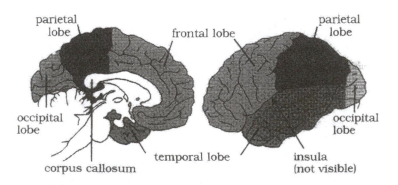

Figure 2.3 Brain lobes diagram

M. Solms and O. Turnbull (2002) *The Brain and the Inner World.* London: Karnac, p. 15.

hallucinations while we sleep. Another example, given by Freud, was a dream evoked in him by his wife, Martha, remarking that their family doctor, Otto, looked strained and tired. In his subsequent dream, wrote Freud, 'My friend Otto was looking ill. His face was brown and he had protruding eyes'. This was impelled, it transpired, by wishful ambitions evoked in Freud by seeing Otto the previous day.[26]

'A daytime thought may very well play the part of entrepreneur for a dream,' Freud observed. But, he went on, 'the entrepreneur, who, as people say, has the idea and the initiative to carry it out, can do nothing without capital'.[27] The entrepreneur, as daytime stimulus, finds its capital, in the case of dreams, argued Freud, in a wish-fulfilling activity of the mind. 'Wishful cathexis to the point of hallucination', he told Fliess, 'are described by us as psychical primary processes; by contrast, those processes which are only made possible by a good cathexis of the ego ... are described as psychical secondary processes.'[28] Primary process, wish-fulfilling hallucinations, Freud maintained, begin developmentally with the hungry baby's 'experience of satisfaction' on being fed. This forms a 'mnemic image' which is revived, in turn, in hallucinatory form when the baby is next hungry. 'Thus the aim of this first psychical activity', Freud claimed, 'was to produce a "perceptual identity" – a repetition of the perception which was linked with the satisfaction of the need.'[29]

Noting that babies continue sucking at the breast when their hunger is satisfied, and noting also that they suck at their lips, fingers, thumbs and at other objects as substitutes, Freud argued that sucking for nourishment at the mother's breast initiates the baby's sexual wishes and fantasies through giving them objective shape and form. 'Sucking at the mother's breast is the starting-point of the whole of sexual life,' he declared, 'the unmatched prototype of every later satisfaction, to which phantasy often enough recurs in times of need.'[30]

The mother feeding her baby thus brings its sexual wishes and desires into being, according to Freud. It also evokes her wishes and desires. She may express them in the way she holds, looks at, and talks to her baby. This too contributes to giving her baby's wishes their first shape and form, and their initial sexual meaning too. Freud claimed:

A child's intercourse with anyone responsible for his care affords him an unending source of sexual excitation and satisfaction, since the person in charge of him, who, after all, is as a rule his mother, herself regards him with feelings that are derived from her own sexual life: she strokes him, kisses him, rocks him and quite clearly treats him as a substitute for a complete sexual object.[31]

This is exacerbated, he added, by the sexual repression of middle-class women. It causes them often to be sexually disappointed in the fathers of their children and to look for sexual satisfaction instead to their children, thus awakening their child's 'sexual precocity'.[32] He also noted the hetero-sexual desires awoken in parents by their children – fathers often being sexually aroused by their daughters, mothers by their sons – this too shaping the child's 'erotic wishes', Freud argued, with sons wanting to take their father's place, daughters that of their mother in their sexual intercourse together.[33]

The sexual wishes and desires of children are also aroused and shaped by other children. They influence each other's wishful fantasies through what they tell each other about sex and prostitution, said Freud. This revives in the schoolboy impressions and wishes from his earliest infancy. Freud wrote:

> He begins to desire his mother herself in the sense with which he has recently become acquainted, and to hate his father anew as a rival who stands in the way of this wish, he comes, as we say, under the dominance of the Oedipus complex.

Thanks to what other children tell him about sex, Freud added to this his first formulation of his Oedipus complex theory of neurosis, the boy may entertain fantasies which, he argued, 'have as their subject his mother's sexual activities under the most diverse circumstances'.[34]

Similar fantasies may occur as hallucinations while we sleep. If the realization of the wishes constituting these hallucinations is unacceptable to consciousness, to what Freud called the secondary processes of the ego, this realization may be disguised so as not to waken us and thus prevent it continuing. It may be disguised by condensing or displacing unacceptable with more acceptable images. Added to these two 'dream-work' disguises of 'condensation' and 'displacement', argued Freud, we also use the disguise afforded by what he called 'pictorial arrangement of the psychical material'.[35] It uses the ambiguous meaning of visual imagery to help conceal from consciousness unacceptable intentions and wishes unconsciously fulfilled in our sleeping hallucinations.

A further dream-work disguise is provided by what Freud called 'second-ary revision'.[36] This is the process by which, once the sleeping hallucination has been transformed into the material of the remembered dream, any remaining gaps, incongruities and irregularities are done away with by the dreamer using prevailing rules of picturing and language so as to see and tell their sleeping hallucinations as a coherent whole. The primary process wish-fulfilments afforded by our sleeping hallucinations are thus disguised, accord-ing to Freud, by dream-work mechanisms of condensation, displacement, pictorial arrangement, and secondary revision, guided by what he later called secondary process or conscious 'attention' to what our 'sense-impressions' tell us about external reality.[37]

Neurotic symptoms, he maintained, are constituted by the same dream-work mechanisms that disguise and transform our wish-fulfilling sleeping hallucinations into the pictures and stories we tell ourselves and others as dreams. Just as our sleeping hallucinations result from inner or external stimuli awakening twinges or squiggles of appetitive interest which then provoke wish-fulfilling hallucinations constructed out of our past experience (recorded in the brain's parietal, occipital and temporal lobes), so too neurotic symptoms result from present experience awakening and giving new meaning to past experience which then operates by deferred action in the present. In so far as this meaning is unacceptable to our conscious ego we subject it to dream-work disguise.

Discovering the unconscious meaning causing the analysand's ills therefore entails the analyst undoing and deconstructing the art- or dream-work disguise constituting these ills, as I mentioned in Chapter 1. This process of deconstruction is the central task of psychoanalytic psychotherapy. Its main method involves undoing the analysand's dream-work disguise of their repressed and unconscious wish-fulfilling fantasies by encouraging them to free associate to bits and pieces of their symptoms, memories and dreams to discover their underlying wishes and meaning. This process of deconstruction entails, according to Freud, persuading the analysand to say whatever comes to mind in association to fragments of what they remember, unhampered by any drive to cohere these fragments into a meaningful or reasonable whole.

> We therefore tell him [the analysand] that the success of the psychoanalysis depends on his noticing and reporting whatever comes into his head and not being misled, for instance, into suppressing an idea because it strikes him as unimportant or irrelevant or because it seems to him meaningless.[38]

This can be illustrated with Freud's case history of a 23-year-old Russian and amateur artist, Sergei Pankieff, specifically with Pankieff's associations to a dream occurring to him on the Christmas Eve of his fourth birthday, to which he attributed his subsequent childhood neuroses. 'I dreamt that it was night and that I was lying in my bed,' he told Freud, adding:

> Suddenly the window opened of its own accord, and I was terrified to see that some white wolves were sitting on the big walnut tree in front of the window. There were six or seven of them. The wolves were quite white, and looked more like foxes or sheep-dogs, for they had big tails like foxes and they had their ears pricked like dogs when they pay attention to something. In great terror, evidently of being eaten up by the wolves, I screamed and woke up.[39]

It was the way the wolves stared at him, said Pankieff, that was most frightening. 'It seemed as though they had riveted their whole attention on me,' he explained. He showed Freud a drawing he had made of this bit of the dream (Figure 2.4).[40] He also made a painting of it.[41]

After the dream, it seems, he became terrified of a picture of a wolf illustrating the folk tale, *The Wolf and the Seven Little Goats*, with which his older sister tormented him. In it, as Freud could see from the reproduction Pankieff found to show him, 'the wolf was standing upright, striding out with one foot, with its claws stretched out and its ears pricked'.[42] Unlike his sister, who provoked Pankieff's anxieties, his mother sought to allay them by telling him Bible stories, this doubtless contributing to his obsessively kissing religious pictures before going to bed at night.

Freud, however, found that the analysand's free associations, such as those of Pankieff to his wolf dream, are often impeded by the analysand equating the analyst with figures from their past, especially from their early childhood. Other 'transferences', as Freud called these equations, 'are more ingeniously constructed,' he said, 'and they may even become conscious, by cleverly taking advantage of some real peculiarity in the physician's person or circumstances and attaching themselves to that'. They are then not 'new impressions', argued Freud, but 'revised editions' of the past.[43] Examples included for Freud his 18-year-old patient, Dora, who, it seems, unconsciously transferred onto him fantasies about her father and about the husband, Herr K, of her father's lover, Frau K. Such transferences, Freud

Figure 2.4 Pankieff: Wolf dream drawing

S. Freud (1918) From the history of an infantile neurosis. *SE* 17: 30. Sigmund Freud, copyrights © The Institute of Psychoanalysis and The Hogarth Press, reprinted by permission of The Random House Group Ltd, and in the United States by permission of Basic Books, a member of Perseus Books, L.L.C.

observed, inhibit the analysand's free associations. At the same time, he asserted, 'they do us the inestimable service of making the patient's hidden and forgotten erotic impulses immediate and manifest'.[44]

How, though, can the analyst discern in these manifestations the unconscious fantasies and wishes impelling them? This entails the analyst adopting a method akin to the analysand's method of free association. 'It is not in the least our business to "understand" a case at once,' Freud told his readers, 'this is only possible at a later stage, when we have received enough impressions of it',[45] he said in introducing his case history of a 5-year-old patient, now known as 'Little Hans'. Freud's impressions of Hans were largely shaped by notes that Hans' father, Max Graf, made about his development. Graf noted for instance his wife telling Hans, then aged 3½, on seeing him touch his penis, 'If you do that, I shall send for Dr. A to cut off your widdler. And then what'll you widdle with?'[46] Graf also noted that, on seeing his 1-week-old sister, Hanna, having a bath, Hans commented, 'But her widdler's still quite small' and 'When she grows up it'll get bigger all right.'[47] Graf furthermore observed that when he drew a picture of a giraffe Hans had seen at the zoo, Hans said, 'Draw its widdler too', to which Graf told Hans to draw this himself, which Hans did, adding a further line to make it bigger (Figure 2.5.1).[48] Freud's other impressions of the case included Graf's observation that, on seeing a horse urinating, Hans said, 'The horse has got its widdler underneath like me', and that, on seeing his 3-month-old sister, Hanna, having her bath, Hans emphasized, 'She has got a tiny little widdler.'[49]

More impressions provided to Freud by Graf included Hans' mother saying that one day, when they were on holiday in Gmunden, and she was drying Hans after his bath, taking care not to touch his penis, Hans asked, 'Why don't you put your finger there?' 'Because that'd be piggish,' she replied. 'What's that? Piggish? Why?' he asked. 'Because it's not proper,' she said. 'But it's great fun,' he laughed.[50]

Hans evidently enjoyed having his mother more to himself when they were on holiday in Gmunden from where Graf returned to work in Vienna. Perhaps this gave Hans the idea of getting rid of Graf altogether. Possibly this caused him to dread lest Graf retaliate by attacking him, and to his displacing and symbolizing this dread in the form of a phobia lest horses attack him. When asked what most frightened him about horses, Hans replied, said Freud, 'that he was particularly bothered by what horses wear in front of their eyes and by the black round their mouths'.[51] At this Freud was struck by the similarity between what Hans described and Graf's spectacles and moustache. Evidently putting these impressions together with his previously formed ideas about murderous Oedipal rivalry between fathers and sons, Freud asked Hans if he was frightened of his father, Graf, being angry with him because he was so fond of his mother. 'But why do you think I'm angry with you?' Graf interrupted, 'Have I ever scolded you or hit you?' 'Oh yes!' said Hans. 'When?' 'This morning.'[52] At this Graf remembered that

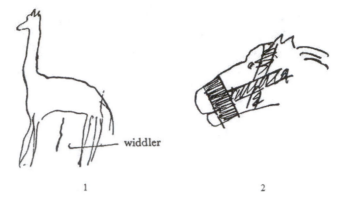

Figure 2.5 Hans: Giraffe and horse's head

he had indeed hit Hans when he had butted him in the stomach earlier that day.

Freud's observations prompted Graf soon after to draw a picture of a horse's head for Hans (Figure 2.5.2),[53] and to ask him whether the 'something black on their mouths' was a moustache so as to make more conscious his otherwise unconscious displacement of his fear of him onto horses.[54] Perhaps this contributed to Hans soon after becoming more conscious of the anger he had displaced from Graf onto a phobia of horses. He played games, for instance, in which he pretended to be a horse biting Graf. And, just as he had asked Graf, when he was 3½, to add a widdler to his drawing of a giraffe and then added one himself, and then made it bigger, he now day-dreamed, aged 5, that a plumber gave him a widdler. 'He gave you a bigger widdler and a bigger behind,' asked Graf. 'Yes.' 'Like Daddy's; because you'd like to be Daddy.' 'Yes, and I'd like to have a moustache like yours,' he said.[55]

In telling all this Freud included his own impressions as well as those of Graf. In analysing adults, however, Freud reduced the impressions he obtained of his patients by not looking at them directly, but by instead sitting behind them as they lay on his consulting room couch. It was, he acknowledged, a remnant of the procedure he had used in treating patients through hypnotism. To this he added, by way of justification, that he could not abide being stared at by patients for eight hours or more each day. Furthermore, he said, 'I do not wish my expressions of face to give the patient material for interpretations or to influence him in what he tells me.'[56]

In doing analysis, Freud warned, analysts must guard against affecting the analysand's free associations by counter-transference reactions evoked in them by 'the patient's influence on [the analyst's] unconscious feelings'. Since, he added, 'no psycho-analyst goes further than his own complexes and internal resistances permit',[57] Freud also emphasized the importance of analysts analysing and continuing to analyse themselves to protect their clinical work from being obstructed by their personal complexes and resistances.

Another means of reducing the analyst's counter-transference influence on the analysand's free associations involves their adopting a stance of 'evenly-suspended attention' free from selection influenced by what they might expect or be inclined to perceive.[58] Although Freud recommended this, he was evidently influenced, in doing analysis, by his own expectations and inclinations, not least by expectations formed on the basis of his previously constructed theories in arriving at constructions of the unconscious cause of his analysands' ills. This can be illustrated with another example, that of a 27-year-old lawyer patient, Ernst Lanzer, who suffered a crippling obsession with whether or not to obey an army captain's command to him, regarding a trifling postal debt, 'You must pay back the 3.80 kronen to Lieutenant A'. This obsession included the thought that, were he to obey this command, a woman he admired, as well as his long-dead father, might be subjected to an Eastern punishment, told Lanzer by the captain, in which rats are put in a basin inverted on the criminal's buttocks so as to gnaw into his anus.[59]

Despite his resistance to free associating to bits and pieces of this and other thoughts, memories and dreams, Lanzer recounted to Freud various associations, including the following: his governess sexually exciting him, as a 5-year-old, by letting him play with her genitals; his touching another governess sexually when he was 7; fear that his parents guessed his thoughts; worry that his sexual thoughts might cause his father to die; his obediently praying 'May God protect him' only to find a 'not' intervening so he quickly recited 'a short formula concocted out of the initial letters or syllables of various prayers' to prevent any countervailing command intervening.[60] Other associations included his thinking, aged 21, when his father died, that this might make him rich enough to marry his lady-love, this then coming into conflict with his mother suggesting he marry a rich cousin instead.

The convergence of these and other associations on father-centred nodal point conflicts about sex, together with Freud's then developing theories about the father-centred infantile and sexual origin of neurosis, led Freud to suggest to Lanzer that, before he was 6, he had been guilty of some misdemeanour connected with masturbation for which his father had punished him. At this Lanzer remembered that his mother had often told a story of how, when he was 3 or 4, he had bitten someone – she thought it might have been his nursemaid – for which his father had beaten him. Furious under his father's blows, the infant Lanzer had apparently hurled abuse at his father. Since he did not know any bad language, he had called him all the names of common objects he knew, screaming, 'You lamp!', 'You towel!', 'You plate!', and so on. At this, it seems, his father was so shaken by Lanzer's fury he stopped beating him, declared 'The child will be either a great man or a great criminal!', and never beat him again.[61] Fearful of what his rage might do to his father, Lanzer thereafter became a coward. Whenever he was enraged and frightened by one of his brothers or sisters being beaten, he said, he crept away and hid.

Lanzer could not recall the event that had led to this 'cringe-and-creep' response.[62] Instead he repeated it in revised form in his analytic sessions with Freud. Just as he had verbally abused his father, he verbally abused Freud. He told him obscene fantasies of seeing Freud and his children eating Freud's mother's genitals, of seeing himself lying on his back on Freud's daughter and 'copulating with her by means of the stool hanging from his anus', of seeing Freud's female relatives being 'choked in a sea of revolting secretions of every kind', and of seeing Freud's 12-year-old daughter cutting a herring stretched between Freud's wife and mother, 'extending from the anus of one to that of the other'.[63] Lanzer cringed in thus regaling Freud with these fantasies. 'How can a gentleman like you, sir,' he asked, 'let yourself be abused in this way by a low, good-for-nothing fellow like me? You ought to turn me out: that's all I deserve.' At this he got up from the couch and paced the room because, he said, he was frightened Freud might beat him. Or, if he stayed on the couch, reported Freud, 'he would bury his head in his hands, cover his face with his arm, jump up suddenly and rush away, his features distorted with pain'.[64] Lanzer attributed this to his father having had such a violent temper he sometimes did not know when to stop.

Lanzer's transference onto Freud of his experience of his father elicited the above recounted fantasies and also made him cringe and inhibited him from telling Freud his free associations. 'If he could have tolerated the situation, it would have been an occasion in which he imbued his feelings with more self-conscious thought. He could, for instance, have talked about his anxiety and his fearful feelings,' comments the US psychoanalyst, Jonathan Lear.[65] 'Psychoanalysis itself is the building up of a practical-cognitive skill of recognising the fractal nature of one's unconscious conflicts as they are unfolding in the here and now,' Lear adds. 'A good interpretation is simply a form of words which accurately describes those conflicts – and which thereby augments this practical skill',[66] a skill which others call 'mentalization'.[67] In Lanzer's case these conflicts included his inhibiting himself from thinking by busying himself with obsessively repeating commands and prayers, and doing and undoing what he did, as part of a tactic whereby, writes Lear, 'when he gets anxious, he cringes and creeps away'.[68]

Lanzer's case history was first published in 1909. The next year Freud's notorious 'case history' of Leonardo da Vinci was published. In it, and obviously without any free associations from Leonardo (dead since 2 May 1519), Freud attributed the inspiration of Leonardo's painting, *Madonna and Child with St Anne*,[69] to a childhood wish in Leonardo to be the adored object of the youthful and idealized gaze of his mother, stepmother and paternal grandmother, with whom he lived with his father when he was 5.

Freud also interpreted the painting as covert realization of another wish, recalled as follows as a memory by Leonardo in thinking about his research, as a young man, into the flight of birds:

> It seems that I was always destined to be so deeply concerned with vultures [sic];[70] for I recall as one of my very earliest memories that while I was in my cradle a vulture came down to me, and opened my mouth with its tail, and struck me many times with its tail against my lips.[71]

To prove that Leonardo's painting, *Madonna and Child with St Anne*, was prompted by this wishful memory, as he understood it, Freud included a 'picture-puzzle' line drawing highlighting, with diagonal lines, a vulture shape which can be seen in this painting, and which, said Freud, quoting Pfister, 'leads to the mouth of the child, i.e. of Leonardo himself' (Figure 2.6).[72]

'An artist is originally a man who turns away from reality because he cannot come to terms with the renunciation of instinctual satisfaction,' Freud wrote the next year.

> [The artist] finds his way back to reality, however, from this world of phantasy, by making use of special gifts to mould his phantasies into truths of a new kind, which are valued by men as precious reflections of reality.[73]

Freud thus allied the artist's transformation of their wishful fantasies into art with our dream-work transformation, as he understood it, of our wish-fulfilling, sleeping hallucinations into the pictures and stories we tell as dreams. Freud also allied art, by implication, with the neurotic's transformation of their repressed unconscious wishes into bodily symptoms as mnemic images of what they repress. Indeed, he mused, the conversion or transformation of their fantasies into bodily symptoms could be regarded as 'a caricature of a work of art'.[74]

This might be true of hysteria. But what about obsessional and phobic neuroses and the paranoia of schizophrenia? Freud attributed the latter in the case of a judge, Daniel Paul Schreber, to Schreber displacing guilt-ridden Oedipal desire for, and hatred of his father onto God,[75] just as he also defensively used, according to Freud, 'the sun as a sublimated "father-symbol" '.[76] As for obsessional neurosis, Freud had linked its ritualistic symptoms in his 2 March 1907 talk to his colleagues in Vienna, as I said at the beginning of Chapter 1, to religious rituals.[77] Following his account of the Little Hans, Lanzer and Schreber cases, Freud detailed further links between phobic and obsessional neurosis and religious rituals. He argued that these rituals result from repression and displacement of murderous Oedipal hatred of the father

Figure 2.6 Leonardo: Picture-puzzle

onto symbols of him, as in the eating of bread and drinking of wine as symbolic of the body and blood of the son of God in Holy Communion.[78]

To the analogy he drew, implicitly and explicitly, between phobic and obsessional neuroses and religious rituals Freud added an analogy between philosophy and schizophrenia. In both, he said, thoughts can become so divorced from 'the residues of perceptions of words', in which they originate, that 'in order to become conscious, [they] need to be reinforced by new [perceptual] qualities'. The divorce and abstraction of thoughts from the perceptual qualities of words and things in which they originate can pose problems for philosophy. They can also pose problems for psychoanalysis, as Freud warned:

When we think in abstractions there is a danger that we may neglect the relations of words to unconscious thing-presentations, and it must be confessed that the expression and content of our philosophizing then begins to acquire an unwelcome resemblance to the mode of operation of schizophrenia.[79]

Guarding against flight from perceptual reality into abstract and pre-conceived ideas is another reason analysts should adopt a stance of evenly-suspended attention free from selection and inclination, as mentioned above. The analyst doing analysis, said Freud, 'should withhold all conscious influences from his capacity to attend, and give himself over completely to his "unconscious memory" '.[80] He recommended the analyst doing analysis

> to avoid so far as possible reflection and the construction of conscious expectations, not to try to fix anything that he heard particularly in his memory, and by these means to catch the drift of the patient's unconscious with his own unconscious.[81]

But this, of course, implies enabling the analyst's unconscious fantasies to operate in psychoanalytic psychotherapy. Freud did not emphasize this. He did however argue that when the analysand's free associations become 'insufficient or fail altogether',[82] or become 'mute',[83] the analyst can usefully supplement these associations with what they suggest in terms of the analyst's already acquired knowledge of dream-symbols and their meanings. Since analysands, in their defensive dream- or art-work constructions, are, said Freud, 'unaware of the meaning of the symbols they use, it is difficult at first sight to discover the source of the connection between the symbols and what they replace'. But, he went on,

> with the help of a knowledge of dream-symbolism, it is possible to understand the meaning of separate elements of the content of a dream, or separate pieces of a dream or in some cases even whole dreams, without having to ask the dreamer for his associations.[84]

Through using their knowledge of dream-symbols, he reported of himself and his fellow-analysts, 'we arrive at a satisfactory sense for the dream, whereas it remains senseless and the chain of thought is interrupted so long as we refrain from intervening in this way'.[85]

The analysand's use of symbolism in their dream-work disguise of their unconscious wishes proves that the analysand has, Freud argued, 'a symbolic mode of expression at his disposal which he does not know in waking life and does not recognize'.[86] Freud related this mode of expression to symbols occurring in myths and fairytales, folk sayings, songs, colloquialisms and poetry. Their occurrence indicated to him the survival of 'an ancient but extinct mode of expression', a 'basic language' of which, he said, 'all these symbolic relations would be residues'.[87]

Many symbols, he observed, are sexual. 'Sharp weapons, long and stiff objects, such as tree-trunks and sticks, stand for the male genital,' he maintained, 'while cupboards, boxes, carriages or ovens may represent the uterus.'[88] Reflecting the importance accorded phallic symbolism by male-dominated, patriarchal societies, such as our own, he wrote:

> The more striking and for both sexes the more interesting components of the genitals, the male organ, finds symbolic substitutes in the first instance in things that resemble it in shape – things, accordingly that are long and up-standing, such as sticks, umbrellas, posts, trees and so on.[89]

By contrast, he argued, female sexuality is often symbolized by what is empty and hollow.

Emphasizing the ancient roots of symbolism, he also noted its continuing development and modification through the incorporation of newly invented objects as symbols. The above-mentioned use of umbrellas to symbolize the penis is one example. He also noted (in addition to the 'famous symbol', the snake, as he put it) 'revolvers ... watering-cans ... extensible pencils ... flying-machines ... and ... Zeppelin airships',[90] this last invention also being mentioned by Proust in discussing symbols in his 1927 book, *Time Regained*, published posthumously as the last part of *Remembrance of Things Past*.

Just as Proust may have known little or nothing about Freud's ideas, Freud, it seems, knew nothing of Proust's work. As for the analyst's use of their knowledge of dream-symbolism, prompted by what the analysand says and does by way of free association in analysis, this can be illustrated with Freud's case history of Dora, specifically his account of interpreting her opening her purse and putting her finger in it during an analytic session as expressing, in symbolically disguised form, her wish to masturbate. The purse functioned as symbolic 'substitute for the shell of Venus,' he said, 'for the female genitals'.[91] Another example, again from this case history, is Dora recalling in association to a dream in which a man told her, 'Two and a half hours more',[92] a memory of remaining 'two hours in front of the *Sistine Madonna*, rapt in silent admiration' on seeing this painting by Raphael in Dresden (Figure 2.7).[93] With this her free associations came to an end. 'When I asked her what had pleased her so much about the picture,' Freud reported, 'she could find no clear answer to make.' Eventually she said, 'The Madonna.'[94] Given the failure of Dora's free associations at this point, Freud supplemented them with the knowledge of dream-symbols which her *Sistine Madonna* association evoked in him, namely the Madonna as symbol of virginity. 'Moreover,' he added, 'the notion of the "Madonna" is a favourite counter-idea in the mind of girls who feel themselves oppressed by imputations of sexual guilt, – which was the case with Dora.'[95]

Figure 2.7 Raphael: *Sistine Madonna*

As well as being influenced in Dora's case by his prior knowledge of and assumptions about the symbolic meaning of purses and the Madonna, Freud was also influenced by his assumption that, as Lacan put it, 'a girl is made to love boys [so that] if something torments her, something repressed, in Freud's eyes it can only be this – she loves Herr K [the husband of her father's lover, Frau K]'.[96] Had Freud 'intervened by allowing the subject to name her desire,' Lacan went on, drawing on Freud's final footnoted afterthought about Dora's repressed desire not for Herr K, but for his wife, Frau K, he might not have left her in hallucinatory identification with her father desiring Frau K as *Sistine Madonna*. Instead, failing to name and enable Dora to become conscious of this desire, Freud left Dora, said Lacan, 'lost deep in contemplation of this painting – the image of the Madonna, before which,' he pointed out, 'a man and a woman stand in adoration'.[97]

Worse was to follow. Freud became increasingly convinced that men's revolt against dread of losing their penis, and women's revolt against penis envy, constitute the Oedipus or, more accurately, the castration complex essence of the ills bringing men and women into analysis.

> We often have the impression that with the wish for a penis and the masculine protest we have penetrated through all the psychological strata and have reached bedrock, and that thus our activities are at an end.

Freud wrote the above in one of his final essays about the clinical practice of psychoanalytic psychotherapy, which he had first founded many years before. 'This is probably true,' he added, 'since, for the psychical field, the biological field does in fact play the part of the underlying bedrock.'[98] With this he bequeathed to some of his followers the reduction of their analysand's free associations to castration complex 'repudiation of femininity' interpretations akin to the formulaic paintings of a hack artist. 'My dear Jung, promise me never to abandon the sexual theory,' Freud had long before told Jung, 'we must make a dogma of it, an unshakeable bulwark.'[99] How did Jung respond?

Chapter 3

Jung

Although Freud became increasingly dogmatic in insisting on his Oedipus and castration complex construction of the psychological ills of children and adults, he retained his method of deconstructing the mythological, symbolic and dream- and art-work disguises which he also believed constitute these ills. Furthermore, despite warning against psychoanalysis, like schizophrenia, overvaluing abstract ideas and losing sight of the sensory and perceptual roots of thinking in talking about things with others, he was suspicious of what could be called sensory or perceptual logic. 'An advance of intellectuality consists in deciding against direct sense-perception,' he wrote, 'in favour of what are known as the higher intellectual processes – that is, memories, reflections and inferences.' He celebrated in these terms the victory of kinship descent reckoned in the name of the father, not the mother, the latter 'established by the evidence of the senses', he said, welcoming the patriarchal rule that, as he put it, 'the child should bear his father's name and be his heir'. He also celebrated the Jewish law against making images of God. As a result, despite having described himself as 'a completely godless Jew',[1] he said, 'our God is the greatest and mightiest, although he is invisible like a gale of wind or like the soul'.[2]

Whereas Freud regarded the work of psychoanalysis as essentially one of analysing and deconstructing the dream- or art-work constructions constituting the analysands' symptoms, as he understood them, Jung's approach centred on completing the analysand's dream- and fantasy-based images into healing constructions in terms of the symbolic meanings these images suggested to him, meanings which he culled from ancient myth, philosophy and religion. In keeping with his medical colleagues at the Burghölzli mental hospital in Zurich, where he first worked as a psychiatrist, he attributed his patients' ills to a repressed 'feeling-toned complex of ideas'. This complex could be identified, he argued, from 'the feeling-tone common to all the individual ideas' in the patient's response to items in the word association tests used in the hospital to diagnose its inmates.[3] Healing the patient from their ill-making feeling-toned complex entails replacing it with a healing complex, Jung maintained. 'A purposive treatment,' he wrote in an essay he sent Freud on beginning their correspondence in 1906, 'is best achieved by introducing some new complex that liberates the ego from domination by the complex of the illness.'[4]

Jung illustrated this process of treating ill-making complexes by introducing new complexes or images in his first book, *Symbols of Transformation*. In it he quoted at length from the report of her self-analysis by a young American woman, Miss Frank Miller.[5] He quoted, for instance, Miller's account of waking from a dream recalling the phrase, 'when the morning stars sang together'. Together with images this suggested to her – which she gleaned from Milton's *Paradise Lost*, the *Book of Job*, and Haydn's *Creation* oratorio – the phrase inspired Miller to write a poem. It began, 'When God had first made Sound', which she changed to 'When the Eternal first made Sound'. She subsequently discovered this image was similar to a myth, of which she had not known at the time, according to which the world was created by a whirlwind which, she said, must have made a great deal of noise and sound. She likened the bringing together of such seemingly inherited, dream-inspired, myth-bequeathed images with more recent culturally given images to the motifs resulting when, she wrote, 'the little bits of coloured glass in a kaleidoscope form marvellous and rare patterns'.[6]

Jung called this process of extending dream and fantasy images in terms of past myths and motifs 'amplification'. It clarifies 'the metaphorical content of dream symbolism,' write his followers. 'Amplification enables the dreamer to abandon a purely personal and individualistic attitude toward the dream image', so that, they argue, 'one consciously experiences oneself within and as part of archetypal energies rather than as their object'.[7]

To amplification Jung added a method he called 'personification'. By this he meant the transformation of aspects of the analysand's psyche into figures also gleaned from myths and philosophical and religious systems from the past. Several examples can be found in his account of his 1913–16 self-analysis following his rejection of Freud's equation of the libido with sex rather than with 'vital energy' or *élan vital*,[8] as he put it, and following his rejection of Freud's 'materially-minded' approach to psychoanalytic psychotherapy in favour of a more introspective, 'spiritually-minded' approach.[9]

Examples of personification included, for Jung, seeing himself in a dream with 'an unknown, brown-skinned man, a savage,' he said, together with the hero of Teutonic legend, Siegfried, whom Jung and the 'savage' shot dead. Siegfried was the personification of Jung's drive to become a hero which now no longer suited him. Hence, he argued, his killing Siegfried in his dream. As for the 'savage', he personified, said Jung, 'the primitive shadow' archetype of his collective unconscious.[10]

In another dream Jung saw two figures – a man who called himself Elijah with a girl called Salome. She was blind. She personified, argued Jung, the anima archetype, an aspect of himself which did not see the meaning of things. She also personified eroticism. The old man, by contrast, personified the archetype of 'the wise old prophet', symbolizing intelligence and knowledge. They were also personified, added Jung, by a figure he called 'Philomen'. He described him as having 'an Egypto-Hellenic atmosphere with a Gnostic coloration'.[11] Jung painted a picture of a dream in which this figure appeared. He also talked with Philomen, and learnt from what he said, reported Jung, that, through personification, he could talk to, and thus think about aspects of himself as separate from himself.

Jung's influential US follower, James Hillman, has written in similar vein about the value of personification. He argues that we can register and know a feeling only through it being personified as a 'fantasy-image'.[12] He calls personification 'soul-making'. He likens it to the ancient Greek and Roman practice of giving names to aspects of the psyche in calling their statues 'Victory', 'Fortune', 'Modesty', 'Mercy', 'Peace', 'Forgetfulness' and so on. Freud, he says, achieved a similar effect in giving conscience the name, 'Superego', just as Jung called aspects of the mind 'Shadow', 'Old Wise Man' and 'Great Mother'. Personifying aspects of the mind makes them into containers for the soul. It is inspired, Hillman adds, by the anima archetype. We can call her 'Angel' 'Daemon' or 'Genius'. Whatever we call her, he insists, this archetype is an impersonal force impelling us to transform brute sensation into personified meaning.

Hillman warns, however, against personifying and giving aspects of the psyche names that reduce them to stereotypes. Perhaps it was to avoid this problem that Jung developed another analytical psychology method of psychotherapy. He called it 'individuation'. It aims to bring out individual aspects of the psyche by relating them to, but not reducing them to culturally given symbols so as to enable the analysand to reconnect with otherwise unknown archetypes inherited, according to Jung, in each of us individually in what he called the collective unconscious. Individuation is geared to enabling the analysand to become 'himself, whole, indivisible and distinct from other people or collective psychology (though also in relation to these)', write Jung's followers. Through individuation, they argue, 'the person becomes conscious in what respects he or she is both a unique human being and, at the same time, no more than a common man or woman'.[13]

This method of analytical psychology psychotherapy, like amplification, can also be illustrated with examples from Jung's 1913–16 self-analysis which included his painting mandalas, starting with one now known as *Mandala of a Modern Man* (Figure 3.1.1).[14] 'My mandalas were cryptograms concerning the state of the self which were presented to me anew each day,' he explained. 'In them I saw the self – that is, my whole being – actively at work.'[15] They culminated in a mandala inspired by a dream in which he found himself, with three younger travelling companions, in Liverpool's harbour area from where they climbed to the upper part of the city. Here, in the city centre, they found a garden. It was square. In the middle was a lake or large pool with a red-flowering magnolia tree. It stood, said Jung, 'in everlasting sunshine', enabling him to understand why it was that a friend of one of his dream companions had made his home there.[16]

In the mandala inspired by this dream (Figure 3.1.2),[17] Jung painted the red-flowering magnolia as 'a sort of rose made of ruby-coloured glass', he said. It shone like a star. The wall surrounding the square-shaped park of his dream became a street from which radiated eight further streets, from each of which eight more streets radiate. They meet in 'a shining red central point,' Jung further explained, 'rather like the Étoile in Paris'. In thus combining the classic motifs of a flower, star, circle, precinct and a city divided in four, his painting pictured, he said, 'a window opening on to eternity'.[18] With its centre as goal, it revealed, he claimed, 'that the self is the principle and archetype of orientation and meaning'.[19] It achieved the goal of his self-analysis, which he had begun in 1913, he said, to discover the myth in which he as an individual lived.

A much more detailed illustration of his method of individuation can be found in his account of his analysis of an American, Miss X. She was 55 when her analysis in Zurich began in late October 1928. Before arriving in Zurich she went to Denmark to discover more about her mother's Danish roots. The scenery inspired her to paint, and she continued painting in Zurich. At her first meeting with Jung she told him a fantasy in which, he wrote,

> she saw herself with the lower half of her body in the earth, stuck fast in a block of rock. The region round about was a beach strewn with boulders. In the background was the sea. She felt caught and helpless. Then she suddenly saw me in the guise of a medieval sorcerer. She shouted for help, I came along and touched the rock with a magic wand. The stone instantly burst open, and she stepped out uninjured.[20]

She showed Jung a picture she had made of this fantasy (Figure 3.2.1, Plate 1).[21] It demonstrated her imprisoned state, he said, 'attached to the earth, in the land of her mother . . . caught in the unconscious . . . still stuck with half her body in Mother Earth'.[22] The boulders of her fantasy featured in her picture as eggs. 'The egg is a germ of life with a lofty symbolical significance', Jung said, adding what, to me at least, seems mystery mongering:

> it is the orphic egg, the world's beginning . . . the vessel from which, at the end of the *opus alchymicum*, the homunculus emerges, that is, the Anthropos, the spiritual, inner and complete man, who in Chinese alchemy is called the *chen-yen* (literally, 'perfect man').[23]

This might seem absurd. Not to Jung.

Urging Miss X to go beyond this mere fantasy-image of freeing herself from the unconscious, he encouraged her to make a picture of liberating

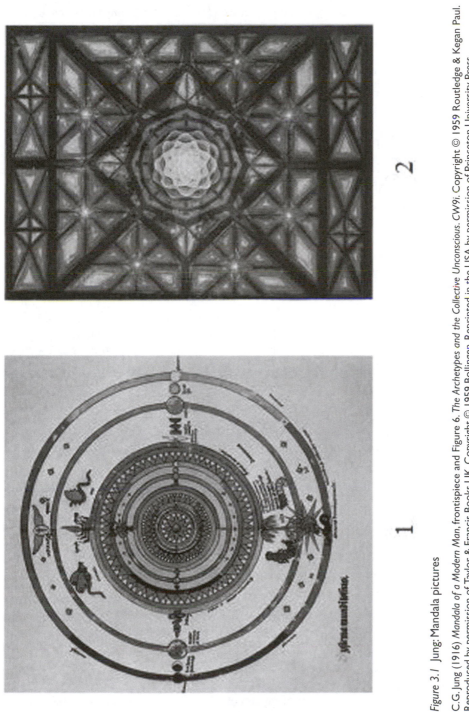

Figure 3.1 Jung: Mandala pictures

herself. This resulted in a second picture (Figure 3.2.2, Plate 1). Its flash of lightning, said Jung, symbolized the freeing of her psyche or spirit. Paracelsus and the alchemists used the same symbol. He also told her about ancient circular symbols of the soul. This doubtless contributed to her including another circular shape in her third painting (Figure 3.2.3, Plate 1). It represented her 'true personality', said Jung. He also related it to the Chinese '*chen-yen*' and to what he called 'the *homo quadratus* of alchemy'.[24]

Alchemy increasingly figured in his interpretations of Miss X's subsequent paintings. She related the snake in her third painting to having seen a snake in a dream. A snake also figured in her next painting (Figure 3.2.4, Plate 1). It could be seen as sexual. But it was more accurate to interpret it as symbolizing, argued Jung, 'a law of life to which sex is subordinated'.[25] It also manifested the animus archetype of her soul. He explained:

> For a woman, the typical danger emanating from the unconscious comes from above, from the 'spiritual' sphere personified by the animus, whereas for a man it comes from the chthonic realm of the 'world and woman,' i.e., the anima projected on to the world.[26]

Perhaps Jung's equation of the snake as symbol of danger contributed to snakes not featuring in any of Miss X's subsequent paintings included by him in his account of her analysis. Instead they all centred on a circular shape in accordance with his interpreting such shapes as symbolizing neither the body nor sexuality but the spirit or soul. He called the circle in her next picture (Figure 3.2.5, Plate 1) the '*benedicta viriditas*' of alchemy.[27] He likewise interpreted her paintings following her return to New York in terms of alchemy, including one of Fifth Avenue (Figure 3.2.6, Plate 1). 'On the blue flower in the centre the *coniunctio* of the "royal" pair is represented by the sacrificial fire burning between them,' he wrote. 'The inner bond should be thought of as a compensating "consolidation" against disintegrating influences from without.'[28]

Such interpretations evidently influenced Miss X's inclusion of circular imagery, similar to Jung's paintings of mandalas, in her paintings. He maintained, however, that her paintings demonstrated 'the spontaneity of the psychic process and the transformation of a personal situation into the problem of individuation'.[29] Her mandala pictures 'rendered visible with pencil and brush,' he argued, a freely emerging 'ideogram of unconscious contents'.[30] Contrary, however, to his insistence on the freedom and spontaneity of the results of his individuation method, the repeated circular shapes in Miss X's later paintings look far from free and spontaneous. Rather they look as if they were the result of her being influenced by Jung's interpretations routinely to include these shapes in all her paintings during and following her analysis with him.

For Jung, however, interpreting and constructing the analysand's images in alchemical and other symbolic terms, rather than deconstructing and exposing the analysand's defensive use of such symbols, as in Freud's free association method of psychoanalysis, is the correct aim of psychoanalytic psycho- therapy. He deplored, in these terms, likening analysis to art. 'The danger of the aesthetic tendency is overvaluation of the formal or "artistic" worth of the fantasy-productions,' he maintained:

> The danger of wanting to understand the meaning is overvaluation of the content, which is subjected to intellectual analysis and interpretation, so that the essentially symbolic character of the product is lost.

The analysand should instead follow the lead of Goethe's Faust, he argued. They should ask of the paintings and imagery they construct in the course of their analysis, 'How am I affected by this sign?'[31]

Jung argued that the value of another analytical psychology method – 'active imagination' – resides in the signs and symbols of, and hence recon- nection of patients with archetypes in their collective unconscious to which, he said, this method leads. The method includes encouraging analysands to imagine themselves into their fantasies and dreams. An example was one of Jung's analysands who recounted a fantasy which Jung reported as follows:

> He sees his fiancée running down the road towards the river. It is winter, and the river is frozen. She runs out on the ice, and he follows her. She goes right out, and then the ice breaks, a dark fissure appears, and he is afraid she is going to jump in. And that is what happens: she jumps into the crack, and he watches her sadly.[32]

Countering the tendency of analysands to submit to, and passively give way to fantasy signs of the unconscious, Jung encouraged them actively to imagine themselves into them. He encouraged this patient to step into his fantasy to save his fiancée, as manifestation of his anima, he said, from slipping away into unconsciousness, manifested as water under the ice.

Jung's method of 'active imagination' also included encouraging analysands to discover the symbols or myths in terms of which they lived by imagining themselves into pictures they happened to see. He illustrated this with the case of an analysand, inhibited in pursuing this method, who, nevertheless, succeeded in imagining himself into an Alpine scene depicted on a poster at the railway station from which he travelled to his therapy sessions with Jung:

> He saw the meadow and the road and walked up the hill among the cows, and then he came up to the top and looked down, and there was the meadow again, sloping down, and below was a hedge with a stile. So he walked down and over the stile, and there was a little footpath that ran round a ravine, and a rock, and when he came round that rock, there was a small chapel, with its door standing a little ajar. He thought he would

like to enter, and so he pushed the door open and went in, and there upon an altar decorated with pretty flowers stood a wooden figure of the Mother of God. He looked up at her face, and in that exact moment something with pointed ears disappeared behind the altar.[33]

We could understand this as revealing more about the analysand's personal rather than collective unconscious. Alternatively we could understand it as defensive flight from what he wanted to repress and not know about in his personal life.

Understood as defensive flight from personal experience, active imagination into pictures one happens to see is akin to an incident in Chekhov's short story, *Three Years*, in which one of the main characters, Yulia, gains refuge from her unhappy marriage by imagining herself into Levitan's painting, *The Quiet Abode*.[34]

[She] imagined herself walking over the little bridge, then the little path, farther and farther, with stillness all around, the sleepy crakes calling, the fire twinkling in the distance. And for some reason, she suddenly felt she had already seen these same clouds which stretched across the red glow in the sky, and the woods, the field long ago and many times; she felt alone and longed to keep walking, walking, and walking down the path; and there, in the glow of the sunset, lay the calm reflection of something unearthly, eternal.[35]

Jung understood similar examples of imagining ourselves into pictures that happen to 'fall into our consciousness', as he put it, not as defensive but as revealing the unconscious forces by which we are lived. Focusing on the resulting fantasies, taking care not to interrupt what happens in them, the unconscious, he promised, 'will produce a series of images which make a complete story'.[36]

Active imagination also included for Jung imagining oneself into pictures one draws or paints oneself. He illustrated this with two pictures by a schizophrenic patient. He described the first picture (Figure 3.3.1)[37] as a vase containing the disparate elements of the patient's psyche so as to hold them together. It was an attempt at self-cure with its magic circle in the middle, he said, 'drawn round something that has to be prevented from escaping or protected against hostile influences'.[38] The circle serves to centre the patient's attention and visually unite the disparate elements of his psyche. Or so Jung claimed, adding that this is undermined by the vase toppling to the left, which he equated with the unconscious.

The second picture (Figure 3.3.2)[39] is more stable, Jung commented. It gathers together 'the living units of his [the patient's] unconscious, in the form of snakes, into the sacred vase', he said. It does not topple. Its inner animal figures have form. 'A most remarkable thing is that he [the patient]

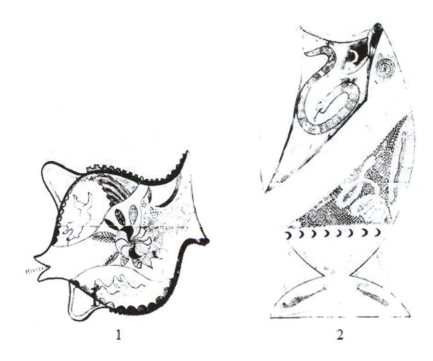

1   2

Figure 3.3 Pictures by unnamed patient

C.G. Jung (1935) The Tavistock Lectures. *The Symbolic Life. CW18*: 177, copyright © 1977 Routledge & Kegan Paul. Reproduced by permission of Taylor & Francis Books UK.

also gathers in the stars', Jung added, saying more about these than about the much more evident snakes in this picture. With the stars, he went on, the patient gathers in 'the cosmos, his world'. He also personifies the unconscious as 'a naked anima-figure who turns her back', her head and arm just visible at the top of this picture. The crescent moons are a further 'symbol of the unconscious', Jung continued.[40] 'The suggestive influence of the picture reacts on the psychological system of the patient and induces the same effect which he put into the picture.' Its healing effect is analogous to that of 'sacred images, of icons,' Jung argued. 'They cast their magic into our system and put us right, provided we put ourselves into them.'[41]

Freud, as I indicated at the beginning of this chapter, was utterly opposed to any such sacred, iconographic or idolatrous use of images. Jung's present-day art therapy followers are often similarly opposed to idolatry. But they are also inspired by his methods of active imagination and personification. Examples include the influential US art therapist, Shaun McNiff, who urges patients actively to imagine themselves into the art they create. Questioning them about it, he asks, 'Can you see red in the picture?', 'Can you touch it?',

'Where is the doorway?', 'How many trees are in the picture on the left?', 'Which color attracts your eye first?', and so on. He also emphasizes the importance of art therapists and their patients becoming skilled in knowing 'how to "feel into" the emerging image in order to help it form itself in ways that realize its potential'.[42]

McNiff does the same with his own art. 'When I paint and interact with the images,' he says, 'I enter the imagination of the picture and the stories that emerge from them.'[43] He urges himself and others to discover their response to the immediately manifest 'colors, textures, bodies, faces, environment' of their art by letting them 'speak', he says.[44] Adopting Jung's personification method, he also encourages patients to speak with details of their art-work as though they were people by asking them questions such as 'What are you feeling?' and 'What do you need?'[45]

Unlike Jung, however, McNiff and other Jung-influenced art therapists stress the importance of attending to the impact of the physical stuff of painting and picture-making. UK art therapist, David Maclagan, calls this 'psychological aesthetics'. By this he means, he says, 'the relation between the actual (aesthetic) qualities of painting, such as line, colour, handling, composition and so on and the inner (psychological) effects that these have on the spectator'.[46]

Examples include the 'impastoed, churned and wiped passages of paint', Maclagan says, of Francis Bacon's paintings, 'compressed into the outlined carcass of the body, so that there is, almost literally, an elision between gestures of painterly making and bodily motions (internal as well as external)'.[47] Writing about Bacon's 1957 painting, *Study for Portrait of Van Gogh IV*,[48] based on Van Gogh's 1888 painting, *The Artist on the Road to Tarascon*,[49] another commentator observes that, after making a preliminary sketch, 'Bacon would then allow chance and accident to intervene. The finished painting would often come about through a process that required the image to be first destroyed and then re-born through the chaos of the paint itself.'[50]

Lucian Freud's paintings, his 1985 self-portrait for instance,[51] similarly convey their impact largely through the substance of paint. Robert Hughes writes:

> The way Freud perceives a form and builds it up from oily mud on a piece of cloth; the way he constructs analysed equivalents to reality – all that, at best, is inspiring. It represents an order of experience totally different from the relatively weightless coming-into-sight of a photographic image or a silkscreen.[52]

The artist and art historian, James Elkins,[53] likewise highlights the thick brushstrokes of Rembrandt's self-portraits.[54] He draws attention to the mud from which pigment is made in likening painting to alchemy and in criticizing Jung's concentration on alchemy's spiritual side to the neglect of the bodily substances – milk, piss, shit and semen included – used by alchemists in seeking to transform base into precious matter. Freud long ago similarly criticized Jung for replacing his sexual theory with a notion of the libido as spirit divorced from the body after having previously warned him not to abandon, in favour of 'occultism', his theory of the libido as a bodily drive.[55]

As well as criticizing Jung for neglecting the body and substance of the materials with which alchemists worked and artists still work, many of his art therapy followers also criticize his focus on interpreting the analysand's dream- and fantasy-images in terms of preconceived archetypes. Maclagan likens this to the art therapy patient's 'inhibition or the refusal of imagination [evident in] stereotyped images, sentimental cliches or in tethered patterns or doodles'. Certainly, Maclagan acknowledges, Jung recognized the value of fantasy- and image-based thinking, unlike Freud who devalued such thinking in favour of verbal abstraction. Jung rightly stressed the importance of 'imaginative fidelity to the image in the course of its elaboration,' Maclagan continues,

> but in his own case studies, and more obviously in those of many of his followers, there is a tendency, once the image has been adequately realized, to tether this elaboration to the hitching posts of archetypal symbolism.

Maclagan, by contrast, favours enabling the image to 'speak' in its own terms, not in terms of preconceived symbols.[56] McNiff similarly criticizes Jung. 'I create from where I am and not from where I think I should be,' he says of his art work. He similarly urges his art therapy readers: 'Trust the process. Relax and follow its lead,' he tells them. 'Let it speak through you. Don't try to control it. Open to that which appears from outside your frame of reference.'[57]

We could understand Jung's rather different approach to active imagination in tying his analysands' images to preconceived, socially given, albeit archaic, symbols as defensive flight from their personal experience akin to the defensive repression of embodied sexual wishes and desires and their displacement into overvaluation of symbols and abstractions as described by Freud in his account of obsessional neurosis and religion. We could also describe this displacement as defence against aggression. It was in these terms that Winnicott criticized Jung's version of psychoanalysis. He noted the importance accorded by Jung in his autobiography to an incident in which, coming out of school near Basle Cathedral, he saw a vision of God sitting high above the world on a golden throne from under which 'an enormous turd falls,' said Jung, 'upon the sparkling new roof, shatters it, and breaks the walls of the cathedral asunder'.[58]

Freud criticized Jung for underestimating the psychological importance of sex. Winnicott criticized him for being 'out of touch with instinct and object-relating', specifically instincts of destruction and aggression towards oneself and others. Taking issue with Jung's account of the above incident, Winnicott wrote:

> We could not expect to find Jung feeling God to be a projection of his own infantile omnipotence and the shitting as a projection of his own hate of the father in the mother; or at a more primitive level, his own destruction of the good object because of its being real in the sense of being outside the area of his omnipotence. Jung describes his playing (which had to be done very much alone till he went to school) as a constant building and rebuilding followed always by the staging of an earthquake and the destruction of the building. What we cannot find in the material Jung provides is imaginative destruction followed by a sense of guilt and then by construction. It seems that the thing that was repressed in Jung's early infancy, that is, before the infantile breakdown [his 'psychotic illness', according to Winnicott], was primitive aggression.[59]

Continuing in this vein, Winnicott argued that Jung's preoccupation with mandala symbolism demonstrated his

> absolute failure to come to terms with destructiveness, and with chaos, disintegration, and the other madnesses. It is an obsessional flight from disintegration . . . in search of the centre of his self . . . [rather than] full and satisfying use of a self that is a unit and is well grounded.[60]

Winnicott was not the first to criticize Jung's neglect of bodily instincts or drives as defensive. So too did Freud. So too, by implication, did Jung's first psychoanalytic patient, Sabina Spielrein, to whose work I will now turn.

Chapter 4

Spielrein

Born in Rostov-on-Don in Russia, in 1885, Sabina Spielrein first met Jung on being admitted by him as an in-patient to the Burghölzli mental hospital in Zurich on 17 August 1904. Case notes from the sanatorium in Interlaken, where she had previously been a patient, included a drawing by her of a man standing over a woman seemingly electrocuting her. Another image below it depicts two doctors – Heller and Hisselbaum – with the word 'devil', in Russian script, under them (Figure 4.1).[1]

'She constantly demands that the writer inflict pain on her, do something to hurt her, treat her badly in some way,' Jung wrote about Spielrein in his Burghölzli notes about her case.[2] Recounting details of her masochism and anal obsessions to Freud, he wrote:

> First trauma between the 3rd and 4th year. Saw her father spanking her older brother on the bare bottom. Powerful impression. Couldn't help thinking afterwards that she had defecated on her father's hand. From the 4th–7th year convulsive attempts to defecate on her own feet, in the following manner: she sat on the floor with one foot beneath her, pressed her heel against her anus and tried to defecate and at the same time to prevent defecation. Often retained the stool for 2 weeks in this way! Has no idea how she hit upon this peculiar business; says it was completely instinctive, and accompanied by blissfully shuddersome feelings. Later this phenomenon was superseded by vigorous masturbation.[3]

Did this anal complex find its twin in Jung, given that he too had anal preoccupations, including still remembering his schoolboy vision of seeing God's turd smashing Basle Cathedral?

Perhaps Spielrein sensed this complex in Jung. She wrote not long after her analysis with Jung began:

> One goes to the doctor because one needs to be free of a complex, one confides in the doctor because one knows, or notices, his interest

Figure 4.1 Spielrein: Drawings

C. Covington and B. Wharton (eds) (2003) *Sabina Spielrein*. London: Routledge, p. 91.

and sympathy; the interest corresponds to understanding, that is to possession of the same complex.

Treatment enables 'the psycho-sexual component of the ego to transform itself,' she continued, 'by means of art or a simple reaction – as you wish'.[4] In her case, she initially agreed with Jung, the transforming and healing complex was provided by the inspiring image of Siegfried, whom Jung later saw as personification of his heroic leanings during his 1913–16 self-analysis. The 'Siegfried symbol', he wrote soon after to her, recalling the role played by this symbol in her analysis, which he now recounted in terms of his then developing method of individuation, was a 'bridge' to her 'individual development'.[5]

After recovering from the hysterical neurosis causing, according to Jung, her 1904 Burghölzli hospitalization, Spielrein qualified as a doctor in Zurich, and then joined Freud's circle in Vienna. By then she had become wary of symbols as cure of psychological illness and distress. Writing about the self-denial of women in oneness with the men with whom they are in love, she described the self-defeating illusory oneness of patients with collectively given symbols as defensive flight from their personal and individual experience. This is particularly evident in *dementia praecox*, she said, a condition which had been renamed 'schizophrenia' by her thesis supervisor, Eugen Bleuler, in his 1911 book about psychiatry. In a paper she presented the same year, 1911, to Freud's psychoanalytic group in Vienna she wrote, as follows, about the schizophrenic's initial battle against losing themselves in oneness with collectively given symbols:

> The collective psyche wants to make the ego-image into an impersonal typical image. The personal psyche tries to restrain this dissolution, causing patients anxiously to transfer the feeling-tone of dissolving complexes to collateral associations that the ego then fixes.[6]

In giving way to this process, she went on, schizophrenics become alienated from themselves. 'Thoughts become depersonalized and "affect" the patient since they come from depths outside the ego, from depths that already have transformed the "I" into a "we" or, perhaps, a "they",' she said. If this defence persists the patient becomes apathetic. 'The life of the psyche also is obliterated . . . the need for differentiation and fulfilment of personal wishes fade away,' she observed, 'ego-differentiated images are assimilated (and dissolved) and transformed into universal images that are typical, archaic, and collective'.[7]

Whereas, in schizophrenia, patients defend against their personal experience by identifying with collectively given symbols, artists, she argued, use symbols in their art to convey their experience to others. Spielrein wrote:

> A personal image-content, derived from material of times past, blends with a similar content and comes into being as a typical collective wish at the expense of the individual. The new content is then projected externally as a work of art.[8]

Or, as she also put it,

> Each image that we share with a neighbour, either directly or as a work of art, is a differentiated product of a primal experience originating in our psyche. . . . In each declaration of a thought, which is a portrait of an image, we establish a generalization in which words are symbols, serving to mould universally human and universally comprehensible ideas around the personal, i.e., the impressions are depersonalized. The purely personal can never be understood by others.[9]

Symbols thus have their uses, alongside personal experience, in creating art.

Whereas the artist uses symbols to convey their personal experience, they can be used in mental illness as a defence against any such recognition, and communication of the patient's personal experience to themselves or others. Following Spielrein's 1911 talk to this effect, Freud wrote of the schizophrenic's defensive flight from personal and perceptual experience to impersonal, collectively given symbols and words. He wrote of their defensively withdrawing, he said, 'instinctual cathexis from the points which represent the unconscious presentation of the object'. This has the effect, he maintained, 'that the part of the presentation of this object which belongs to the system *Pcs.* [preconscious] – namely the word-presentations corresponding to it – . . . receive a more intense cathexis'.[10]

Far from attending to the defensive use of symbols and words in mental illness, Jung regarded them – particularly names of symbolic figures – as means of connecting, via personification, with archetypes in the collective unconscious. He told Spielrein:

> You know perhaps that I distinguish a personal unconscious (the domain of the repressed personal contents) from an absolute or 'collective' unconscious. The latter contains primal images. The hieroglyphs are symbols of these. The new development that will come announces itself in an old language, in symbolic signs.[11]

Spielrein, however, located symbols not in the collective unconscious but in the subconscious. She described this aspect of the mind in terms similar to those used by Freud to describe the preconscious as storehouse of words mediating drive-based unconscious hallucinations and fantasies to consciousness. 'Whenever fatigue, narcosis, or any other form of intoxication weakens "directed" thought – "symbolic" thought sets in,' Spielrein told Jung, 'the subliminal thought process converts thoughts into symbols, not only visual symbols but also acoustical, dynamic "thought symbols," etc.'[12] Banished into unconsciousness, she added, the instincts resort to 'subliminal symbolic languages' mediated by the subconscious. These symbolic languages reveal, she continued, 'possibilities and likelihoods that are "in the air," i.e., very close to realization'. But they can also 'err', because, she said, 'the subconscious is suggestible'.[13] Asking Jung what he meant by calling subliminal symbols 'semiotic signs', she also referred to Freud's account of symbols as defensive dream-work 'disguise for instinctive desire'.[14]

How, though, do we learn the symbols and words of the culture into which we are born? Spielrein provided a beginning answer to this question in a talk she gave at the International Congress of Psychoanalysis held in The Hague in 1920. In her talk she described infants acquiring words through repeating the sounds associated with the pleasurable sounds they make with their lips during breast-feeding. These sounds evoke preconceptions in those looking after them.

[M]others and nurses adapt themselves instinctively to the kinds of language that the child is ready to produce, they feel into the young psyche,
finding material in the depths of their own mind, in their own earlier
stages of development, and allowing this to speak to the child in an
unconscious way.[15]

She illustrated this with various examples, including an 8-month-old baby girl
making the sound 'p', this reminding adults around her of the word 'Papa',
which they said. To this she responded by first repeating her 'p' sound, and by
then, after a few minutes' pause, saying something similar to what they had
said, namely 'Pa-pa-pa'.[16]

The same year, 1920, as Spielrein gave this talk, Freud quoted approvingly
from the 1911 talk she had given to his psychoanalytic group in Vienna,
in which she had described not only schizophrenic defensiveness but also
women's self-destructive oneness with those with whom they are in love.
Freud called the latter evidence of 'primary masochism'. He linked it with the
'Nirvana principle',[17] the term used by another early woman psychoanalyst,
Barbara Low, to describe 'the desire of the newborn creature to return to that
stage of omnipotence,' she said, 'where there are no non-filled desires, in
which it existed in the mother's womb'.[18] Freud attributed this desire to the
existence of a death instinct impelling us to repeat stimulation so as to reduce
its arousing effect to zero, equivalent to the zero stimulation preceding birth
and following our death.

He illustrated this death instinct motivated repetition compulsion, as
he understood it, with the example of his 18-month-old grandson, Ernst,
repeatedly throwing things away from him, saying 'o-o-o-o' as he did so.
Rejecting the possibility that this 'o-o-o-o' sound was meaningless – 'a mere
interjection', as he put it – Freud assumed, as did his daughter, Ernst's
mother, Sophie, that, in saying 'o-o-o-o', Ernst meant 'fort' (the German for
'gone').[19] This, together with Freud's evident preconceptions about children's
upset about being separated from their mothers, doubtless contributed to his
interpreting Ernst's repeated throwing things away from him, saying 'o-o-o-o'
as he did so, as means by which Ernst tried to reduce to zero the upset caused
him by sometimes being separated from his mother. Freud likewise interpreted Ernst telling his mother, 'Baby o-o-o-o', after he had been separated
from her longer than usual. He understood this as referring to the fact that,
while she was gone, Ernst had made his reflected image in a mirror gone by
lowering himself below it so as to make his reflection disappear.

Ernst also represented his father as gone. Or so Freud claimed in interpreting Ernst's play a year later when, having learnt that his father had gone to
the war, he threw down toys which annoyed him, saying 'Go to the fwont!'
This evidently evoked in Freud his now developing ideas about the Oedipal
rivalry of boys with their fathers for sexual possession of their mothers. He
accordingly interpreted Ernst telling his offending toys to go to the front as

signifying his equating them with his father whom, said Freud, '[Ernst] had no desire to be disturbed [by] in his sole possession of his mother'.[20]

I recount these examples in some detail because they nicely illustrate ways in which, just as in Spielrein's account of the infant's early acquisition of words, the child's talk and play evokes already existing ideas in adults around them. This, in turn, shapes the child's developing use of words, and their formation of symbols and fantasies. This is particularly evident in Melanie Klein's child analysis development of psychoanalysis, beginning with a talk she gave to psychoanalytic colleagues in Budapest in 1919.

Chapter 5

Klein

In her 1919 talk Klein detailed conversations with her 4-year-old son, Erich, whom she presented as though he were an unrelated analytic patient of hers. She referred to him as Fritz. Their talk together, as she detailed it, was similar to the interactions between babies and those looking after them described by Spielrein. It was also similar to Freud's account of his and his daughter Sophie's interaction with her son, Ernst, in interpreting his 'o-o-o-o' sounds, accompanying his throwing things away from him, as meaning 'gone'. Just as Freud recommended analysts to supplement the analysand's free associations, when they prove insufficient or fail, with the knowledge of dream-symbolism which these associations evoke in them, Klein supplemented Erich's free associations, when they became inhibited, with the knowledge and ideas which they evoked in her.

She attributed Erich's inhibition, aged 4, to unconscious anxiety about the role of his father in his conception since, when he asked her, 'Where was I before I was born?', and 'How is a person made?', she had told him about the baby's growth in the mother's body but had not mentioned the father's role because, she said, 'he had not at that time asked directly about it'.[1] To free his subsequent imaginative talk and play from inhibition she supplemented, as follows, a fragment of fantasy he happened to utter while sitting on his chamber pot early one morning:

Erich: The kakis [faeces] are on the balcony already, [they] have run upstairs again and don't want to go into the garden [pot].
Klein: They are the children then that grow in the stomach? The kakis are made from food; real children are not made from food.
Erich: I know that, they are made of milk.
Klein: Oh no, they are made of something that papa makes and the egg that is inside mamma.
Erich: I know that.
Klein: Papa can make something with his wiwi that really looks rather like milk and is called seed; he makes it like doing wiwi only not so much. Mamma's wiwi is different to papa's.

Erich: I know that!
Klein: Mamma's wiwi is like a hole. If papa puts his wiwi into mamma's wiwi and makes the seed there, then the seed runs in deeper into her body and when it meets with one of the little eggs that are inside mamma, then that little egg begins to grow and it becomes a child.
Erich: I would so much like to see how a child is made inside like that.
Klein: That is impossible until you are big, because it can't be done till then, but then you can do it yourself.
Erich: But then I would like to do it to mamma.
Klein: That can't be, mamma can't be your wife for she is the wife of your papa, and then papa would have no wife.
Erich: But we could both do it to her.
Klein: No, that can't be. Every man has only one wife. When you are big your mamma will be old. Then you will marry a beautiful young girl and she will be your wife.
Erich: (nearly in tears) But shan't we live in the same house together with mamma?
Klein: Certainly, and your mamma will always love you but she can't be your wife.
Erich: But I would just once like to see how the child gets in and out.[2]

Klein's response to Erich's talk was influenced, she acknowledged, both by determination to avoid the ills resulting from repressing children's knowledge of sex as described by Freud, and by mindfulness of the psychoanalyst, Anton Freund, emphasizing to her the importance of addressing the child's unconscious anxieties in analysing them.

Her above-quoted supplementing of Erich's fragment of fantasy with ideas and images it evoked in her freed his talk, play and imagination from its previous inhibition. Soon after he told her a 'dream-phantasy',[3] she said, about a little car getting between two other cars, each of which had a connecting-rod. She interpreted this as signifying his getting between her and his father in their sexual intercourse together. Erich then told her a dream in which he imagined himself, together with his brother and sister, being pursued by men with sticks, guns, and bayonets from whom they hid in a woman's house even though she told them not to. Supplementing this with the version of Freudian theory that it evoked in her, Klein told Erich that the sticks, guns and bayonets of his dream represented 'his father's big wiwi that he both wishes for and is afraid of'.[4] Further fragments of fantasy included his telling her:

There is a room in the stomach, in it there are tables and chairs. Someone sits down on a chair and lays his head on the table and then the whole house falls down, the ceiling on to the floor, the table too tumbles down, the house tumbles down.

'Who is the someone and how did he get inside?', asked Klein. 'A little stick came through the wiwi into the belly and into the stomach that way,' Erich explained. To this Klein told him, 'he had imagined himself in his mamma's place and wished his papa might do with him what he does with her'. He was afraid, she said, 'that if this stick – papa's wiwi – gets into his wiwi he will be hurt and then inside his belly, in his stomach, everything will be destroyed, too'.[5]

Overlooking her contribution, as Erich's mother, to the development of his fantasies, and to those of her two older children, Hans and Melitta, Klein also overlooked the wider social factors, mediated by mothers and others, which shape the development of children's fantasies and capacity for symbolization. She doubtless also rejected Jung's notion of inherited 'anthropological symbolism', and his assumption that symbols express 'a striving for a higher ethical ideal . . . implicit in the symbol and . . . symbolized by it', as described by her London colleague, Ernest Jones, in detailing two forms of symbolism – personal and social.[6]

Social progress in the development of symbols in religion and science involves, Jones said,

> the constant unmasking of previous symbolisms, the recognition that these, though previously thought to be literally true, were really only aspects or representations of the truth, the only ones of which our minds were – for either affective or intellectual reasons – at the time capable.[7]

To this the art historian, Ernst Gombrich, added that this could equally characterize the development of symbolism in art. He attributed Jones' neglect of this to the fact that, as he put it, 'the aspect of art that attracted most [psychoanalytic] attention was not so much the historical progress of modes of representation, which is so admirably summed up [by Jones], as its expressive significance'.[8]

This was also the case with Klein's account of symbolism. Not mentioning Jones' attention to the social development of symbols in religion and science, and overlooking, as I have said, her contribution, as a mother, to the development of her children's use of symbols, she adopted Jones' account of what he called 'true symbolism',[9] by which he meant symbols generated by children and adults in repressing and displacing 'unconscious material' onto more acceptable objects to symbolize it.[10] He illustrated this with the example of Freud's 18-year-old patient, Dora, using the defence of 'displacement from below upwards', as Jones put it, in repressing and displacing to her mouth the genital excitement supposed by Freud to have been aroused in her by her father's friend, Herr K, embracing her. This was one source, according to Freud, of her oral symptoms, including anorexia. 'Only what is repressed is symbolized,' Jones emphasized, 'only what is repressed needs to be symbolized.'[11]

What, then, is the difference between the defensive generation of symbols supposed by Freud to be involved in the genesis of neurotic symptoms, anorexia included, and the social and historical development of symbols in science and art, which Freud called sublimation? Are all symbols individually generated – whether in neurosis, science, or art – as effect of defensive repression and displacement? Do they all involve displacement? Freud suggested this in describing sublimation as only different from the displacement occurring in neurosis in involving the adaptive and creative capacity of the sexual instinct, as he put it, 'to exchange its originally sexual aim for another one, which is no longer sexual but which is psychically related to the first aim'.[12] Adopting this characterization of sublimation, Klein attributed the genius of Leonardo to his displacing sexual or libidinal interest in the breast, penis, and in a bird's tail, evident from his remembering or imagining (see p. 23) a bird opening his mouth with its tail when he was a baby, onto scientific interest in the flight of birds. Klein argued:

> In Leonardo's case not only was an identification established between nipple, penis and bird's tail, but this identification became merged into an interest in the motion of this object, in the bird itself and its flight and the space in which it flew.[13]

In neurosis, by contrast, displacement is inhibited by fixation and repression, she argued. This calls for the analyst to address the unconscious anxiety causing this inhibition. Or so she suggested, using children's drawings to illustrate the point. She noted, for instance, Erich's inhibited drawings, aged 9, of 'railway-lines with stations and towns'.[14] She also described a 9-year-old patient, Werner's drawing of a motor-cycle with an enormous motor, 'clearly drawn as a penis', she said. On it, she added, 'sat a woman who sets the motor-cycle in motion', its cranking sounds falling in pointed rays on a 'poor little man'. Werner then drew 'a giant with huge eyes and a head containing aerials and wireless sets' together with a tiny man climbing up the Eiffel Tower, represented by a skyscraper, to see the giant.[15] Together these drawings symbolized, said Klein, Werner's admiration for his mother through which he came to admire his father.

Freud's psychoanalyst daughter, Anna Freud, however, took issue with Klein thus translating what her child patients did in analysis as symbolizing unconscious fantasies about their parents.

> If the child overturns a lamp-post or a toy figure she interprets it as something of an aggressive impulse against the father; a deliberate collision between two cars as evidence of an observation of sexual union between the parents. Her procedure consists in accompanying the child's activities with translations and interpretations, which themselves – like the

interpretations of the adult's free associations – exert a further influence upon the patient.[16]

To this Anna Freud added:

> The child who upsets a toy lamp-post may on its walk the day before have come across some incident in connection with such an object; the car collision may be reproducing some happening in the street; and the child who runs towards a lady visitor and opens her handbag is not necessarily, as Mrs. Klein maintains, thereby symbolically expressing its curiosity as to whether its mother's womb conceals another little brother or sister, but may be connecting some experience of the previous day when someone brought it a little present in a similar receptacle.[17]

Rejecting Klein's interpretation of what children do in analysis as symbolizing fantasies about their parents, Anna Freud also rejected her interpreting what they do in analysis as symbolizing their transference of these fantasies onto the analyst: 'the behaviour of the children's analyst, as we have described him,' she maintained, 'is not such as to produce a transference that can be well interpreted'.[18]

Meanwhile Freud had argued that children resolve love and hate of one parent in Oedipal rivalry with them for sexual possession of the opposite-sex parent by identifying with their rival, specifically with the father as superego representative of society's law against incest. This figure, he maintained, is formed on the basis of two contradictory orders: first, 'You ought to be like this (like your father)' in obeying his commands; second, 'You may not be like this (like your father) – that is, you may not do all that he does; some things are his prerogative'.[19] You cannot sexually possess your mother as he does.

Anna Freud concluded from this that, since in early childhood the child's ego and superego are weak, the work of the child analyst entails strengthening their child patients' ego and superego by educating them, and by persuading them to identify with, and act in accordance with their ego and superego. Examples from Anna Freud's psychoanalytic practice included a 6-year-old girl, Adelaide Sweetzer, who, in the course of her analysis, said Anna Freud, 'began to communicate to me a large number of anal fantasies'. This was fine. But then, to the disgust of others in the household where she was staying, Adelaide regaled them with these fantasies. Determined to strengthen Adelaide's superego inhibitions against doing this, Anna Freud told Adelaide that, if she continued telling her anal fantasies at home, her analysis would end. Her analysis could continue on condition that she told these things, said Anna Freud, 'only to me and to no one else'.[20] The child analyst's role is 'to analyse and educate,' she maintained, 'that is to say in the same breath he must allow and forbid, loosen and bind again'.[21]

Klein argued the reverse. Child analysis, she insisted, should focus on freeing children from the inhibiting effects on their ego development of over-harsh and vengeful superego representations of their parents avenging themselves on their oral, anal, and genital attacks on their sexual coupling. Far from strengthening these superego figures, the task of the analyst entails making conscious so as to deconstruct and dispel the fantasies making them so harsh and inhibiting.[22]

Klein illustrated the ills done children by over-harsh superego versions of their parents with examples from her child analysis development of psycho-analysis. She also illustrated these ills with the example of a Scandinavian painter, Ruth Kjär, who, in severe bouts of depression, complained of an empty space inside her. Klein attributed this to supposed persisting childhood fantasies in Kjär of destroying her mother's sexual coupling with her father,[23] and of her mother revenging herself by attacking and emptying Kjär of her sexuality. Klein went on implicitly to argue that Kjär became a painter through facing inner emptiness, symbolized by the space left empty on a wall of her home by her artist brother-in-law removing a painting of his which had been hanging there, and to her filling the space with a painting of a woman, and with other paintings of women, including one of a woman destroyed, recently identified as a painting by an artist, Ruth Weber, alias Ruth Kjär.[24] This painting was followed by Kjär painting a portrait of her mother as magnificently repaired, at least as Klein interpreted it on the basis of a newspaper article about Kjär.[25]

What is to be done, though, when fantasy- and symbol-formation, let alone painting, comes to a standstill in inhibited imagination and free association? Freud argued, in effect, that this calls, in analysis, for analysts to supplement the analysand's stalled associations with the symbolic meanings these associations evoke in the analyst. Striking examples of Klein doing precisely this can be found in her case history of a 4-year-old patient, whom she referred to as Dick, and who might be diagnosed nowadays as a case of autism or Asperger syndrome.

Klein preceded her account of Dick's analysis by adding to her previous theory of symbol-formation the claim that, just as children displace libidinal impulses from their original objects onto symbols standing for them, they also displace destructive impulses from their original objects (specifically the sexual coupling of their mothers with their fathers) onto relatively neutral objects. 'Since the child desires to destroy the organs (penis, vagina, breasts) which stand for the objects, he conceives a dread of the latter. This anxiety contributes to make him equate the organs in question with other things,' she maintained. To this she added:

> owing to this equation these in their turn become objects of anxiety, and so he [the child] is impelled constantly to make other and new equations, which form the basis of his interest in the new objects and of symbolism.

Klein described these individually generated symbols, in effect, in circular terms as both effect and cause of fantasy- and symbol-formation. '[Not] only does symbolism come to be the foundation of all phantasy and sublimation but, more than that,' she also argued, 'it is the basis of the subject's relation to the outside world and to reality in general'.[26]

The individually generated displacement and sublimation Klein described as contributing to symbol- and fantasy-formation can, she argued, become inhibited if the child is over-anxious. Freud had written of the inhibiting effect of the 'anxiety-idea' of castration in the case of his 5-year-old patient, Little Hans, and in the case of his Russian artist patient, Sergei Pankieff, when they were 4.[27] To this Klein added that symbol-formation can become inhibited by fixation due to limits in 'the ego's capacity at a very early period to tolerate the pressure of the earliest anxiety-situations'.[28]

In Dick's case this tolerance was evidently very limited. He had acquired some symbols. But his symbol-formation had become severely impeded by destructive fantasies, said Klein, as evidenced by his refusing to bite food, and by his inability, aged 4, to hold scissors, knives or tools. His curiosity was also inhibited. He showed little interest in anything. He strung sounds together meaninglessly. He repeated words mechanically. And he seemed not to grasp the purpose or meaning of things around him. Almost his only interest, it seems, was an obsession with trains and stations, door-handles, and the opening and shutting of doors.

Given his mute and aimless running around her consulting room at their first meeting, Klein supplemented what she knew of this obsession with the Oedipal ideas it evoked in her. Getting two toy trains, she called one 'Daddy', the other 'Dick', and put them side by side. When Dick responded by making the Dick train roll to the window, saying 'station', she interpreted, 'The station is mummy; Dick is going into mummy'.[29] 'She slams the symbolism on him with complete brutality,' Lacan later commented. 'She hits him a brutal verbalisation of the Oedipal myth, almost as revolting for us as for any reader – You are the little train, you want to fuck your mother.'[30] Kristeva is more approving. In her biography of Klein she lauds the method of child analysis which Klein pioneered as forwarding a technique in which, Kristeva writes, 'the therapist's named fantasy, which interprets the proto-fantasy enacted by the child, raises the child's emergent thought to a third level: a level that shall be termed symbolic'.[31]

As for Klein's analysis of Dick, her interpreting and putting into words what his train and station obsession might unconsciously symbolize for him, was followed by his previously repressed anxiety coming more to the fore. After she made this interpretation he ran into the space between the doors of her room, shut himself in, said 'dark', and ran out again. 'It is dark inside mummy. Dick is inside dark mummy,' commented Klein. At this he asked, 'Nurse?', to which she replied, 'Nurse is soon coming', which he repeated. The next day he again and again asked, 'Nurse coming?' He also put the Dick train in Klein's dark entrance hall and insisted it stay there. He did much the same in his third session with Klein. On this occasion he also ran behind a chest of drawers, repeatedly asked for his nurse, and, for the first time, was evidently interested in Klein saying, 'Nurse is coming soon'.[32] He also pointed at a toy coal cart, said 'Cut', and tried to scratch at pieces of black wood on the cart representing coal. Because he was unable to hold the scissors he looked to Klein to do the cutting for him, which she did, and which she interpreted as symbolizing cutting faeces from his mother after he threw the damaged cart into a drawer, saying 'Gone'.[33]

His destructive fantasies now became increasingly conscious and available for him to put into words. Examples included his raising a little toy man to his mouth, gnashing his teeth, and saying, 'Tea daddy', meaning, said Klein, 'Eat daddy'.[34] This was followed with remorse and with his putting the toy man into Klein's hand. Another time, seeing pencil shavings in her lap, he said, 'Poor Mrs Klein'. Still another time, he said, 'Poor curtain'. It was his 'premature empathy' with his surroundings, Klein argued, that had been decisive in bringing his destructive impulses and their symbolic and fantasy development and sublimation to a halt by taking refuge in, the phantasies of the dark, empty mother's body',[35] symbolized by his hiding in the dark space between the doors of her room.

Klein's account, in these terms, of Dick's analysis was published in 1930. Previously she had described boys defending against conflict between love and hate of their mothers with 'excessive protestations of masculinity' and with 'narcissistic over-estimation of the penis'. She had described girls defending against analogous conflicts by 'turning to the father' and identifying with him.[36] Citing Klein's article to this effect, Freud wrote of girls being impelled to shift from Oedipal desire for the mother to Oedipal desire for the father by their intensely ambivalent love and hate of her. 'The very surprising sexual activity of little girls in relation to their mother is manifested chronologically in oral, sadistic, and finally even in phallic trends directed towards her,' he wrote. These trends are expressed, he added, 'in a form forced on them by early repression, a fear of being killed by the mother'.[37]

Freud followed this by replacing, to some extent, his previous terminology of unconscious and conscious, primary and secondary mental process with an account of three agencies of the mind – id, ego and superego. He likened the id to 'a chaos, a cauldron full of seething excitations'. He also abandoned, to some extent, his earlier treatment aim of undoing the analysand's art- and dream-work defensive disguise of the unconscious wishes he believed constituted their symptoms in favour of reviewing and shoring up the ego's defences. 'Where id was there shall ego be,' he now declared. 'It is a work of culture – not unlike the draining of the Zuider Zee.'[38]

Anna Freud, in turn, developed this treatment goal in a book published to coincide with his eightieth birthday. Again emphasizing, as she had in her earlier book about child analysis, the value of the analyst strengthening the analysand's ego by fostering their identification with the analyst's ego and superego, she also illustrated the adaptive value of identification with others in everyday life. A major example, reiterated by her followers, is the defence she called 'identification with the aggressor', by which she meant identification with the authority of those with whom the child or adult is otherwise in conflict.[39]

Adherents of Klein's approach to psychoanalysis adopted a different tack. An important example was the emphasis by the psychoanalyst, James Strachey, on the value of psychoanalytic interpretations to the extent that, far from fostering the analysand's transference identification with the analyst as seemingly personifying their superego fantasies, the analyst recognizes and puts this identification into words so it can become conscious, deconstructed and dispelled.[40] These fantasies can involve manic delusions of grandeur as described by Klein's Berlin analyst, Karl Abraham,[41] and as subsequently described by her as a defence against grief and depression.

Klein's first major essay about this was published in 1935. In it she described mania as a defence against 'depressive position' recognition of ambivalence, and remorse for the harm done those we love by also hating them. Alternatively we may defend against recognition of ambivalence by splitting love and hate apart, with the risk of this leading to 'persecution-anxiety', she said, due to what is split off and hated being projected into others who are then experienced as persecuting and attacking us.[42]

Persecution-anxiety and mania are thus two effects, according to Klein, of inability to withstand what she described as depressive position anxieties. Her colleague, Joan Riviere, said:

> The content of the depressive position is the situation in which all one's loved ones within are dead and destroyed, all goodness is dispersed, lost, in fragments, wasted and scattered to the winds; nothing is left within but utter desolation.[43]

Riviere followed this with an account, as follows, of the destructive fantasies of early infancy:

> Limbs shall trample, kick and hit; lips, fingers and hands shall suck, twist, pinch; teeth shall bite, gnaw, mangle and cut, mouth shall devour, swallow and 'kill' (annihilate); yes kill by a look, pierce and penetrate; breath and mouth hurt by noise, as the child's own sensitive ears have experienced.[44]

Together with Klein, Riviere wrote about responding to depressive position recognition of the destruction wrought by these hateful impulses by repairing their devastating effects.[45]

Riviere's book, with Klein, about this was followed by the Edinburgh-based psychoanalytic psychotherapist, W.R.D. Fairbairn, writing similarly about art in terms of destruction and its repair. He noted the destruction impelling art. He gave the examples of Goya's painting, *Disasters of War*,[46] and Francis Picabia's *La Nuit espagnole*.[47] He also noted the violence of Van Gogh's brushwork in his paintings of cypress trees.[48] Fairbairn argued:

> Since the chief source of inner tension is found to lie in the pressure of destructive urges, and since artistic activity both relieves this inner tension and is essentially creative, we are justified in concluding that the principle of restitution is the governing principle in art.[49]

Instances of such restitution included for Fairbairn the meticulous painting by Vermeer of domestic interiors which give, he said, 'a very definite impression of the integrity of the object'. He went on to describe Paul Klee's *Dynamics of a Head* (similar to his 1922 painting, *Senecio*),[50] and Picasso's painting, *Woman in a Chemise Sitting in an Armchair*. It was included, like Picabia's *La Nuit espagnole*, and Klee's *Dynamics of a Head*, but with the title, *The Woman with the Golden Breasts*, in Herbert Read's celebration of the 1936 London exhibition of surrealism (Figure 5.1).[51] For Fairbairn this painting by Picasso showed both sadistic and destructive 'tearing in pieces' and integrating repair of 'objects reduced to fragments'.[52] In this, wittingly or unwittingly, Fairbairn reiterated an account of art-making similar to that of the surrealist writer, Georges Bataille, who described art as developing out of 'progressive destruction' and the childish impulse evoked by a blank piece of paper to cover it in scribbles.[53]

Klein's analysand, John Rickman, like Fairbairn, similarly explained art as effect of destruction and its psychological ramifications in the form of depressive position states of mind. The artist, he said, 'goes behind the veil which screens the source of our dejection and brings back evidence for the triumph of the creative impulse over the forces of destruction'.[54] Painting, he argued, begins with a destructive attack by artists in making marks on their canvas. These persist in their finished art-work with the effect of evoking similar fantasies of destruction and its repair in the minds of the artist's public.

Children, he argued, express similar fantasies in their drawings. Then, driven by anxiety about the fate of their external world's inner counterparts, said Rickman, they try to depict faithfully what is outside them. This is followed by their art showing more measured composition aimed at synthesizing elements which have been destroyed and torn apart. Rickman continued:

> [If] we reckon with the fact that the child goes through periods when the face of familiar things is changed and all that it loves and trusts is

Figure 5.1 Picasso: *The Woman with the Golden Breasts*

crushed by its own violence and befouled by its hate, and if with all this
we reckon with the influence and power of infantile phantasy and experience upon our adult perception and emotion: then we may see how the
artist can lead us into and out of the world of suffering.

The artist's 'creative activity is the Beginning of a New World built on the
ruins of the old,' he maintained, 'those strokes of the brush in his phantasy
build up bit by bit the good objects which he has destroyed and makes them
come to life'. This implies, Rickman continued, that 'unless the artist can
reach down to the experience of deep anxiety and find the way out his work
will not give us a deeper understanding of ourselves or a fuller enjoyment
of life'.[55]

This was published in 1940. Early the next year Klein began a four-month,
six-day-a-week analysis of a 10-year-old school-phobic patient, Richard. It
centred largely on drawings Richard did during his analysis. Klein's account
of his treatment makes evident her increasingly centring her ideas about
child and adult psychology not so much on the Oedipus and castration complex but on notions about death instinct impelled destructive, persecutory,
manic and depressive states of mind which she theorized as preceding and
conditioning this complex.[56]

Richard came into analysis, according to Klein's account of it, with fantasies about other children which made him so anxious with the onset of war,
in which his family home suffered bomb damage, that he had been completely
unable to attend school for the previous two years. At his first meeting with
Klein he indicated some of his anxiety-making fantasies in talking to her
about the dreadful things Hitler did to the Austrians even though, like Klein,
he said, Hitler too was Austrian. Supplementing this with her now retelling
Freud's Oedipus and castration complex theory in terms of maternally
centred depressive position destructive fantasy, Klein asked Richard if he was
also worried about his mother. Yes, he said, he worried a tramp might attack
and kidnap her at night. He imagined rescuing her by scalding the tramp with
hot water to make him unconscious. This suggested, said Klein, that he had
forgotten that his father was with his mother at night, that he could protect
her. Perhaps he had forgotten, she continued, because he felt his father acted
destructively towards his mother when he was in bed with her just as Hitler
was destructive towards Austrians like her.

Maybe this and other interpretations contributed to Richard becoming
increasingly taciturn and inhibited about talking with Klein in the following
days. To undo this inhibition Klein brought paper and pencils for him to draw
with. '[He] did not start out with any deliberate plan and was often surprised
to see the result',[57] she observed. His first drawing (Figure 5.2.1, Plate 2)[58] also
made him conscious of factors of which he was previously unconscious. He
was surprised, for instance, to discover that he had given two German
U-boats the numbers '10' and '16' corresponding to his own age and that of

his cousin, John, also in analysis with Klein. Prompted by her describing the U-boats as symbolizing himself and his 18-year-old brother, Paul, attacking their parents (represented by the British warships, *Truant* and *Sunfish*, of this drawing, as Klein put it), Richard observed that the periscope of the *Sunfish* was poking into the *Truant* warship. This evoked further parentally, specifically maternally centred ideas in Klein. She said the periscope stood for Richard penetrating into his mother.

This might have contributed to his repeating this theme in another drawing in which he drew *Sunfish*'s periscope sticking into another warship, *Rodney* (Figure 5.2.29, Plate 2). Interpreting this in terms of her depressive position theory about fantasies of destruction and its repair, which the drawing evidently evoked in her, Klein said the *Sunfish* warship stood for

> Richard when he took away Daddy's genital and made himself into an adult. . . . At the same time, he was sorry for Daddy and wanted to make reparation by putting the 'grown-up' starfish-Daddy between the plants and make him into a gratified child.[59]

He also drew many starfish shapes which he divided into different coloured sections like those on the map of the wall of the room in which he met with Klein, and on which he anxiously followed the then advance of Hitler's German empire across Europe. Learning from Klein's interpretations that the differently coloured sections of his starfish map drawings symbolized different members of his family, Richard said of one of these drawings (Figure 5.2.12, Plate 2) that the nasty black bits were his brother, the light blue bits his mother, and the purple bits the maid and cook in the hotel where he and his mother stayed in Pitlochry, Scotland, so he could attend his sessions with Klein, who was then staying there, away from the wartime bombing of London. The very small blue bit in the middle, he said, was himself. The red was his father. And the whole picture was, he announced, 'a greedy starfish full of big teeth'.[60]

The next day he coloured several bits of another starfish or empire drawing red (Figure 5.2.14, Plate 2). 'This is me, and you will see what a large part of the empire I get,' he told Klein. Then he coloured some sections light blue, saying happily, 'Can you see how Mummy has spread herself. She has got much more of the empire.'[61] After this he coloured other sections purple to symbolize his brother helping him. The black bits symbolized his father, he indicated. Supplementing this with what it evoked in her, Klein said that, since she was wearing a light-blue cardigan, and since Richard had previously depicted himself as a greedy starfish, this drawing symbolized himself swallowing everyone to get her as 'more and more of the good Mummy into himself'.[62]

His drawings of battleships and of empire- or map-like starfish were interspersed with drawings of German and British railway tracks. They included one on which he wrote, 'Map of Raillray' (Figure 5.3.54). He drew it after a weekend when, he said, he had been glad to recover his toy train from his family's bomb-damaged home. The same weekend he had also suffered the shock of finding his father suffering a heart attack on the bathroom floor. He was glad to have his toy train back, said Klein, because it stood for himself as alive and feeding from his mother's breasts. He had represented them, she argued, with the two circles of his 'Raillray' drawing. He needed them, she added, because his father's heart attack had made him frightened of dying. 'Daddy is very ill,' he agreed, climbing onto a box to look out of the window. He then asked Klein to help him down because, she explained, he wanted 'to make her into a good Mummy'.

Meanwhile he marched up and down, shouting, stamping and goose-stepping. This symbolized, she said,

> his feelings that he had bombed and soiled Daddy with his faeces and urine, that he was like Hitler marching and goose-stepping. He was afraid and very worried that he had made Daddy ill, and so also injured Mummy, who, he felt, contained Daddy.[63]

Evidently, she indicated, he felt remorseful for his manic identification with Hitler as an idealized superego figure attacking others, his father included.

Richard may well have had Hitler in mind in making his next drawing (Figure 5.3.55). He called it 'Mrs M. Klein' and gave her 'goggle eyes', thereby making her look like Hitler, observes one commentator.[64] Acquiescing, however, with Klein's breast interpretation of the circles of his 'Raillray' drawing, Richard said that what might look to us like Hitler's goggle eyes were breasts. Saying this, he kissed one of them. Breasts again and again featured in Klein's interpretations of his subsequent drawings, just as circular images as symbols of the soul again and again featured in Jung's interpretations of the paintings of Miss X (see p. 34).

Like some of Richard's other drawings, the last drawing included in Klein's book about his treatment, which he did a few days before his analysis ended, depicted railway lines. As he drew them (Figure 5.3.74), he explained that his pencil travelling along the line was a train. He wanted to become an explorer, he said, and read travel books. But this evoked rather different ideas in Klein. She saw the line as depicting the shape of a woman's body. He was exploring her body and that of his mother, she said. Acquiescing with this interpretation, Richard told Klein the circle at the top of the drawing was a breast with a nipple inside. Then, furiously making a dot in the middle, he restrained himself from making further dots, because, although he was angry with her about his analysis ending, Klein interpreted, he wanted to keep her and his mother 'safe'.[65]

We could argue that this simply proves Anna Freud's criticism of Klein that, by 'accompanying the child's activities with translations and interpretations'

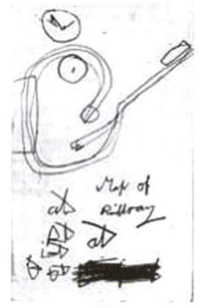

54

55

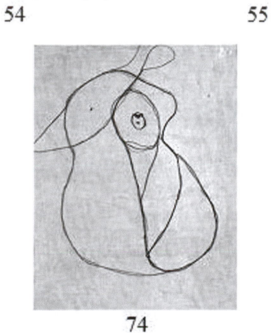

74

Figure 5.3 Richard: 'Mrs M. Klein' and 'Raillray' drawings

(see p. 50), Klein unduly influenced them. Yet, in arguably shifting Richard from inhibited and repetitive drawings of war and destruction to facing love and hate of her as symbolic image of his mother as both loved and hated, good and bad, she contributed to the reduction of the anxiety-making unconscious fantasies resulting from this image being split apart which had arguably contributed to the anxieties preventing him going to school. Certainly he returned to school after his analysis with Klein ended. But his return was short-lived. Nevertheless, perhaps his analysis helped him overcome the 'inhibition of his faculties and interests',[66] which, said Klein, marked the beginning of his treatment with her. After his return to school failed, and after being taught at home, he succeeded in going to university. 'The result of this analysis was', Klein however acknowledged, 'only a partial one.'[67] Her analysis of the art historian, Adrian Stokes, from 1929 to 1936, and again briefly in 1938 and 1946, was arguably more successful.

Chapter 6

Stokes

Stokes's biographer, Richard Read,[1] maintains that Stokes is the patient referred to by Klein as Mr B in her 1932 book, *The Psychoanalysis of Children*. Whether or not Mr B is Stokes, Klein depicts Mr B's writing in much the same terms as she depicted Kjär's paintings (see p. 52), namely as means of repairing the writer's or artist's inner world. She attributed his symptoms, by contrast, to his fleeing inner for outer reality. And she interpreted his homosexuality, which was one of the factors bringing Stokes into analysis with Klein (his first appointment was 5 December 1929), to this too involving defensive flight from inner to outer reality. Displacing fears about inner destruction and emptiness onto women, she argued, Mr B's homosexuality was due to his defensively fleeing from conflicted love and hate of his mother and women generally into idealizing men and masculinity. 'To him,' she wrote, 'only the male, in whom all was manifest and clearly visible and who concealed no secrets within himself, was the natural and beautiful object.'[2] As well as contributing to his homosexuality, 'displacement of his fears of internal dangers into the external world,' she said, also led to him feeling persecuted.[3]

To this she added that Mr B fled woman-centred destructiveness and gloom by going abroad. In his autobiography, *Inside Out*, published after his analysis with Klein had ended, Stokes described gloomy-making women from his early childhood: 'a very strict governess, a most patriotic Irish lady,' for instance, 'dismissed for maltreating me,' he said; and 'a morbidly religious middle-aged woman', whom he depicted as making even the sheep in Hyde Park look 'wicked and guilty'.[4] He contrasted this with the transforming revelation, as he recalled it, of emerging on New Year's Day, 1922, as a 19-year-old Oxford undergraduate, from Northern Europe into Italy's Southern light:

> As the train came out of the Mont Cenis tunnel, the sun shone, the sky was a deep, deep, bold blue. . . . At the stations before Turin, the pure note of the guard's horn but sustained and reinforced the process by which time was here laid out as ever-present space . . . Italians . . . talked

like Romans. Their warm precipitation of life sustained, as it seemed to me, by the glowing reflected light of thousands of sunlit years, banished memories of Hyde Park. . . . There was a revealing of things in the Mediterranean sunlight, beyond any previous experience; I had the new sensation that the air was touching things; that the space between things touched them, belonged in common; that space itself was utterly revealed. . . . It seemed that for the first time things were happening entirely outside me. Existence was enlarged by the miracle of the neat defining light. Here was an open and naked world. I could not then fear for the hidden, for what might be hidden inside me and those I loved. I had, in fact, incorporated this objective-seeming world and proved myself constructed by the general refulgence. Nothing, for the time, lurked, nothing bit, nothing lurched.[5]

Just as Stokes thus contrasted the gloom of London with the light of Italy, Klein said of Mr B:

In contrast to his native town, which he thought of as a dark, lifeless and ruined place . . . he pictured an imaginary city full of life, light and beauty, and sometimes found his vision realized, though only for a short time, in the cities he visited in other countries.[6]

She described Mr B's creativity, by contrast, as repairing his inner world. 'His work in writing his book and the whole process of mental production entailed by it were linked in his unconscious to restoring the inside of his body and creating children', she said.[7] It was through analysing and thus countering his flight to outer reality in, for instance, idealizing the penis of his male lovers, that she enabled Mr B, as she understood it, to focus on his inner world and thus helped him to recover from the ills bringing him into analysis with her. As soon as his persecutory and other fears had been analysed, she reported, his 'capacity for work was still further increased and his heterosexual position reinforced'.[8]

As well as identifying Mr B with Stokes, Richard Read argues that Stokes is also the patient referred to by Klein as 'C' in the essay in which she first developed her theory of depressive position states of mind. To illustrate defensive flight from depression into manic and dominating control and domination over others (we could call it phallic omnipotence, to use Freud's penis-centred terminology) she recounted, as follows, one of C's dreams:

he was travelling with his parents in a railway-carriage . . . felt that he was 'managing the whole thing', taking care of the parents . . . [he] urinated . . . into a basin . . . [on finishing] he noticed that his penis was very large and he had an uncomfortable feeling about this – as if his father ought not to see it, since he would feel beaten by him and he did not want to humiliate his father. At the same time he felt that by urinating he was sparing his father the trouble of getting out of bed and urinating himself.[9]

This was followed by his worrying that Klein's match might fly off and hit him as she lit her cigarette. She did it wrong, he said, 'like his father, who served the balls the wrong way at tennis'.[10]

C went on to tell her a dream in which he heard 'the frizzling sound of something which was frying in the oven'. The noise sounded like the 'crying of a tiny voice', he said. It made him feel 'a live creature was being fried'. He tried to draw his mother's attention to this. But he could not make her understand that, as he put it, 'to fry something alive was much the worst thing to do, worse than boiling or cooking it . . . more torturing since the hot fat prevented it from burning altogether and kept it alive while skinning it'. Klein interpreted this as symbolizing his fantasy of his 'mother containing the burning penis and dying children (the oven with frying pan)' and other 'anxiety-situations' impelling his defensive 'manic control over his parents', she said, referring to his previous dream.[11]

If Klein's patients, Mr B and C, were indeed Stokes, perhaps her analysis of his manic omnipotence as defence against depressive position recognition of ambivalence (of loving what we also hate) contributed to Stokes recovering from the writing block from which he suffered following the publication of his first two books, *The Thread of Ariadne* in 1925, and *Sunrise in the West* in 1926. Perhaps it also contributed to his criticizing artists who exercise manic or omnipotent control over their material by imposing their preconceived feelings and fantasies on it. In books published during his 1929–36 analysis with Klein, he deplored as 'modelling' the dominance of artists over the materials with which they work. Modelling, he said, involves artists not allowing their medium any 'rights' of its own. It involves artists treating their material as 'formless mud' from which a shape is not 'uncovered but created', he said. 'The modeller realizes his design with clay,' he continued, 'he does not envisage that conception as enclosed in his raw material.'[12]

Modelled forms 'can well be the perfect embodiment of conception', he acknowledged. But they result from ideas 'untrammeled by the restraint that reverence for objects as solid space inspires'. Objects in modelling are 'consciously impressed with the associative and transitional qualities of the mind's processes,' he went on. Modellers begin their art-making with their own ideas and fantasies, not with ideas and fantasies which they find and which are revealed to them by the material with which they work. 'Characteristic of modelling is an effect of the preconceived,' he maintained.[13] It results from the artist's projection of their fantasies onto the material with which they work.

By contrast, he argued, artists who adopt a 'carving' approach respond to what they find in their material. Carving can thus serve as an emblem, we could add, of psychoanalysts responding to what they find in what their analysands say and do by way of free association in arriving at an interpretation of the unconscious cause of their analysands' ills. It also serves as an emblem of analysts adjusting their interpretations to take account of what emerges from the analysand's subsequent free associations in their work together. We can understand in these terms Stokes' description of carving as involving 'conception all the time [being] adjusted to the life that the sculptor feels beneath his tool'.[14]

Initially appalled by Michelangelo's dominating imposition of his preconceived ideas on the marble with which he worked, Stokes illustrated the quite different carving approach to art-making, of which he approved, by quoting approvingly Michelangelo's poem (unfortunately translated as doggerel): 'The best of artists hath no thought to show / Which the rough stone in its superfluous shell / Doth not include: to break the marble spell / Is all the hand that serves the brain can do.'[15] And, of course, we can easily see Michelangelo's work as what Stokes called carving and as thus revealing what he found in the marble he carved in his final works, including his unfinished *Pieta* in Milan,[16] and his *Slaves*,[17] now in the Accademia in Florence.

Not only does carving, as understood by Stokes, serve as emblem of analysts responding to what they find in their analysands' material in formulating their interpretations. It also serves as emblem of analysts externalizing in what they say the unconscious fantasies they discern and find in their analysands' free associations, just as artists externalize in their art what they find in their medium. The best examples of just such externalization in art can be found, according to Stokes, in Quattro Cento Italian architecture, sculpture and painting. He defined Quattro Cento as whatever in early Italian Renaissance art externalizes 'humanistic fantasies' and 'southern compulsion to throw life outward, to objectify'. He included the process by which, he wrote, 'Renaissance sculptors made stone to bloom'.[18] He praised Quattro Cento art as emblematic of the 'process of living', of 'a turning outward into definite form of inner ferment'.[19]

Quattro Cento art includes 'mass-effect', claimed Stokes, in which, he said, 'every temporal or flux element was transformed into a spatial steadiness'. This was facilitated by the light of Southern Europe which, he argued, 'induces even a Northerner to contemplate things in their positional or spatial aspect, as objects revealed, as symbols of objective realization'. He lauded instances of Quattro Cento art which achieve outward opening, unifying, full flowering blossoming. 'For what else is civilization,' he asked, 'but a converting of formless power to organized show, to outwardness?'[20]

Carving is life. 'For living is externalization', Stokes explained, 'throwing an inner ferment outward into definite act and thought.'[21] Reiterating this equation of life with making the inner world outward, massive, and manifest, he proclaimed:

Wherever you find relief forms, be they ornament or figure, arabesque or swag, wherever you find these shapes, whatever their position, turning to show to you their maximum, like flowers that thrust and open their faces to the sun, wherever that is the salient point about them, then that sculpture is Quattro Cento as I define it.[22]

Examples for Stokes included dolphins carved by the school of Francesco di Giorgio over a window of the Palazzo Letimi in Rimini (Figure 6.1).[23] He described them as 'swimming out of the brick', as 'incrustation' magnetically drawn up from the sea to the surface'.[24]

Most of all he illustrated Quattro Cento carving with the example of the early Renaissance transformation, in the 1450s, of a Gothic church in Rimini into a humanist, quasi-secular, pagan even, temple – the Tempio Malatestiano. He described the Tempio's façade, designed by Alberti, as 'sudden like a glimpse, firm like a flower in full bloom . . . pent-up to instant manifestation . . . mass all at once like mountains in sunlight'.[25] Its 'stone-blossom' and 'incrustation' convey, he claimed, 'organic connexion between architectural members and between background and ornament'. Its pilasters look as if they had 'grown from the wall-space . . . steadfastly like a flower'.[26]

He also drew attention to ways in which marble carvings by Agostino in the Tempio symbolize the externalization of inner feeling and fantasy into outward form. Marble, he pointed out, is made by the action of water on shells making them into limestone. Agostino externalized and made this, marble's inner watery essence, outwardly manifest in waves of water, and in the folds of cloth of his carving of *Diana*, which, he said, 'open and close like the rhythmic washing to and fro of tresses of seaweed clothing a far rock beneath clear water'.[27] This example also illustrates Agostino's use of the classical tradition to externalize inner feelings by personifying and naming them – in this instance its tradition of giving the name 'Diana', to what Stokes described as 'female seductiveness, magnetic, a form of indiscriminate suction drawing in diverse material'.[28]

Further instances of Quattro Cento carving serving as emblem of the externalization of inner feelings involved in analysis making conscious what is otherwise unconscious include Agostino's use of the 'equal diffusion of light' emanating from marble,[29] and his graduating, thinning, rounding, and polishing it to reveal its translucence. As a result, we feel, said Stokes, 'that not the figure, but the stone through the medium of the figure, has come to life'.[30] We can also see this in Agostino's sculpture, *Madonna and Child with Angels* (Figure 6.2).[31] Stokes wrote of this sculpture:

The further into the stone the more pronounced becomes the flattening of shapes: yet the inner and background shapes suggest no less contour than the other shapes, with the result that they are luminous even

Figure 6.1 School of Francesco di Giorgio: Window of Palazzo Letimi, Rimini

CWAS I, Plate 2.

in the dimmest light, as if their contours were indeed the face of the stone-block itself.[32]

His account of this sculpture also highlights ways in which art can serve as emblem of the condensation of different fantasies which the analyst might seek to externalize and make conscious in interpreting them. He noted, for

Figure 6.2 Agostino: *Madonna and Child with Angels*

instance, 'the poignancy of the child's curving shoulder juxtaposed upon the face of an angel behind, from which the shoulder's roundness graduates [so as to] give each other shape'.[33] He also noted ways in which this sculpture brings different perspectives together into a whole as an analyst might also seek to do in bringing different aspects of the analysand's psyche together in an interpretation.

Examples of unifying different aspects or perspectives within the same art-work included, for Stokes, the following details of this sculpture:

The child's face is seen definitely from below, whereas the angels' heads adjoining, and those on the other side of the relief, are on eye-level. Moreover whereas we see the child's face from below, we see the top of his head and even parts of the back of it from above. Otherwise so much of the head could not be represented. This transition from one perspective to another passes muster because the head is tilted to the side and downwards, while the eyes look slightly up. Yet the perspective is even more complicated than this. Parts of the face we see on eye-level, and the ear, like the ear of the Virgin, is represented in complete profile.[34]

Stokes called this unifying of different perspectives and aspects 'identity in difference',[35] a term he borrowed from the neo-Hegelian philosopher, Bradley, whose book, *Appearance and Reality*, very much influenced Stokes' understanding of art.

Perhaps mindful of Klein's theory of depressive position integration of the infant's initial part-object fantasies about its mother's breast, faeces and the penis of the father imagined inside her into whole object images of her, Stokes wrote admiringly of the identity in difference, of the unification of different elements achieved by the architect Luciano Laurana in the courtyard he designed for the ducal palace in Urbino.[36]

Luciano did not stucco his brick. He left it rough. In the second place his stone is white; pilasters are thin, plain, unfluted, immeasurably straight and smooth. Archivolts have a few deep lines. The stone, then, lies on the brick in low relief, yet stands out simple, distinct, a white magic, *nitidezza*. The unpassable space between window-frame and pilaster along the storey, or the exact framing of a window that lies back on the wall – for the colonnade beneath is broad – give so supreme an individuality to each stone shape (though every pilaster, for example, except for his place, is the same as the next), that one appears to witness a miraculous concurrence of masterpieces of sculpture, each designed to show the beauties of his neighbour as unique. There is no other traffic among them. Their positions are untraversable, and no hand shall dare to touch two stone forms at a time. They flower from the brick, a Whole made up of Ones each as single as the Whole.[37]

This unification of 'Ones' into a 'Whole' was an instance of what Stokes called Quattro Cento mass effect. It enables, he said, 'the instantaneous synthesis that the eye alone of the senses can perform'.[38]

Although Stokes illustrated identity in difference with examples from sculpture and architecture, he first introduced the term into his account of the visual arts in writing about painting. 'The colours of a picture are fine when one feels that not the colours but each and every form through the medium of their colours has come to an equal fruition,' he said, explaining the value of colour in enhancing identity in difference. A supreme example for him was Giogione's painting, *The Tempest*.[39] Having applauded the immediacy of painting celebrated by Giorgione in terms of it being assimilable as a whole at 'a single glance' (*una sola occhiata*),[40] Stokes wrote of *The Tempest*:

> Giorgione chooses a moment of utmost revelation, in visual terms sunrise or sunset when things stand 'as they really are' and when the hush of this revelation induces a contemplative mood. At such time relationship and affinity between objects become an essential part of their meaning: every clearly seen object appears to possess equal importance, equal insistence whatever the size, owing to the interlocking palpability of local colour.[41]

The immediacy of this effect also nicely captures Klein's version of psychoanalysis. Unlike Freud, she focused less on interpreting unconscious fantasies from the past and their deferred action in the present. Rather, she focused on the immediacy of the here-and-now transference by analysands of their fantasies onto their analysts.

On the other hand, and paradoxically, it might take time for the analyst to discover the impact of these fantasies on them. Art can also serve as emblem of this. Exceeding the fifty-minute time-frame of the psychoanalytic 'hour', Stokes' friend and follower, the philosopher, Richard Wollheim, said of his experience of looking at paintings:

> I came to recognize that it often took the first hour or so in front of a painting for stray associations or motivated misperceptions to settle down, and it was only then, with the same amount of time or more to spend looking at it, that the picture could be relied upon to disclose itself as it was.[42]

Wollheim also showed how paintings can convey attention to what is going on in the mind of another in writing as follows of Bellini's depiction of Noah's son on the right-hand side of his painting, *The Drunkenness of Noah*:[43]

> without looking either pruriently at, or angrily away from his father's genitals, [he] draws the wine-coloured, blood-coloured, shroud across them . . . the features are blurred. Layers of glazes veil his head, as if to suggest (no more than that) that this is where it is all taking place. It is his reverie that we observe, and the connection of this fact with corporeality, evident enough in the presence of the picture, is that it ensures that it is under his conception, his conception and not that of either of his brothers, under, in other words, a benign conception, of the old patriarch's body that the picture gains corporeality.

This painting too is an instance of identity in difference. Wollheim drew attention to this in writing, for instance, of Bellini's 'use of colour, simplified now to white and the near-complementaries of pink and green, but with a wide tonal range'.[44]

Identity in difference is also realized in Northern Renaissance painting. Instances for Stokes included Bruegel's painting, *The Tower of Babel* (Figure 6.3, Plate 3).[45] He wrote, as follows, for instance, about the path leading from the seashore in the lower half of the painting:

> The pink arch is the goal; to the eyes of the waggoners it represents the sum and total of this yellow-green, blue-green hill. For our eyes the very shape of the wall as well as its hue, grows from the green. Or conversely, this arching wall distinguishes for us each cognate green substance and form. And again, the pink is not sudden or isolated. The horses and the carters' clothes, the colours of them who make this journey, seem to reproduce a mixture of the green with the pink. The rest of the section prepares us for the wall, for this pink form of green, yes, pink form of green. A pink-brown lunch basket lies upon the foreground green bank, near to a yellow cleft: there is some neutralizing warmth in all the bluish greens.[46]

Arguing with potential critics who might say that Bruegel himself had no intention of achieving identity in difference, Stokes added:

> Bruegel's preoccupation with such relationships and of those fantasies of which it is the vehicle, appears proved by the fact that in some of his pictures one may detect a small and isolated area of colour, crimson, for instance, amid tree roots, that serves no representational purpose whatsoever, but which is essential to the mosaic of the whole.[47]

Perhaps, nevertheless, it was not Bruegel's paintings but those of Picasso which alerted Stokes into seeing mosaic-like identity in difference in *The Tower of Babel*.

Certainly he cited Picasso's paintings in writing about identity in difference. He wrote of Picasso's 1925 painting, *Woman with a Mandolin* (Figure 6.4.1, Plate 4),[48] for instance:

> one will perceive immediately that there exists some integrating relation . . . between the figure and the chair on which she sits. This relationship depends upon a little addition sum that the eye unconsciously performs . . . take this red and blue, their respective areas and shapes, and we shall find that the purple-brown part of her head-dress gives some sort of equivalent, both in form and in colour. . . . In terms of two forms 'going into' a third, of one texture as the sum of another of larger area and so

on, there is perhaps expressed the wished-for stabilizing, not so much of our personalities as of its qualification by those miscellaneous mixed-up archetypal figures within us, absorbed in childhood, that are by no means at peace among themselves.[49]

He wrote similarly, many years later, about another 1925 painting by Picasso, *The Dance* (Figure 6.4.2, Plate 5).[50] 'It shows that every piece of the canvas is emotive, contributing to the whole', to which he added:

we are instantaneously convinced by this agitated scene . . . we see that every line and tone and division helps in the setting up of various relationships across and down the face of the canvas . . . an emotive or poetic whole is there expressed, since the expressiveness is transmitted by a rich language of form . . . [which] encourages further meaning because it is itself the container of a sum of meanings.[51]

Possibly influenced by Picasso's paintings, Stokes also emphasized identity in difference in describing the paintings of his friend, Ben Nicholson. They invite synthesis between eye and brain so that, he argued, 'basic fantasies of inner disorder find their calm and come to be identified with an objective harmony'.[52] Stokes illustrated the point with Nicholson's *1934–6 (Painting – Still Life)* (Figure 6.5.1, Plate 6).[53] Using ekphrasis – 'the creation of verbal equivalents that brings art works to the imaginative eye'[54] – just as, one could say, the analyst's creation of verbal equivalents of the analysand's unconscious fantasies makes them available to the ear – Stokes wrote of this painting:

one has the sense of a piece of colour, a red segment, for instance, containing all the other colours and tones and so, of course, the areas in which they figure. These latter seem to be an extension or elaboration of the former, a division of the rays that go to make this red, and into this red one feels they may be folded up again. Colour thus employed expresses identity under the form of a maximum difference. . . . Particularly remarkable are the relative positions of the saturated blue shape and of the red. The blue seems to come swiftly forward and as swiftly to retire. Beyond the saturated colours with white and black, there extend grayish and brownish zones of equivocal hue . . . they suggest to the fantasy an organic progression, as if they were potent to contain the seed of the saturated hues and even of the white, sum of all the colours.[55]

Something similar could be said of Stokes' 1937 painting, *Penwith Moor* (Figure 6.5.2, Plate 7).[56]

Very much better known, of course, is Picasso's 1937 painting, *Guernica*.[57] It movingly illustrates (albeit Stokes might not have agreed, according to his biographer, Richard Read) ways in which painting can serve as an emblem of the analyst bringing together the analysand's fragmentary free associations into an interpretation. *Guernica*'s fragments include an image of a horse of which the Kleinian analyst, Hanna Segal, writes, 'The horse is a dying victim, yet it is his enormous teeth that stand out, symbolizing, I think, its own, and our own, oral aggression'.[58] What makes the painting different from a photograph of the destruction by Franco's forces of the Basque capital, Guernica, which the painting memorializes, is the unity of the destroyed fragments. 'The shattered elements, the broken-up limbs are composed into formal wholes,' Segal explains. In this painting, she reiterates, 'there is a constant work of integration establishing connections, creating formal wholes, finding a rhythm'.[59] She also claims that paintings like *Guernica* impel the viewer to become conscious of otherwise unconscious fantasies of destruction and its repair which the artist depicts. 'Not only does the recipient identify with the creator, thereby reaching deeper feelings than he could do by himself,' she adds, 'he also feels that it is left for him to look for completion.'[60]

Stokes wrote at length of openings in walls of everyday buildings likewise leaving the viewer to see and consciously experience fantasies of part-object fragmentation and destruction evoking also their whole-object protective and reparative completion.

> [I]t is as if those apertures had been torn in that body by our revengeful teeth so that we experience as a beautiful form, and indeed as indispensable shelter also, the outcome of sadistic attacks, fierce yet smoothed, healed into a source of health, which we would take inside us and preserve there unharmed for the source of our goodness.

It is also as if, he continued,

> the smooth body of the wall-face, or the smooth vacancy within the apertures, were the shining breast, while the mouldings, the projections, the rustications, the tiles, were the head, the feeding nipple of that breast. Such is the return of the mourned mother in all her calm and beauty and magnificence. She was mourned owing to the strength of greed, owing to the wealth of attacks that have been made on her attributes whenever there has been frustration. Greed is excited once more but achieves a guiltless catharsis on this sublimated level. And so, we welcome the appearance or re-appearance of the whole object which by contradistinction has helped to unify the ego; the joining, under one head, of love and of apparent neglect which thereby may become less fantastic; the entire object, self-subsistent in opposing attributes.[61]

Some may find this implausible and off-putting. Not so Stokes' abovementioned friend and follower, the philosopher and art historian, Richard Wollheim. Referring approvingly to Stokes' book, *Smooth and Rough*, in which this lengthy passage occurs, Wollheim showed that it helps explain the inviting effect of townscapes by the Welsh painter, Thomas Jones – *Houses in Naples* (Figure 6.6),[62] for instance – of which Wollheim wrote:

> [Jones] gets timeless, discoloured buildings of great dignity and humble materials to revive the infant's perception of the body: the body, stretched out, close up, palpable, taken in through the eyes of desire or destruction. . . . phantasies . . . which assure us that we have the power to restore, to remake, to rebuild, that which we have damaged.[63]

Jones thus captures, claimed Wollheim,

> a particular uncertainty that surrounds many southern buildings, which is whether, at the moment we catch sight of them, they are going up or coming down: whether we see them in the course of construction or demolition.

He contrives 'to transform visual ambiguity into emotional condensation,' Wollheim continued.

> These buildings, having come down, or once destroyed, are next restored: they grow up again. They rise against a little boy's sky, of clear morning blue or liverish grey, flecked with clouds of cotton wool.[64]

The art of ancient Greece can have a similar effect. It gives, said Stokes, 'form to each manifestation of the psyche, however primitive, to contemplate it from a distance without super-abundant aid of mystical identification, and to discover for it an integrative role'.[65] Art, he also wrote, invites oneness with its 'object-otherness'. As such, he said, it is 'an emblem of the state of being in love'.[66] It is emblematic of 'self-subsistent or whole objects' together with 'connexions that blur'. One could also call the latter, he said, 'the homogeneous experience of the "oceanic feeling"'.[67]

He borrowed this 'oceanic feeling' term from Freud, who also used it to connote the illusory oneness of 'ego' and 'object', 'I' and 'you' occurring at 'the height of being in love'. Freud attributed this feeling of inner-outer oneness to persistence into adulthood of the illusory 'primary ego-feeling' of the breast-feeding baby of oneness with its mother's body.[68]

Emphasizing art as inspired by the external world inviting oneness with its object-otherness, Stokes claimed

> an impression occupies real salience for an artist when it suggests an entire and separate unity, though, at the same time, it seems to be joined to the heart of other, diverse, experiences, to possess with them a pulse in common: that is the feeling the artist strives to re-create.[69]

Figure 6.6 Jones: *Houses in Naples*

To highlight the inviting power of the artist's resulting art, Stokes took his readers on an imagined tour of Rembrandt's portraits in London's National Gallery,[70] saying:

> Here, on the walls, faces come softly but vividly from dark backgrounds, faces and hands that 'realize' the sitters. Drawing, texture, disposition, echoing toppling shape, seem to be a rich fructification of character rather than the physical representatives. Such an effect depends on eliciting from us muscular response to the drawing and an increase of the usual correlating activities of vision.[71]

The oneness thus invited by Rembrandt's portrait paintings with those they depict is visceral.

Stokes also noted the limits imposed by the external reality of what the artist creates and shows us in inviting our illusory oneness with it. The sky also limits what we can project and feel at one with in it. 'I find in the clouds today the splendid shapes of T'ang figures', Stokes mused. But just as the shape, sex, age, voice, ethnicity, and so on of analysts limits the analysand's illusory oneness of their fantasies with them, so too the clouds limit what we can see of our fantasies in them. Detailing the point, Stokes wrote:

> Anyone who, looking at the clouds, with or without conscious phantasy, is increasingly arrested by their shape, tone, disposition, or the spaces between them, by every detail and its interrelation, experiences an aesthetic sensation. In asserting this I am presuming that conscious phantasy, if it makes an appearance, does not merely use the condition of the clouds as a point of departure but that, on the contrary, the movements of phantasy or of judgment have been transposed into, and therefore restricted by, the very particular visual and tactile terms of these cloudy forms . . . in such kind of apprehension we are as one with the *virtu* of the object while at the same time we, in turn, are giving to its intrinsic structure in bodily terms, to its actuality or distinctiveness, to its separateness from ourselves, full value.[72]

Works of art likewise invite and exercise an 'incantatory' and 'empathic, identificatory, pull upon adepts', he said, which we are all the more willing to go along with in so far as they convey, 'self-sufficiency as restored, whole objects'.[73] This also has its parallel with psychoanalysis, with Klein's theory that children and analysands progress from insecure identification with others as part-objects – breast, faeces, penis and so on – to identification with others as whole, self-sufficient, loved and hated, good and bad figures beginning with those who first mother us.

Stokes illustrated the power of art to invite oneness with both primitive part-object and more integrated whole-object fantasies with J.M.W. Turner's poem, *Fallacies of Hope*, from which Turner quoted in exhibition catalogues of his paintings. The poem conveys, said Stokes,

> the conception, in one aspect, of the infant who believes in the omnipotent and scalding propensity that belongs to his stream of yellow urine as it envelops the object so closely attached to himself, an object split off in his mind from the good breast with which he is also one.[74]

Similar enveloping oneness is invited by Turner's late paintings – his 1843 painting, *Light and Colour*,[75] for instance. Stokes wrote of these paintings:

> In the great last period, not only is the world washed clean by light, but humidity is sucked from water, the core of fire from flame, leaving an iridescence through which we witness an object's ceremonious identity: whereupon space and light envelop them and us . . . whirlpool of fire and water . . . beneficence in space.[76]

Wollheim conveyed something similar. He contrasted painting with verbal metaphors such as 'Religion is the opium of the people' in which one term highlights an aspect of what is conveyed by another term by being paired with it.[77] Paintings, by contrast, he argued, invite oneness with them without any such pairing. As such art is arguably akin to the dream-work process not so much of pairing one term 'as if' it were another which displaces it, but of condensing one thing with another, just as the analytic setting invites analysands to condense and identify their fantasies about those who are important to them with their analysts, without pairing or displacing one with the other.

To illustrate ways in which painting invites just such condensation and 'metaphorizes the body',[78] Wollheim cited Wilhelm de Kooning's late 1970s abstract paintings – his *Untitled XIX* (1977)[79] and *Untitled III* (1979)[80] paintings, for example. In a passage reminiscent of Riviere's account of the destructive fantasies of earliest infancy (see p. 55), Wollheim wrote of these paintings:

> [De Kooning] crams his pictures with infantile experiences of sucking, touching, biting, excreting, retaining, smearing, sniffing, swallowing, gurgling, stroking, wetting. These experiences, it will be noticed, extend across the sense modalities, sometimes fusing them, sometimes subdividing them: in almost all cases they combine sensations of sense with sensations of activity.[81]

Emphasizing the embodied character of these fantasies, often overlooked in the abstractions of much psychoanalytic writing, Wollheim also noted 'the lusciousness of the paint, and . . . the fat and gaudy substance into which he [de Kooning] works it up', and the way this is contained within a near-square frame, evoking and symbolizing, Wollheim claimed, 'the simplicity and the fragility of the rudimentary self'.[82]

Much more inviting, arguably, as refuge from primitive, mother- and woman-centred part-object fantasies is the intact, whole-object separateness symbolized by men and masculinity, as recounted by Klein in her analysis of Mr B and C, alias Stokes, according to his biographer, Richard Read, with which I began this chapter. Klein, however, overlooked the male-dominated or patriarchal social factors contributing to flight from mother-centred part-object fantasy to identification with what presents and is symbolized by the penis or phallus as Freud and his follower, the French psychoanalyst, Jacques Lacan put it. In this, and much more explicitly than Stokes and Wollheim, Lacan described examples from the visual arts in conjunction with the clinical practice of psychoanalysis.

Chapter 7

Lacan

Klein, as I have said, opposed Anna Freud's method of fostering the child analysand's identification with the ego and superego of the analyst. Others were less averse to this method of psychoanalysis. They included Anna Freud's so-called ego psychology followers in the United States. Examples include Ralph Greenson in California who emphasized the importance of boys dis-identifying from their mothers and identifying instead with men and masculinity to develop a strong, male-based ego and identity.[1] The influential feminist psychoanalyst, Nancy Chodorow, in turn adopted Greenson's theory in developing her critique of existing sexual inequalities and differences.[2]

Meanwhile Anna Freud had many years before attributed the psychological ills of adolescents to the weakening, with sexual maturation, of their identification with the superego of their parents.[3] This was followed by her analysand, the analyst, Erik Erikson, emphasizing the adaptive value for teenagers of resolving their adolescent identity crisis, as he understood it, by identifying with group leaders and others in forming their adult identity.[4] His friend, the psychoanalyst, Peter Blos, likewise emphasized the importance of adolescents strengthening their ego by reworking their separation and individuation from their mothers as infants through identifying with male pop stars and sports idols.[5] These theories have, in turn, been reiterated by present-day followers of Erikison and Blos.[6]

Long before this, Ernst Kris, who, together with Heinz Hartmann and Lacan's analyst, Rudolph Loewenstein, pioneered the US development of ego psychology, famously advocated 'regression in the service of the ego' as inspiration of art and creativity. 'But,' Kris went on, 'regression [in the direction of the id] in the case of aesthetic creations . . . is purposive and controlled.' Otherwise, he warned, 'the [artist's] symbols become private, perhaps unintelligible even, to the reflective self'.[7] He recommended, in keeping with the celebration of the ego by his US psychoanalytic colleagues, that, even in the throes of artistic creation, the ego should remain in relative control. As for the clinical practice of US ego psychology, its leading exponent during the 1960s and 1970s, Heinz Kohut,[8] advocated that, in cases of narcissistic personality disorder, the analyst should strengthen the analysand's ego by fostering their mirroring and idealizing transference identification with them.

Just as Klein opposed Anna Freud's tactic of encouraging her child analysands to identify with her superego authority, Lacan opposed the US ego psychology development of Freud's later work. The job of the analyst, he argued, is to expose as illusory and self-alienating the analysand's identification and oneness with the analyst's ego or superego. Their task is not to reinforce it. Klein initially theorized the superego as first coming into being in the infant in the form of a vengeful witch-like figure retaliating against the infant's oral and anal, as well as genital, Oedipal attacks on the mother's sexual coupling with the father.[9] Klein later described identification with superego figures as manic defence against recognizing the destruction done those we love by also hating them. Lacan, by contrast, conceptualized the ego, ego-ideal or ideal-I as seductive effect of others, artists included, showing and inviting us to lose ourselves in identification with what they show us to desire and see. This centres, he said, on phallic symbolism in the patriarchally structured societies which, along with the anthropologist, Claude Lévi-Strauss,[10] he argued has always characterized human society, both past and present.

Lacan's development of psychoanalysis in these terms, however, is wilfully obscure. One way of understanding his approach is to begin with surrealist art which particularly influenced him, specifically Salvador Dali's self-styled method of 'paranoia-criticism'. This, in turn, can be understood as an outcome of the adoption by André Breton and other surrealists of Freud's free association method in rebelling against the ego and superego demands of the art establishment of their time. In this they were also inspired by the nightmare paintings of Hieronymus Bosch; by the dream-inspired writing of the poet and novelist, Gérard de Nerval; and by the poet and writer, Ducasse, also known as Lautréamont, whose nonsense construction, '*Beau comme la rencontre fortuite sur une table de dissection d'une machine à coudre et d'un parapluie*' ('the fortuitous encounter of an umbrella and a sewing machine on a dissecting table'), became a slogan of surrealist rebellion against orthodoxy.[11]

Crediting the then recently deceased poet, Guillaume Apollinaire, with inventing the term 'surrealism', Breton defined it as

> Psychic automatism in its pure state, by which one proposes to express – verbally, by means of the written word, or in any other manner – the actual functioning of thought. Dictated by thought, in the absence of any control exercised by reason, exempt from any aesthetic or moral concern.[12]

Urging fellow surrealists to adopt Freud's method of free association, he wrote:

Put yourself in as passive, or receptive, a state of mind as you can. Forget about your genius, your talents, and the talents of everybody else. . . . Write quickly, without any preconceived subject. . . . Go on as long as you like. Put your trust in the inexhaustible nature of the murmur.[13]

Breton and his fellow-surrealists also used as inspiration a pastime like the squiggle game in which, instead of making pencilled or painted squiggles or doodles, players take turns improvising on each other's words by supplying words which they suggest. Particularly celebrated within the history of surrealism is the absurd symbolic linkages of the collage-like construction: '*Le cadavre / exquis / boira / le vin / nouveau*' ('The exquisite / corpse / shall drink / the bubbling / wine').[14]

Breton also advocated the use of séances to inspire surrealist art. Influenced by his mental hospital work during the First World War, explains one commentator, he 'encouraged colleagues gifted with the power to generate fabulous images while asleep (Desnos, Crevel and Péret), to do so in the presence of the group and to report their dreams as they occurred'.[15] They were hopeful that this séance-based method would provide an unlimited source of artistic inspiration.

Influenced by de Nerval, surrealists in the 1920s also used their privately occurring dreams to inspire their art. Breton gave the example of the following phrase occurring to him as he slept: 'There is a man cut in two by the window'. The phrase was accompanied, he said, 'by the faint visual image of a man walking cut half way up by a window perpendicular to the axis of his body'.[16] Noting such images, he speculated,

With a pencil and white sheet of paper to hand, I could easily trace their outlines . . . a tree, a wave, a musical instrument, all manner of things of which I am presently incapable of providing even the roughest sketch.[17]

Examples of just such dream-inspired art included, for Breton, drawings and paintings by Desnos and Masson.

But there was a problem. 'No one is unaware any more that there is no Surrealist painting,' wrote Breton's critic, Naville. 'Neither the random marks of the pencil, nor the image retracing dream figures, nor imaginative fantasies, of course, can be so characterized.'[18] To this Desnos replied that, just as painting requires skill, so too does writing. But this does not preclude both being inspired by spontaneously occurring dreams and free associations:

the great problem for a Surrealist painting has been the application of the definition of Surrealism to pictorial processes. . . . Doubtless the error consisted in the excessive importance unwittingly given to craft. The Surrealist poet makes use of known words and writes with familiar letters. Painters can paint, in terms of craft, as they wish.

He added:

> What counts is the first conception, whether they have a vision of the whole painting and record this vision, or, being venturesome, they allow the inspiration to renew itself by fits and starts and to get stronger with each brushstroke until the painting is completed.[19]

The fact that painting, like writing, depends on socially acquired skills does not prevent it being inspired by 'the first conception', free of social convention, with which the painter, like the writer, can begin each new work of art. The problem is particularly obvious in painting because, while we learn the skill of writing as young children so we can have the impression of practising it entirely freely and automatically as adults, painters usually learn the skill involved in painting relatively late in life so that they are much more aware than writers of the social conventions governing their art-making.

One way of achieving freedom in painting is not by making random or free association doodles or scribbles but by using the freedom enabled by the ambiguity of visual imagery. Freud had noted the use we make of the 'pictorial arrangement of the psychical material',[20] as he put it, in effecting the dream- or art-work disguise of unconscious wishes he believed impel neurotic symptoms. Salvador Dali similarly exploited the ambiguity of visual imagery. He used what he called a 'double image' to impose whatever meanings he wanted on his public. Celebrating this freedom, he declared:

> I believe the moment is at hand when, by a paranoiac and active advance of the mind, it will be possible (simultaneously with automatism and other passive states) to systematize confusion and thus help to discredit completely the world of reality.[21]

'Paranoia', he explained, 'uses the external world in order to assert its dominating idea and has the disturbing characteristic of making others accept this idea's reality.' It does this by using details of external reality for 'illustration and proof,' he added, 'and so comes to serve the reality of our mind'.[22]

To illustrate the freedom of his self-styled 'paranoia-criticism' method Dali cited his 1930 painting, *Invisible Sleeping Woman*.[23] He painted it to make its beholders see a horse, a woman, a lion, or other figures. His freedom in making his art's recipients see these different meanings was limited, he argued, only 'by the mind's degree of paranoiac capacity'.[24] An earlier example was his 1928 painting, *The Stinking Ass*,[25] which can be seen 'covered with thousands of flies and ants' or as 'the hard and blinding flash of new gems'. We are thus 'brought to desire ideal objects,' he argued in contending that such paintings contribute, just as the free association creations of the poet and novelist can contribute, to the surrealist revolution in bringing about 'the imminent crisis of consciousness'.[26]

Impressed by Dali's 'stinking ass' article, Lacan phoned him to arrange their first meeting. Like Dali, he too was interested in paranoia. Freud had attributed it in Schreber (see p. 23) to Schreber displacing his repressed love and hate of his father onto his doctor, Flechsig, and onto God, both of whom he experienced as persecuting him with their hatred. In a subsequently published essay,[27] Freud argued more generally that paranoia involves the patient mis-locating their feelings of hatred in others whom they then experience as attacking them. Lacan's translation of this essay was published in 1931. On 18 June that year he examined, as a medical student, a 38-year-old patient, Marguerite Pantaine-Anzieu, following her hospitalization in Sainte-Anne after stabbing an actress, Huguette Duflos, in a fit of paranoia.

As far as I can gather Marguerite's paranoia stemmed from displacing hatred of her mother onto one of her sisters to whose care her 7-year-old son had been consigned to protect him from the ills done him by Marguerite's obsessive fear for his life. Having identified her sister, not herself, as locus of the hatred she bore others, Marguerite then displaced her hateful image of her sister onto a close woman friend, whose mother knew the actress, Sarah Bernhardt, from whom Marguerite then shifted her hateful fantasies onto Bernhardt's actress friend, Duflos. Questioned by the police after stabbing Duflos, Marguerite explained that Duflos had been spreading malicious rumours about her, and that she had felt compelled to look her in the eye lest Duflos think ill of her for not defending her son from her. That was why she had gone to the theatre where Duflos worked. That was why she stabbed her.

Why is it, though, that an actress in the case of Marguerite's paranoid obsession with Duflos, and that celebrities and others more generally can become figures in whom we misidentify our hateful feelings and fantasies as though they were their locus and cause? Describing the early childhood origins of just such misidentification, Lacan noted ways in which children misidentify feelings and fantasies with their toys as though they embodied them. Their toys thereby become hated and hateful objects of their revengeful attack just as Duflos became the object of Marguerite's revenge due to her misidentifying her hatred as coming from Duflos not her. Lacan observed:

> One need but listen to the stories and games made up by two to five year olds, alone or together, to know that pulling off heads and cutting open bellies are spontaneous themes of their imagination, which the experience of a busted-up doll merely fulfils.[28]

We can see similar projection of hatred into painted images of its destructive and fragmenting effect. 'One must leaf through a book of Hieronymus Bosch's work, including views of whole works as well as details, to see an atlas of all the aggressive images that torment mankind', Lacan noted, adding:

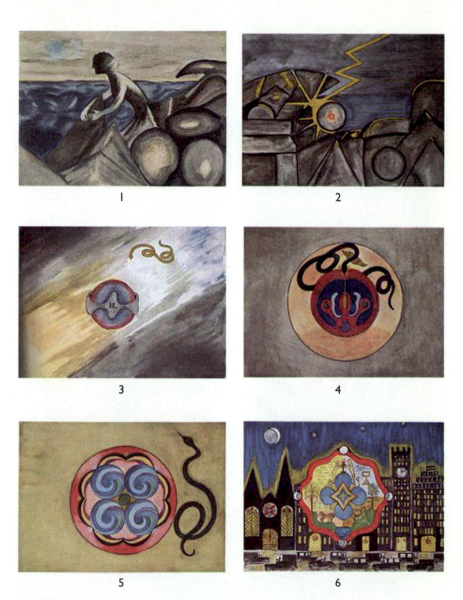

Figure 3.2 (Plate 1) Miss X: Paintings

These images from Miss X's analysis can be found in C.G. Jung (1933) A study in the process of individuation. *The Archetypes and the Collective Unconscious. CW9i.* Copyright © 1959 Routledge & Kegan Paul. Reproduced by permission of Taylor & Francis Books UK.

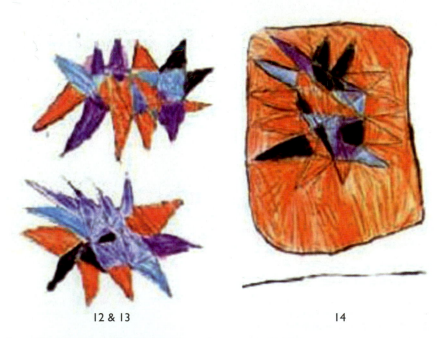

1 29

12 & 13 14

Figure 5.2 (Plate 2) Richard: Battleship and empire drawings

Figure 6.3 (Plate 3) Bruegel: The Tower of Babel

Figure 6.4.1 (Plate 4) Picasso: *Woman with a Mandolin*

Figure 6.4.2 (Plate 5) Picasso: *The Dance*

Copyrights © Tate, London, 2006, © Succession Picasso/DACS, London, 2006.

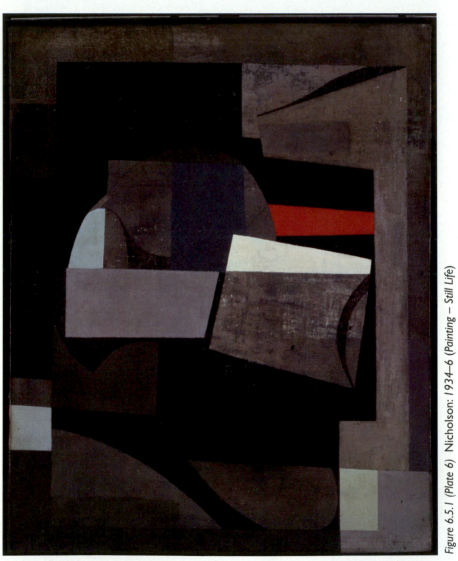

Figure 6.5.1 (Plate 6) Nicholson: *1934–6 (Painting – Still Life)*

Figure 6.5.2 (Plate 7) Stokes: Penwith Moor

Figure 7.1 (Plate 8) Bosch: *The Garden of Earthly Delights* (detail)

Copyright © Museo Nacional del Prado, Madrid.

Figure 7.3 (Plate 8) Holbein: *The Ambassadors*

Figure 8.2.2 (Plate 10) Milner: *Dragon*

J. Field (1934) *A Life of One's Own.* London: Chatto & Windus, p. 155.

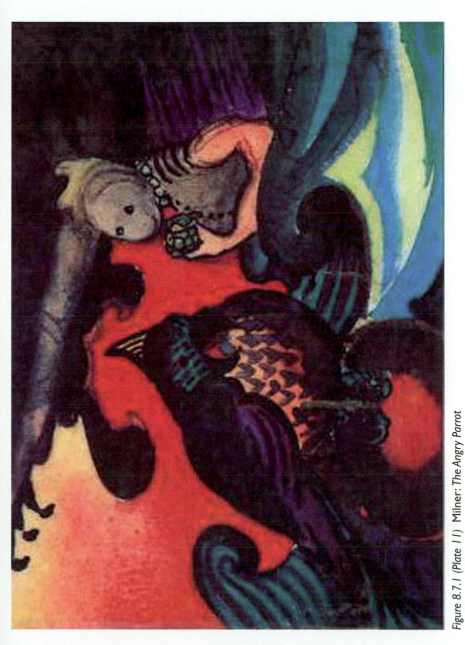

Figure 8.7.1 (Plate 11) Milner: The Angry Parrot

M. Milner (1950) *On Not Being Able to Paint*. Oxford: Heinemann, 1971, front cover.

Figure 8.7.2 (Plate 12) Milner: *The Angry Ape*

M. Podro (1990) The landscape thinks itself in me. *International Review of Psycho-Analysis 17*: 401–12, Figure 2.

Figure 11.3 (Plate 13) Bion: Norfolk, Dordogne and Oxfordshire paintings

Figure 11.4 (Plate 14) Bion: Redcourt paintings

2

1

Figure 11.5 (Plate 15) Bion: Swanage and California paintings

Figure 13.2 (Plate 16) Holbein: *The Dead Christ in the Tomb*

Copyright © photo: Martin Bühler, Kunstmuseum, Basel.

The prevalence that psychoanalysis has discovered among them of images based on a primitive autoscopy of the oral organs and organs derived from the cloaca is what gives rise to the shapes of the demons in Bosch's work. Even the ogee of the *angustiae* of birth can be found in the gates to the abyss through which they thrust the damned; and even narcissistic structure may be glimpsed in the glass spheres in which the exhausted partners of the 'Garden of Delights' [Figure 7.1, Plate 8][29] are held captive.[30]

The same phantasmagorias occur in the dreams of analysands when their analysis, Lacan said, 'appears to reflect off the backdrop of the most archaic fixations'. He illustrated this with the case of a patient who dreamt he was in a car with a woman with whom he was having a difficult love-affair. In the dream the patient was pursued, said Lacan, 'by a flying-fish, whose balloon-like body was so transparent that one could see the horizontal level of liquid it contained: an image of vesical persecution of great anatomical clarity'.[31]

Lacan had previously claimed:

> After the repeated failures encountered by classical psychology in its attempt to account for the mental phenomena known as 'images', psy-choanalysis proved itself capable of accounting for the concrete reality they represent . . . because it began with their formative function in the subject.[32]

This was, of course, achieved first and foremost by Freud's attention to dream-images. It was also achieved by Klein's emphasis on fantasy in her child analysis development of psychoanalysis. Commending her account of drawings by her 10-year-old school phobic patient, Richard,[33] Lacan observed:

> through her we have the mapping, drawn by children's own hands, of the mother's inner empire, and the historical atlas of the internal divisions in which the imagos of the father and siblings – whether real or virtual – and the subject's own voracious aggression dispute their deleterious hold over her sacred regions.

Klein enables us to see in children's drawings the outward, inverse image, '*Urbild*',[34] he said, of the self in bits and pieces which makes so attractive identification of ourselves with others, or with whatever presents as intact and whole.

The fragmented self – the image of the self in bits and pieces – arises, according to Klein's findings, from the infant's libidinal and destructive part-object relations to its mother's breast, faeces and the father's penis imagined inside her. It results in 'a mosaic structure like that of a stained-glass window', said Lacan. It may resemble 'a jig-saw puzzle, with the separate parts of the body of a man or an animal in disorderly array'. Bosch makes us see this too, he added, with his paintings featuring

> the incongruous images in which disjointed limbs are rearranged as strange trophies; trunks cut up in slices and stuffed with the most unlikely fillings, strange appendages in eccentric positions, reduplications of the penis, images of the cloaca represented as a surgical excision, often accompanied in male patients by fantasies of pregnancy.[35]

If these are the images through which our identity is first formed then no wonder, Lacan speculated, 'the jubilant interest shown by the infant over eight months at the sight of his own image in a mirror'. For the mirror shows the infant an image of itself which is whole and thus particularly seductive given its initial 'organic disturbance and discord [in] the image of the "body in bits and pieces" '.[36]

'In comparison with the still very profound lack of coordination in his own motor functioning,' the image of another child, like 'the visual gestalt of his own body' in the mirror, serves as 'an ideal unity, a salutary imago'. Its value is also 'heightened', Lacan added, 'by all the early distress resulting from the child's intra-organic and relational discordance during the first six months of life, when he bears the neurological and humoral signs of a physiological prematurity at birth'. It is the toddler's confusion of its feelings with those reflected to it by others that accounts for its in-feeling (*Einfühlung*) empathy with them. This is evident in the fact that, at this age, a 'child who beats another child says that he himself was beaten', or, as Lacan also noted, 'a child who sees another child fall, cries'.[37]

As further evidence of the impact on the child of seeing what others do, he quoted St Augustine recalling in his *Confessions*, 'I myself have seen and known an infant to be jealous even though it could not speak. It became pale, and cast bitter looks on its foster-brother'. St Augustine thereby located, Lacan commented, 'spectacular absorption (the child absorbed), the emotional reaction (pale), and the reactivation of images of primordial frustration (with an envenomed look) [as] psychical and somatic coordinates of the earliest aggressiveness'.[38]

The invitation by what is shown us by others into imagined, albeit false, identification with the images they present is the precondition of the infant similarly identifying with what is not itself in identifying with the first person pronoun, 'I', of language. Herein lies the origin of the ego, ego-ideal or 'ideal-I', argued Lacan. Identification with the ego or I offers the infant a means of stabilizing and idealizing what is otherwise inwardly unstable and far from ideal. The baby's reflected mirror image is similarly inviting. It offers the infant, Lacan argued, 'the contour of his stature that freezes it and in a symmetry that reverses it, in opposition to the turbulent movements with which the subject feels he animates it'.[39]

Writing about the aftermath of this development in adults in analysis, Lacan observed:

> the I formation is symbolized in dreams by a fortified camp, or even a stadium – distributing, between the arena within its walls and its outer border of gravel-pits and marshes, two opposed fields of battle where the subject bogs down in his quest for the proud, remote inner castle whose form (sometimes juxtaposed in the same scenario) strikingly symbolizes the id.[40]

Such dreams pictured for Lacan the split between the id and ego introduced, in his view, by the inviting allure of escaping the id, likened by Freud to 'a cauldron full of seething excitations',[41] or the fragmentation of what Klein called the 'paranoid-schizoid position',[42] for identification or, rather, misidentification with the socially given ego or 'I' of language.

Taking refuge from the introjected 'partial objects' characterizing earliest infancy, according to Klein,[43] in the wholeness of the socially given 'I' or ego is understandable. So too is the appeal of 'the stability of the standing posture, the prestige of stature, the impressiveness of statues, which,' said Lacan, 'set the style for the identification in which the ego finds its starting-point and leave their imprint on it for ever'.[44] These images give to each of us in early infancy an anticipated 'illusion of unity', of 'self-mastery', while also conveying, he argued, 'constant danger of sliding back into the chaos from which he [the subject] started'.[45]

Klein similarly noted the flight of children from mother-centred fantasies of fragmentation and destruction into celebrating, desiring, or identifying with men and masculinity (see p. 54). Freud also described defensive flight from ambivalent love and hate of our parents into identification with others as source not only of the superego but also of the ego as 'precipitate of abandoned object-cathexes'.[46] But if we remain stuck in identification and oneness with these figures there is no space between us and them for wishing and desiring to come into being through their acquiring an object, 'a local habitation and a name', as Shakespeare put it in explaining how, in art, specifically poetry, imagination bodies forth what is otherwise 'airy nothing and things unknown'.[47]

Collapsing the space between oneself and what is given us to see by what is outside us risks the fate of the mythical Narcissus fixated and rigidified in adoring his mirrored reflection, bereft of any companion, save Echo mirroring what he said, to enable him to name and know that the object of his desire, his reflected image in a pool of water, was not someone else but an inverted image of himself. Perhaps Lacan intended to say something about this with his paper, 'The mirror phase', which he presented to the International Congress of Psychoanalysis in Marienbad in August 1936. But he left when Ernest Jones interrupted him ten minutes after his talk began, and the paper Lacan intended presenting was never published.

The next year Salvador Dali completed a painting, *The Metamorphosis of Narcissus* (Figure 7.2).[48] He called his fate 'death and fossilization'. Explaining its title, he said, 'if one looks for some time, from a slight distance and with a certain "absent-minded intentness", at the hypnotically motionless figure of Narcissus, it gradually disappears until it becomes absolutely invisible'.[49] Freud was evidently impressed when Dali showed him this painting when they met. Thanking Stefan Zweig for introducing Dali to him, Freud told Zweig:

> I had been tempted to regard the Surrealists, who have apparently chosen me as their patron saint, as complete madmen (let us say 95 percent, like 'absolute' alcohol). The young Spaniard, with his candid fanatic's eyes and his undeniable technical mastery, has impelled me to reconsider my opinion. It would in fact be quite interesting to study the genesis of a painting of this kind analytically.[50]

Freud had earlier been puzzled why, despite the infant's desire first being evoked by body-parts – its mother's breast and its fingers and thumb, anus and genitals – so that, as Freud put it, 'a unity comparable to the ego cannot exist in the individual from the start', the infant nevertheless comes to fall in love, like Narcissus, with itself as a whole.[51]

Klein rooted the child's development from part- to whole-object relating to the development of life and death instincts with which she assumed the child is born. She regarded identification with a whole, loved and hated image of the mother, and with the analyst in her stead, as key to mental health. US ego psychologists have argued something similar in advocating the analysand's mirroring or idealizing identification with the analyst as means of countering the ego weaknesses associated with what the Chicago-based analyst, Heinz Kohut, called 'narcissistic personality disorders'.[52] Lacan, by contrast, argued that such identification with what is presented to us by the world and others to identify with – reflections in mirrors, water, and painting included – is self-alienating. He also argued, like Dali, that it is fossilizing.

It can also risk murder, as in the case of Lacan's patient, Marguerite. She recovered from the delusional identification of her fantasies with the actress, Duflos, impelling her to stab her, through the intervention of the law. Three weeks after being arrested and punished for stabbing Duflos, Marguerite's delusional identification with her ended. Lacan's study of 'paranoiac knowledge' in such cases contributed, he said, to his discovery of 'paranoiac alienation of the ego'. It led, he said, to his discovery that just such self-alienating identification with what is given to us by others to see and desire is the precondition of the three-cornered – child, mother, father – Oedipus complex. He described it as a 'triangular relationship between the ego, the object

Figure 7.2 Dali: *The Metamorphosis of Narcissus*

and "someone else" '.[53] The 'someone else' is given by the fact that among humans, he maintained, what we desire is determined by what others desire. We desire what they desire. Seeing what they wish for and desire brings our wishing and desiring into being. It gives wishing and desiring an object and thus knowable shape and form.

It is the child's discovery that the main object of its mother's desire is not itself but someone else that gives its desire an object – its father, say – and a name – the father's name, say, given the continuing prevalence of patrilineal systems of descent in most societies today. This helps explain the frequent symbolization of objects of desire in dreams in paternal or male-centred and phallic terms, as long ago noted by Freud (see p. 26). It also helps explain his observation that, in childhood, sexual difference centres on 'having a male genital and being castrated'.[54]

Denying this castration meaning of sexual difference can lead to it returning as a hallucination. An example was Freud's patient, Sergei Pankieff, who, it seems, unconsciously identified as a child with his mother and with wanting to take her place in sexual intercourse with his father. Not wanting to acknowledge that her lack of a penis might mean that taking her place entailed being castrated as she seemed to him to be, this meaning returned as a hallucination. One day when he was 5, Pankieff told Freud, he was playing in the garden, carving with his pocket-knife when, suddenly, he said, 'I noticed that I had cut through the little finger of my (right or left?) hand, so that it was only hanging on by its skin.' Appalled he sat down, unable to look at his finger. 'At last I calmed down, took a look at the finger,' he continued, 'and saw it was entirely uninjured.'[55] It was an instance, said Lacan, of what is excluded from imaginary and symbolic meaning returning as 'real'.[56]

The child, perceiving the object of the mother's desire as phallic, might identify with this object of her desire. 'The whole problem of the perversions', argued Lacan, 'consists in conceiving how the child, in its relationship with its mother . . . identifies with the imaginary object of her desire insofar as the mother herself symbolizes it in the phallus.'[57] The phallic imagery, in terms of which parents may well symbolize their desire, shapes and gives form to the child's desire. 'If the mother's desire is for the phallus,' Lacan maintained, 'the child wants to be the phallus in order to satisfy her desire.'[58] The child becomes free from paralysing and ossifying identification with the phallic object of her desire only by the intervention of others, by the child's father say, imposing his authority, according to Lacan, saying 'No, you won't sleep with your mother' and to the mother 'No, the child is not your phallus, I have it'.[59]

Seeing the boy's or man's penis might impel the girl to construe this as the object of her mother's desire. She might therefore want to have one too. Certainly Freud claimed that the sight of the penis evokes the girl's envy. She might respond, he said, by disavowing her lack of a penis. Or she might imagine she will acquire one and become a man. Or she may abandon sex. Or, to use Lacan's words, 'insofar as the mother herself symbolizes it in the phallus',[60] she may adopt the same phallic object of desire as her mother. She may adopt her father, for instance, and others in his stead, as main object of her desire. It is the sight of the penis, 'strikingly visible and of large proportions', wrote Freud, that reorients the girl from Oedipal desire for the mother to Oedipal desire for the father. Overlooking the social factors privileging the penis or phallus as symbol of sex and desire, and overlooking women's role in childbearing, Freud attributed the 'extraordinarily high narcissistic cathexis' accorded the penis 'to its organic significance for the propagation of the species'.[61]

Freud, and Lacan after him, were not the first, of course, to observe that our desires are shaped by what others desire, and that our identity and self-consciousness too are shaped by others. Hegel long ago argued that our self-consciousness comes into being through the recognition conferred on us by others. He gave the example of the master's consciousness of himself coming from his servant's recognition of him as master. The servant is free to confer this recognition, he added, only through transcending himself and realizing his free will through the work he does for his master.[62] We could also liken the origin of self-consciousness to the imagined scene, described by Sartre, in which, looking through a keyhole, so intent on what one sees one forgets oneself, one suddenly becomes acutely self-conscious in becoming aware of being the object of another's gaze. 'All that is necessary', said Lacan, commenting on this scenario, 'is for something to signify to me that there may be others there.'[63]

We do not even have to see others seeing us for them to make us self-conscious. Seeing, however, highlights the point. Lacan illustrated it with the example of a fisherman pointing out a sardine can glittering in the sea, telling him, 'You see that can? Do you see it? Well, it doesn't see you!' Yet, Lacan insisted, 'it was looking at me, all the same. It was looking at me at the level of the point of light, the point at which everything that looks at me is situated.'[64] Light looks at us. By means of the light which is in the depths of our eyes, he added, 'something is painted . . . something that is an impression, the shimmering of a surface that is not, in advance, situated for me in its distance . . . grasps me at every moment'.[65]

He also highlighted ways in which our self-consciousness comes into being through artists showing us what to see and desire. He emphasized the point with the example of Holbein's painting, *The Ambassadors* (Figure 7.3, Plate 9).[66] Like an advertisement, this picture, painted in 1533, says John Berger, 'demonstrates the desirability of what money could buy . . . the visual desirability of what can be bought lies in its tangibility, in how it will reward the touch, the hand, of the owner'. A similar painting, *Portrait of Georg Gisze of Danzig*,[67] completed by Holbein the previous year, resulted in the Turkish rug depicted in it being subsequently marketed as a Holbein carpet.

But what about the odd shape in the foreground of *The Ambassadors* painting? Does it market and whet our appetite for buying what it depicts? Why is it depicted, according to Berger, 'in a (literally) quite different optic from everything else in the picture'?[68] We could use it to highlight ways in which what might seem a meaningless bodily as opposed to a meaningful psychological symptom can be seen as meaningful if only it is looked at differently. The philosopher, John Wisdom, theorized analysis similarly in likening the analyst seeing the analysand unconsciously seeing meaning in what they see – 'a snake in the grass', for instance – even though the analysand is unconscious of seeing any such meaning.[69] Similarly on looking at this painting straight ahead we see a different meaning, as in Salvador Dali's double images, from what we see looking at the painting from its right-hand edge. Then we see that this object is not depicted to whet our appetite for buying what it depicts but that it is a skull signifying the non-existence of death.

Looked at straight on, this shape suggested to Lacan, he said, 'that loaf composed of two books which Dali was once pleased to place on the head of an old woman'.[70] This was subsequently reconstructed into the piece known as *Retrospective Bust of a Woman*,[71] now in the New York Museum of Modern Art. Perhaps referring to Dali's picture, *The Persistence of Memory*,[72] Lacan said the loaf-shape reminded him of 'Dali's paintings of soft watches, whose signification', he said, 'is obviously less phallic'.[73]

Revealed as a skull, we can see that the enigmatic shape in Holbein's *The Ambassadors* is the result of distorting geometric projection. Lacan argued:

> All this shows that at the very heart of the period in which the subject emerged and geometral optics was an object of research, Holbein makes visible for us here something that is simply the subject as annihilated, annihilated in the form that is, strictly speaking, the image embodiment of the *minus-phi* $[(-f)]$ of castration.[74]

Like all paintings, *The Ambassadors* is 'simply what any picture is, a trap for the gaze'.[75] We lose ourselves in being trapped into identifying with what the painter invites us to see. 'In Holbein's picture,' Lacan emphasized, 'we are literally called into the picture, and represented as caught', as nothing, reflecting as the picture does our 'nothingness', as he put it, 'in the figure of the death's head'.[76]

Something similar occurs in analysis. Analysands become nothing in losing themselves in mis-recognizing and misidentifying themselves and their fantasies, desires, or 'signifiers', to use Lacan's term, with the analyst. The analyst's job is not to reinforce this misidentification and add to the analysand's self-alienation through encouraging their identification with them as ego-ideal, as advocated by US ego psychologists such as Heinz Kohut. The analyst's task, according to Lacan, entails discerning and putting into words this identification at the moment it begins to emerge from unconsciousness so it can be exposed, deconstructed and dispelled.

Achieving this outcome depends on the analyst operating as a quasi-mirror. We can illustrate this using the following diagram borrowed by Lacan from a 1934 book about optics by Bouasse (Figure 7.4).[77] If we represent the analyst by the vertical mirror 'A', and the unconscious meaning or fantasy in the analysand, '$', by the vase containing the flowers on the right-hand side of the diagram, then this can be seen and become conscious as such in $ only by virtue of the flowers and the inverted vase on the left-hand side of the diagram being inverted and brought together by the convex mirror, 'xy', as reflected and mediated by the analyst as mirror, 'A'.

Just as paintings, or popular celebrities such as the actress, Duflos, in the case of Lacan's patient, Marguerite, invite misidentification with them, so too the analytic situation invites the analysand's mistaken identification of their fantasies with the analyst. The analyst's ability to put this misidentification into words depends on their following the rule according to which, said Lacan, 'we [analysts] avoid all expression of personal taste, we conceal whatever might betray them, we become depersonalized, and try to represent for the other an ideal of impassability'. The slightest pretext, he said, is enough to arouse the analysand's aggressive intent, thereby reactualizing the unconscious fantasies bringing them into analysis. These are revealed only to the extent that the analyst becomes 'as devoid as possible of individual characteristics', argued Lacan, and 'offers the subject the pure mirror of a smooth surface'.[78]

The analysand's unconscious fantasies, intentions and meanings are first brought into being as they are in all of us by others mediating the patriarchal social order, the 'Other' with a big 'O', said Lacan, into which we are born,

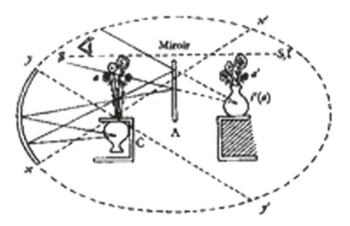

Figure 7.4 Bouasse: Optical diagram

and in which we live. It is through analysis inviting the analysand into mistakenly identifying their unconscious fantasies with the analyst, and through the analyst putting this into words that the analysand discovers who, said Lacan, 'he is truly addressing, without knowing it'.[79] Freud did this by following the analysand's free associations, the nodal points in which they converged, and the symbolic meanings which this suggested in arriving at his interpretations of the unconscious wishes disguised in the analysand's symptoms. Klein traced back from what the analysand said or did in analysis – drawings in the case of her 10-year-old school phobic patient, Richard – the unconscious fantasies they thereby symbolize and displace.

In his 1928 novella, *The Story of the Eye*, written after he had been in analysis, the surrealist writer, Georges Bataille, depicted a succession of objects displacing each other as objects of desire, including a saucer of milk, eggs, bull's balls and a bull-fighter's eyes.[80] Lacan, in turn, likened the analyst's work to that of the detective in Edgar Allan Poe's short story, *The Purloined Letter*, who retraces the successive displacements of a love letter in seeking to discover who had stolen it from its original addressee.[81] Most of all, Lacan argued, the analyst's task involves deciphering the analysand's self-alienation resulting from their misidentifying with others and with their idealised phallic objects of desire. The ills resulting from such misidentification are illuminatingly illustrated by another psychoanalyst, Marion Milner, in developing a different version of psychoanalysis, as I will detail next.

Chapter 8

Milner

Milner's development of psychoanalysis can be traced back to the findings of her self-analysis, beginning in the 1920s, and reported by her in books published in the 1930s under the pen-name, Joanna Field. In these books she described ills she suffered from identifying with a narrowly focused male drive, as she understood it, geared, she said, to doing and getting things done. She contrasted this with wide attention to, and oneness with the world around her, which she equated with feminine receptivity.

She described experiences of this latter stance during the year, 1927, she married Denis Milner. 'I have felt life flowing all around me and over my head – and I am happy to be immersed,' she wrote in her 1927 diary. Another time, she recalled, 'I felt a sudden immense reality with D. The swans and reeds [in Golders Hill Gardens] had a "thusness", "so and no otherwise" existing in an entirely different sphere from the world of opinion.'[1] She also wrote of her pleasure in wide-open attention to music, putting herself into it as she listened to it at a concert, as she illustrated with a doodle (Figure 8.1).[2]

Other examples of receptive, feminine or wide as opposed to narrow, male-driven attention included, for Milner, her becoming engrossed in looking at a Cézanne still-life depicting a white plate with green apples on a cloth.

Figure 8.1 Milner: Concert doodle

J. Field (1934) *A Life of One's Own*. London: Virago, 1986, p. 74. This and other Milner images are reproduced by kind permission of Margaret Walters.

I simply sat and looked, too inert to remember whether I ought to like it or not. Slowly then I became aware that something was pulling me out of my vacant stare and the colours were coming alive, gripping my gaze till I was soaking myself in their vitality.[3]

She found herself becoming similarly drawn into another painting. Looking at it, she noted:

my mind settled down to complete absorption, oblivious to all but the harmonies of shape and colour which took on a life of their own and continued to grow out of the paint the longer I looked . . . so that I could see the whole all at the same time.[4]

Something similar occurred when she sketched an animal in London's Regent's Park Zoo (Figure 8.2.1).[5] '[It] posed itself upon the rocks,' she explained, 'and the shape of him so seized hold of me that there was no room for thought of my own incapacity, I just began to draw in frantic haste'.[6]

Other times, however, she became alienated by 'blind thinking' equation or identification, as she called it,[7] of her wishes and fears with people and things around her. Freud had described something similar. He had described the hallucinatory 'perceptual identity' between past and present occurring, he said, in the hungry baby imagining itself sucking for nourishment at its mother's breast for satisfaction as it has before.[8] To enable analysands to discover the content of similar hallucinatory thinking lying at the root of their ills, he encouraged them to free associate, as I have said, to bits and pieces of their memories and dreams. Milner adopted this technique in her self-analysis. Since the sea often occurred in her dreams, she decided to write down ideas it suggested to her:

mother . . . feeling ashamed when they laughed at Miss R.'s and they said I'd painted the sea blue . . . cool green water to dive into . . . no bathing-dress and people watching . . . lose myself . . . fear.[9]

She also followed Jung's method of active imagination and his doctrine, which she quoted approvingly, 'The image is equally an expression of the unconscious as of the conscious situation of the moment'.[10]

Impressed by the value of visual imagery as means of self-analysis, she remembered herself, aged 15, making a picture of a dragon (Figure 8.2.2, Plate 10).[11]

For in those days I used to listen to several sermons in every week and took the moral exhortations of a girls' boarding-school rather seriously, my dragon became a picture of my own faults, something I hated, something to be pinned up on the wall to spur me on to struggle against them.[12]

1

Figure 8.2.1 Milner: Zoo sketch

J. Field (1934) *A Life of One's Own*. London: Virago, 1986, p. 70.

Free associating to her picture reminded her of the dragon, Fafnir, killed by Siegfried, 'the jaws of death', and 'fear', she said, 'that my personal identity would be swallowed up'.

It was this fear of being swallowed up, and losing herself that paradoxically drove her to alienate herself from herself in obeying the 'purpose-driven' male drive, as she put it, 'always to be getting things done to prove to myself that I existed as a person at all'.[13] She also noted her disquiet about male figures. She found herself mis-seeing William Blake's picture, *The Ancient of Days*,[14] as 'a drunken clown peering down from the clouds, with wisps of hair falling about his besotted face and immense false nose'. It revealed to her an unconscious or subconscious image of God, as originator of the world, motivated by 'malevolent intention', which could be borne only by forgetting this 'with the help of drugs: drink, noise, and hilarity'.[15]

As well as adopting Freud's method of free association, and Jung's method of active imagination, Milner was also influenced in her self-analysis by E.M. Forster's quip, in discussing Gide's psychoanalytic novel, *The Counterfeiters*, 'How can I tell what I think till I see what I say?'[16] She accordingly supplemented her free association writing with free association doodling so as to see what she said and thought. 'I simply followed my impulse and drew unquestioningly what I felt to be important,' she explained, 'my thought took to itself material from anywhere and everywhere in order to find a form in which to become clothed and visible.'[17] She located what was invisible and unknown, which she sought to see, in the 'IT', theorized by Groddeck, and described by Freud as evidence that 'we are "lived" by unknown and uncontrollable forces'.[18] Noting this, Milner described the images resulting from her free association doodling as informed by 'flickering movements of the mind' evoking an 'answering activity,' she said, 'a knowing that was nothing to do with me'.[19]

Sometimes this answering activity seemed benign. Other times quite the reverse. 'The way is to the destructive element submit yourself,' she wrote, quoting Conrad.[20] But what was this destructive force which alienated Milner from herself? Something of its character emerged for Milner in images occurring to her in trying to illustrate Robert Louis Stevenson's verse, 'Whenever the moon and the stars are set, / Whenever the wind is high, / All night long in the dark and the wet, / A man goes riding by.'[21] Trying to illustrate these lines, she found herself drawing sweeping curves (Figure 8.3).[22]

One of these curves reminded her of a dream of a tidal wave, standing, she said, 'for the panic dread of being overwhelmed by the boundless sea of what was not myself'.[23] The last curve reminded her of 'a looming fear of thunder', 'St Martha's Chapel which crowns the Pilgrim's Way', and the hymn 'There is a green hill far away, / Without a city wall'. It also reminded her of an 'electric machine in my father's study,' she said, 'of parental and divine anger, of guilt and primitive fear and my own emotional urges'.[24]

These urges could be male or female. She identified the former urge, as I have said, with a narrowly focused stance, impelled, she said, by a 'questing beast [which] saw items according to whether they served its purposes, saw them as a means to its own ends, not interested in them at all for their own sake'.[25] She pictured this drive as a male-like 'sharp-shooter girl on horseback' in contrast to the 'striking femaleness of the swooningly passive figure' of a doodle she did one day in New York (Figure 8.4).[26]

She was fearful of this swooningly female aspect of herself being overwhelmed by what was not herself. But she also courted this in acquiescing, surprisingly, with the misogynist writer, Otto Weininger's dictum that woman is 'fusion with everything she knows' and with his assertion, 'Women have no existence and no essence; they are not, they are nothing.'[27] The psychoanalyst,

Figure 8.3 Milner: Curves

J. Field (1934) *A Life of One's Own.* London: Virago, 1986, pp. 163–4.

Sabina Spielrein, had long before noted women's self-destruction, as she put it, in imagining themselves to be one with the men with whom they are in love.[28] She courted this self-destruction. So did Milner. 'I am nothing, I know nothing, I want nothing', she told herself,[29] just as St Paul said, apropos of achieving oneness with God, 'Only when I become as nothing can God enter in.'[30]

Figure 8.4 Milner: New York doodle

J. Field (1934) *A Life of One's Own*. London: Virago, 1986, p. 89.

She also courted the masochistic surrender to others which Freud,[31] and his immediate followers, Helene Deutsch,[32] for instance, equated with femininity.

'After the misery of the week-end I came to see you, submerged and hoping nothing,' Milner wrote to her lover,

> I'd come empty, expecting nothing – is that why you were able to fill me? . . . Is this the losing of oneself, the self-forgetfulness that so many hunt after? My blood is not mine, it is a gloriously alive thing, something with purposes not mine, that may even destroy me. But I'm glad . . . glad to be possessed, possessed by something that has no consideration for my good. I feel exultant because my good has been wiped out, for I was utterly tired of striving for my own good.[33]

But, as this makes explicit, such surrender carries the risk of being taken over, possessed by what is alien, and no good for oneself.

Men could have this effect on Milner. So too could women as mediators of the purpose-driven, male-dominated society in which we live. Finding herself speechless with rage on hearing the front door shut as the man in her life left after an angry quarrel between them, she wildly scribbled. 'At first what I was drawing seemed to be a snake around a tree-trunk,' she recalled, 'and I was still angry and hopeless'. But then a drawing emerged (Figure 8.5). It led to the following associations:

> at first I thought it was a sort of female Punch, and then suddenly saw that it was also the Duchess in *Alice in Wonderland* who always screamed 'Off with her head'. At once . . . I remembered all the people from my childhood upwards, mostly women, since I had been educated by women, who by sheer force of a loud voice or a show of anger or sarcasm, had had the power to make me 'lose my head', to wipe out from me all sense of my own identity, not only to thwart me in what I wanted, but to produce such a state that I no longer knew what I wanted at all, I was aware only of them, utterly possessed by them.[34]

Milner's account of these figures is reminiscent of the terrifying viragos peopling the destructive fantasies of the case histories recounted by Melanie Klein, who supervised Milner in the 1940s.

Destructive fantasies also emerged from Milner's free association doodling with paint. She wrote of one such experiment:

> I had provided myself with a pile of rough paper, filled my brush with whatever colour seemed most attractive at the moment, and then begun

Figure 8.5 Milner: Female Punch

J. Field (1934) *A Life of One's Own.* London: Virago, 1986, p. 198.

idly to spread the colour over the paper. I had had no preconceived plan, but had let my brush follow any shape that was suggested by the first dab of paint.[35]

The resulting images included

the head of a sheep . . . a dragon dancing a jig . . . a wolf in the dark . . . some snake in the Bible that was good, not evil . . . Shadrach, Meschach and Abed-nego, who were cast bound into the burning fiery furnace and were not burned.[36]

She also found destructive or potentially destructive images emerging when she tried to depict a misty morning on the Sussex Downs:

I concentrated on the mood of the scene, the peace and softness of the colouring, the gentle curves of the Downs, and began to scribble in charcoal, letting hand and eye do what they liked. Gradually a definite form had emerged and there, instead of the peaceful summer landscape, was a blazing heath fire [Figure 8.6.1], its roaring flames leaping from the earth in a funnel of fire, its black smoke blotting out the sky.[37]

To this image she added another initially intended to convey, she said, 'the over-arching beeches spreading protecting arms in the still summer air [of a] perfect June morning'. The result (Figure 8.6.2), however, showed 'two stunted bushes on a snowy crag, blasted by a raging storm'.[38]

Other images conveyed hatred of authority as well as submission to it. An example was a picture she called *The Angry Parrot* (Figure 8.7.1, Plate 11).[39] It prompted the following thoughts:

1   2

Figure 8.6 Milner: Heath fire and stunted bushes

M. Milner (1950) *On Not Being Able to Paint*. London: Heinemann, pp. 7, 8.

The parrot certainly seems to be me. What then is the way out, how is it going to escape being drowned in those stormy seas of feeling? For if it gives in to what 'they' want, the grabbing Thunder-god and the Grey Lady, if it lets them take its precious egg, it feels it will lose its identity altogether and never be a separate person at all. And yet if it does not give in they may destroy it as a punishment or go away altogether and leave it to drown.[40]

Something similar emerged from another doodle (Figure 8.7.2, Plate 12).[41] She called it *The Angry Ape*. It began, she said, 'from a scribbled shaded line that had turned itself into an ape-like creature . . . terrified of something'. To this she added

he is turning his head away from his own hands, hands which are red with blood and aching to attack the two serpents. The serpents are chatting happily together, it is their garden, Adam and Eve, parents, and they can't be bothered with the ape, in fact they have no idea how awful he feels . . . the ape is turning away because he cannot bear to look at them and face the jealousy and rage and fury they arouse: fury partly because he is shut out . . . partly because they own the garden and can order him about.[42]

Other destructive images included a drawing, *The Farmer's Wife* (Figure 8.8.1),[43] this title being suggested to Milner by the drawing reminding her of the castrating female figure in the nursery rhyme: 'Three blind mice, three blind mice / They all ran after the farmer's wife / She cut off their tails with a carving knife . . .'. She also wrote about destructive confusion akin to Freud's likening of the id to 'a chaos, a cauldron full of seething excitations'.[44] Perhaps it was dread of this confusion signalling destruction that led to some of her doodles remaining chaotic scribbling. Or perhaps, she speculated,

some internal forbidding, based on fear of instinctive forces within, had succeeded in isolating the particular area of feeling and idea stirring at the moment, with the result that it could not become fused with recognisable images and socially meaningful symbols, but would remain private and incommunicable. Or possibly it had so fused with images but they were too instinctively direct and primitive to be acceptable to the conscious self.[45]

She was also particularly struck by a doodle she surrounded with words (Figure 8.8.2).[46] It indicated, she said, that naming chaos – framing it with words – can make it bearable. Or she evaded what chaos might signify by impatiently making a doodle become 'a recognisable object too soon'.[47]

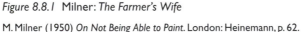

1

Figure 8.8.1 Milner: *The Farmer's Wife*

M. Milner (1950) *On Not Being Able to Paint.* London: Heinemann, p. 62.

This is not dissimilar to Klein's postscript to her essay introducing her theory of 'paranoid-schizoid' states of mind. In it she noted Freud's emphasis, in his analysis of Schreber's schizophrenic breakdown, that it involved Schreber imagining his doctor, Flechsig, as fragmented into 'forty to sixty sub-divisions' from which he took refuge in obsession with God.[48] Milner's flight from inner fragmentation and chaos, and its scribbled manifestations, into making her doodled images into readily recognizable, stereotyped figures is arguably similar to this. Picasso, by contrast, made her see, she said, that

> here was someone who had the courage to recognise and admit such inner chaos; whatever his position as an artist, he at least showed how deceptive the external wholeness of bodies can be, how one can look to the outside world like a whole person and yet be all in bits inside, full of conflicting wishes and chaotic standards, one's self can be nothing but a caddis-worm shell of bits and pieces, picked up anywhere and stuck on anyhow. And he had managed to show this with a kindness and humour,

2

Figure 8.8.2 Milner: Chaos doodle

M. Milner (1950) *On Not Being Able to Paint.* London: Heinemann, p. 75.

at least in some of the pictures, which made it a much less intolerable fact to face.[49]

Picasso, she suggested, enabled his public to tolerate the plunge evoked, for Milner, by Cézanne reputedly saying, 'Descend with the painter into the dim tangled roots of things, and rise again from them in colours, be steeped in the light of them'.[50] But this plunge can evoke dread of destruction, Milner pointed out, 'fears of embracing, becoming one with, something infinitely suffering, fears of plunging into a sea of pain in which both could become drowned'.[51]

Yet this self-same plunge can also be inspiring. It is the stuff of falling and being in love. Just as Freud described being in love as evoking the illusion of oneness with what is other than oneself, so did Milner. She had described this oneness with otherness the year she married her husband, Denis, as I illustrated at the beginning of this chapter. She described this self-same oneness with otherness occurring in art:

[The] experience of outer and inner coinciding, which we blindly undergo when we fall in love, is consciously brought about in the arts, through the conscious acceptance of the as-if-ness of the experience and the conscious manipulation of a malleable material.[52]

Precursors of this account of art-making can be found in the account by the artist-turned-philosopher, William James, of mystical 'oneness' with 'the Absolute' or with God as inspiration of religion.[53] The Nobel prize-winning writer, Romain Rolland, similarly wrote to Freud of the inspiration he derived from the feeling of the 'eternal . . . without perceptible limits, and like oceanic, as it were'.[54] The art historian, Bernard Berenson, wrote too of oneness with the otherness of art. He called it 'the aesthetic feeling . . . that fleeting instant, so brief as to be almost timeless, when the spectator is at one with the work of art he is looking at'.[55]

Unlike Lacan, Milner approved of analysts fostering oneness of their analysands with them. She likened this illusory oneness to the oneness she experienced with the materials she used in drawing and painting. They gave her, she said, 'a public reality that was very pliant and undemanding . . . pencil and chalk and paper provided a simplified situation in which the other gave of itself easily and immediately to take the form of the dream'.[56] A similar oneness is rightly promoted by analysis, she argued, 'through the analyst acting as a pliant medium, giving back the patient's own thought to him, in a clarified form, rather than intruding his own needs and ideas'.[57] Whereas Lacan regarded the task of analysts as that of exposing, deconstructing and dispelling the analysand's illusory oneness of their fantasies with them, rather than acquiescing in, or reinforcing this oneness, and whereas Milner had deplored the self-alienating effect of identifying with the male drive inculcated in her by her teachers and others, she nevertheless argued that analysis, like art, is helpful in enabling recovery of what she understood as female openness to, and oneness with what is other than oneself. She asked:

> Could one say that by finding a bit of the outside world, whether in chalk or paper, or in one's analyst, that was willing temporarily to fit in with one's dreams, a moment of illusion was made possible, a moment in which inner and outer seemed to coincide?[58]

But in celebrating the oneness of analysands with their analysts, Milner lost sight of the self-alienation involved. She also lost sight of the two-way conversational essence of talking cure psychoanalytic psychotherapy. Yet she also recognized this in likening it to painting, drawing and doodling. As she said of her doodling:

> Quite often there was some conscious intention of what to draw, at the beginning, but the point was that one had to be willing to give up this first

idea as soon as the lines drawn suggested something else, it was almost like playing a game of psycho-analyst and patient with oneself, one's hand 'talked' at random, the watching part of one's mind made running comments on what was being produced.[59]

Milner also observed that her art-making was particularly satisfying in so far as it involved 'a dialogue relationship between thought and the bit of the external world represented by the marks made on the paper'.[60] Her close friend and colleague, Donald Winnicott, likewise described psychoanalytic psychotherapy as a form of dialogue. He called it playing. He described it as taking place in the space created by the overlap, dialogue, or interplay of the analysand's world of experience with that of the analyst. Generously crediting Milner with helping him become aware of this,[61] Winnicott wrote of conversations with her in the early 1940s conveying to him, he said, 'the tremendous significance that there can be in the interplay of the edges of two curtains, or of the surface of a jug that is placed in front of another jug',[62] as in the following sketch by her (Figure 8.9).[63]

Milner nevertheless persisted in emphasizing the value of analysis enabling the analysand to recover the 'primary ego-feeling', as Freud called the breast-feeding baby's illusory oneness with its mother's body.[64] She also likened this oneness to the equation of inner and outer reality resulting, according to Ernest Jones,[65] from our equating the first incestuous objects of our desire with symbols we use to disguise and represent them to ourselves in a form more acceptable to consciousness. The psychoanalyst, Otto Fenichel, similarly described the infant initially treating objects as one with what they symbolize:

Whereas in distortion the idea of penis is avoided through disguising it

Figure 8.9 Milner: Jugs sketch

M. Milner (1950) *On Not Being Able to Paint.* London: Heinemann, p. 16.

by the idea of snake, in prelogical thinking penis and snake are one and the same, they are perceived by a common conception; the sight of the snake provokes penis emotions; and this fact is later utilized when the conscious idea of snake replaces the unconscious one of penis.[66]

This is akin to Wollheim's account of paintings 'metaphorizing' bodily experience without any intervening or mediating link.[67] Milner had previously deplored the self-alienating effect of identifying with, and acquiescing in the male-centred drive of her education – a drive that can be readily symbolized in phallic terms as a penis or snake, to use Fenichel's example. She had also deplored the self-alienating effect of persisting in an infantile tendency toward 'blind thinking' equation of inner and outer reality.[68] Yet in the 1950s she argued that analysis should enable analysands to recover this self-same equation in so far as it is akin to the infant's initial primary ego-feeling of oneness with its mother in breast-feeding as described by Freud. Indeed, she argued, modern conceptions of art had entailed a shift from his initial account of primary process thinking as constituted by wish-fulfilling hallucinations constituting the unconscious to equating it with the illusory oneness of the breast-feeding baby with its mother's body. 'I think there are signs that a revision of the concept of "primary process" is already in the air,' she reported in 1956, 'a revision that has been partly stimulated by problems raised by the nature of art.'[69]

She illustrated the value of analysis enabling analysands to recover illusory oneness with otherness, akin to illusory oneness with their mothers' bodies as babies, with the case of an 11-year-old patient, Simon, whose problems included deteriorating interest in school which Milner attributed to its 'unmitigated not-me-ness'.[70] He did much better when the school went along with his wishes in letting him and his friends hold their photography club in a schoolroom during school hours. He likewise did much better in analysis when, instead of interpreting the defensive repression and displacement of the original objects of his destructive fantasies onto objects symbolizing them, Milner went along with these fantasies.

This included her indulging, rather than interpreting, the destructive fantasies involved in his melting down a toy soldier in a metal cup which he heated over an electric fire in her consulting room. She understood this as his melting down his male or god-like ego which, she theorized, made him drearily conform with the demands of external reality, this being the cause, in her view, of his deteriorating interest in his schoolwork. She attributed his ego conformity with external reality to his having insufficient experience of the 'cosmic bliss' of oneness with his mother in breast-feeding from her as a baby because this was interrupted by his supplementary bottle feed not being ready in time. This could have led to 'catastrophic chaos'.[71] Instead, said Milner, it led to premature ego development, and to his premature ego compliance with external reality.

Klein had described flight to male-centred ego development, and Lacan described flight to illusory oneness with otherness, as defences against destructive fragmentation calling for interpretation of this flight as defence. Milner, by contrast, argued that analysis, at least in Simon's case, entailed enabling him to recover infantile illusory oneness with otherness. More generally she speculated that, for analysands and non-analysands alike, our finding 'the familiar in the unfamiliar' depends on recovery of 'states of illusion of oneness [as] a recurrently necessary phase in the continued growth of the sense of twoness'.[72]

She also recognized the defensive character of ego-directed compliance with external reality in the case of Simon, and also in the case of a patient, Susan, who was 23 when she first came into analysis with Milner after being hospitalized with schizophrenia following an episode when she had fallen in love and felt one with the world around her. Her mother triumphantly reacted to her hospitalization by proclaiming, 'Now you are mad and so am I!'[73] Imagining herself to be one with this hostile external figure was hardly inviting. Doubtless this contributed to Susan keeping inner and outer reality rigidly apart, and to her rejecting Milner's interpretation of the symbolic meaning of what she said and did in analysis by insisting, 'A thing is what it is and can't be anything else.'[74]

She was nevertheless able to draw imaginatively during her analysis with Milner. The results included a drawing of a baby seal (Figure 8.10.1),[75] for instance, contained in what, at first, looked to Milner like 'a cosy nest'. But she soon after recognized that the containing shape was a threateningly ensnaring snake, expressing, she said, Susan's 'urgent need to keep a watchful eye on her surroundings'.[76] Treatment, she indicated, entailed enabling Susan to become less suspicious and more at one with others, without becoming mad as had happened on becoming one with what was around her prior to her hospitalization.

Evidence, for Milner, of Susan's need to recover this oneness included another drawing (Figure 8.10.2).[77] Milner wrote:

> What strikes me about the picture is that although all the aggressive spiked forms are directed outwards, while she is safe inside, almost even herself being the breast, this does not seem to be a stable position, since the central circle face constantly divides into the two faces in profile, which again constantly interact, first one becoming a whole circle which 'bites' a bit out of the other, and then the reverse happening.[78]

What was needed, she argued, was a situation in which Susan could recover oneness with otherness without this aggressive interchange occurring.

This treatment goal was linked for Milner, it seems, with Winnicott's treatment goal of 'regression in search of the true self'.[79] But its achievement might well be defended against in so far as it involves 'merged boundaries' or

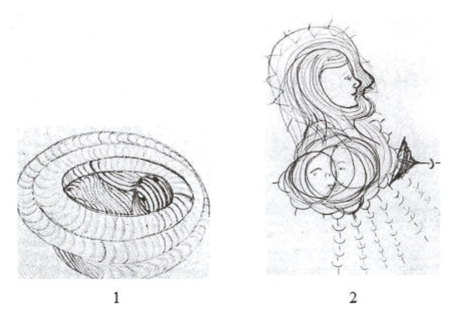

1   2

Figure 8.10 Susan: Drawings

M. Milner (1969) *The Hands of the Living God.* London: Virago, pp. 154, 164.

fusion with others. This resistance arises, said Milner, 'partly out of fear, fear that it means some kind of loss of definition, loss of identity, even loss of sanity'.[80] In such instances, and more particularly when the analysand's sense of themselves is precarious, wrote Milner's psychoanalytic colleague, Nina Coltart, it is more appropriate that the analyst rather than the analysand seek to achieve oneness with otherness through what Milner called wide attention. Coltart called it 'bare attention' in likening the analyst's evenly-suspended attention, as described by Freud, to the attention sought by herself and others in practising Buddhist meditation.[81]

The analyst, Joseph Sandler, similarly wrote of the value of the analyst's oneness with the analysand. He illustrated it with the following anecdote:

> I was walking along a crowded street in London, along the edge of the pavement, when suddenly a man who was walking a yard or two in front of me slipped off the edge of the pavement. I immediately righted myself, just as if I were about to stumble into the street.[82]

He noted the frequency with which, 'when we are not on our guard,' as he put it, 'we mirror the movements we perceive in others'.[83] He attributed this tendency to survival from earliest infancy of the 'direct and immediate identification' which Freud said 'takes place earlier than any object-cathexis'.[84]

He called it 'primary identification',[85] and demonstrated its persistence into adulthood by appeal to the oneness with what is outside us evoked by advertising and art.

But the analyst's oneness with the analysand is not all that counts in analysis. Indeed it can lead to problems akin to Sandler stumbling in too closely following, and identifying with the man ahead of him on the street. Translating what they discover through oneness with the analysand into an interpretation depends on analysts not only experiencing this oneness but also distancing themselves sufficiently so as not only to 'feel *with* the patient but *about* him', said Sandler.[86] In this the analyst's task is similar to that of the painter in cultivating oneness with their emerging painting in bringing it to fruition as theorized by the artist and art education lecturer, Anton Ehrenzweig, with whom Milner worked very closely, and for whom she helped out with the editing of his posthumously published book, *The Hidden Order of Art*.

Chapter 9

Ehrenzweig

Ehrenzweig arrived at his account of the oneness of painters with their emerging paintings in articles first published in the late 1940s. In these articles he drew on Klein's then relatively recently published accounts of 'depressive'[1] and 'paranoid-schizoid'[2] states of mind. His articles began, however, with the seeming revolutionary oneness of different shapes, forms, and perspectives achieved by Picasso in his painting, *Les Demoiselles d'Avignon*, and in cubist paintings beginning with those by Braque in 1909. Later commentators have argued that Picasso was indirectly influenced in helping bring about this revolution in art by the mathematician, Henri Poincaré, and his suggestion that the fourth dimension can be envisaged in terms of uniting a succession of images each seen from a different perspective. Picasso's revolutionary move involved demonstrating, according to one commentator, 'that the different perspectives should be shown in spatial simultaneity'.[3]

The result is that, in Picasso's cubist paintings, as Ehrenzweig put it, 'we might find a guitar superimposed upon a human limb', this recalling 'another set of adjoining forms to which it is juxtaposable'. He illustrated the resulting integration of different shapes with a sketch of a Picasso painting showing its 'form ambiguity' (Figure 9.1.1).[4] 'As the eye glides over the superimposed and overlapping forms the whole structure of the picture seems to shift continually as each form calls up a new juxtaposition of forms,' Ehrenzweig declared.[5] He also noted approvingly Picasso's superimposition of different perspectives in depicting faces. He conveyed this too with a schematic sketch to illustrate Picasso's condensation together of a front- and profile-view of a face (Figure 9.1.2).[6]

Condensed and overlapping perspectives and forms invite the onlooker's eyes to wander in and out of the picture plane. Or so Ehrenzweig claimed. Noting this effect of modern painting, he also noted Herbert Read's observation that this is not peculiar to modern art. 'It is possible to maintain that when we look at an object with the intention of appreciating its form – that is to say, its extension in space – we deliberately avoid such a wandering of attention,' Read suggested. In fact, he added, 'most works of art do not admit of any possible fixed focus – they deliberately invite a wandering eye'.[7]

Figure 9.1 Ehrenzweig: Form ambiguity and Picasso face

A. Ehrenzweig (1953) *The Psycho-Analysis of Artistic Vision and Hearing.* London: Routledge, pp. 24, 188.

Agreeing with Read, Ehrenzweig observed that, long before Picasso, artists brought together different perspectives as one in their art. We often overlook this, Ehrenzweig argued, because we repress it from consciousness in obedience to the repressive superego and secondary revision processes of the mind governed by prevailing conventions regarding perspective, *chiaroscuro*, truth to nature, 'open-air colours', and so on.[8]

Cubism punctured this repression. It led to greater recognition of the unification of different perspectives in art from ancient Egyptian times to our own. The art historian, Ernst Gombrich, recognized this in describing as follows the ancient Egyptian *Portrait of Hesire* (Figure 9.2):

> The head was most easily seen in profile so they drew it sideways. But if we think of the human eye we think of it as seen from the front. Accordingly, a full-face eye was planted into the side view of the face. The top half of the body, the shoulders and chest, are best seen from the front, for then we see how the arms are hinged to the body. But arms and legs in movement are much more clearly seen sideways. [Artists in ancient Egypt] preferred the clear outline from the big toe upwards. So both feet are seen from the inside [in following] a rule which allowed them to include everything in the human form that they considered important.[9]

Ehrenzweig, however, said less about unification of different perspectives in

Figure 9.2 Portrait of Hesire
Egyptian Museum, Cairo.

this example than in later examples of European and American painting and the visual arts. He focused at length, for instance, on the unification of different perspectives in Mantegna's painting, *The Dead Christ* (Figure 9.3.1).[10] He pointed out, with a line drawing (Figure 9.3.2),[11] the dynamic tension resulting from Mantegna's extreme foreshortening of the prostrate body and upturned head of Christ. It evokes the image of an upturned head as symbol, he said, 'of ecstatic devotion in persons who look upwards to heaven or as the antithetic symbol of blasphemy and sneer in scenes of the crucifixion'.[12] He also highlighted the unification of different perspectives in this painting with a diagram (Figure 9.3.3),[13] showing one fixation point centring on the intersection of two diagonals half-way up the left-hand side of the painting, and another centring on the emotional fixation point, Christ's head. To this Mantegna added, Ehrenzweig claimed, further foreshortening so as to crumple Christ's body into a shapeless mass, and so as to telescope his rigid

1

Figure 9.3.1 Mantegna: *The Dead Christ*

face towards his feet, thus conveying utter destruction and death, while also leaving ambiguous whether the squashing of Christ's body is real or simply an effect of his play with perspective.

But the unification of different meanings and perspectives, following rules developed during the early Italian Renaissance, is often credited not to Mantegna but to Cézanne. Certainly his paintings are often regarded as one of the immediate inspirations of the cubist revolution in art inaugurated by Braque and Picasso. Impressed by the dynamic effects of uniting different perspectives, Ehrenzweig detailed this unity in terms of a schematic sketch of one of Cézanne's still life paintings (Figure 9.4).[14]

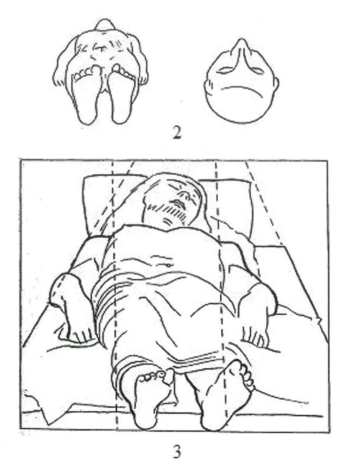

2

3

Figures 9.3.2 and 9.3.3 Ehrenzweig: Diagrams

A. Ehrenzweig (1953) *The Psycho-Analysis of Artistic Vision and Hearing.* London: Routledge, pp. 181, 201.

In traditional art it makes no difference in which sequence we view the single form details of a painting, whether they are the principal eye-catching features or mere background forms. It offers a *static* image corresponding to the final composite memory image which emerges into consciousness after the eyes' initial oscillation. Cézanne's composition would be more exacting; it imposes definite fixation points and definite directions upon our eyes' movements. His distortions are – and this is nothing new in artistic form innovations – ambiguous; different fixation points require different distortions and if there were several fixation points in a painting the distortions can only be a compromise between conflicting influences issuing from the different fixation points.[15]

Figure 9.4 Ehrenzweig: Cézanne sketch

A. Ehrenzweig (1953) *The Psycho-Analysis of Artistic Vision and Hearing.* London: Routledge, p. 194.

Cézanne's unification of different perspectives within a single painting might threaten socially imposed rules of perspective governing our conscious experience and aimed at securing reassuringly stable, safe, and constant perception. But it is more true to reality than these rules, argued Ehrenzweig, again referring to his Cézanne sketch:

> If in one of his still-life paintings the table-cloth hangs over the front edge and seems to break the edge into two, the left half, if traced through the overhanging piece of tablecloth, does not join into the right half, but appears to be shifted to a higher or lower level. But a table edge does in fact appear broken in this way if we focus on the interrupting bit of tablecloth as we would naturally do. That tracing of the two halves into a continuous line, on the other hand, does not correspond to an eye movement suggested by the linear composition of the picture; it would have had no visual reality for Cézanne. There are other cases where an

eye-catching form feature breaks an otherwise continuous line. In the same way the line of the two shoulders of a human figure is broken by the neck in between.[16]

Cézanne's paintings highlight, Ehrenzweig argued, ways in which good art has always dynamically unified not necessarily different perspectives, but the differences of unconscious and conscious perception.

We are affected by this dynamic in appreciating painting. Our appreciation is also affected by the unity of negative and positive spaces achieved by the painter. Arguing in this vein, Ehrenzweig illustrated the point with the unification of the shapes of the heads and the space between the figures in Georges de la Tour in his painting, *The Nativity*, in Rennes.[17] Since we are not usually conscious of the dynamic effect of such bringing together of different shapes, forms, and perspectives, Ehrenzweig claimed, this effect must operate unconsciously. So too with the scribbles of artists on their chosen medium. These too affect our appreciation of their art. When they are absent in copies and mannerist or pastiche imitations of the innovative artist's work, the dynamic and aesthetic effect of the original is lost. Since we are not consciously aware of the contribution of the innovative artist's scribbling to our aesthetic experience of their art, we must unconsciously unite its perception with what is more obvious to conscious perception.

Dreams, Ehrenzweig maintained, involve a similar dynamic in uniting unconscious perception with consciously perceived gestalts. He related unconscious depth perception to the loss of sharp and well-defined focus in dreamlike states of mind in which, he said, forms intermingle and separate in continuous flux, condensing and bringing different images together. He gave the example of a pram, hearse and cannon combining into a single dreamelement. He also related this to Nietzsche's account of art uniting Dionysian chaos and Apollonian order, and to William James' emphasis on ways in which thinking involves both vagueness and clarity.

Opposing the philosophy of Berkeley and Hume, who characterized thinking as consisting solely of clear and distinct ideas, and in contrast to Freud's account of neurotic and defensive forgetting of names and words (see e.g. p. 12), James argued that when we try to recall a name or word, nothing distinct and clear at first occurs. Instead a 'sort of wraith of the name' appears which we forget as soon as 'we "twig" it', he said. Thinking begins in vagueness, in what is incoherent, unclear and diffuse. 'It is,' he continued, in forwarding his theory of thinking as a continuous stream of consciousness, 'the reinstatement of the vague and inarticulate to its proper place in our mental life which I am so anxious to press on the attention.'[18]

Quoting this approvingly on the title page of his 1953 book, *The Psycho-Analysis of Artistic Vision and Hearing*, in which his earlier articles about the oneness of unconscious and conscious perception were included, Ehrenzweig observed that James' emphasis on the emergence from vagueness of clear and distinct ideas was consistent with his later account of religious ideas and institutions emerging out of, and being inspired by vague, inarticulate, intuitive, and beyond words ineffable mystical experience.[19] Freud similarly likened the emergence of the analyst's interpretations from the vagueness of the analysand's free associations to Schiller's dictum: 'where there is a creative mind, Reason . . . relaxes its watch upon the gates, and the ideas rush in pell-mell, and only then does it look them through and examine them in a mass'.[20]

Just as psychoanalytic interpretation begins with vagueness, with the analysand's more or less vague free associations, so does art. 'At the beginning [the artist] knows only vaguely, if at all, what he is going to produce; his mind is curiously empty while he watches passively the forms growing from under his brush,' Ehrenzweig claimed, adding

> Automatic form-control means that the depth mind has taken over the form-production which therefore now reflects the gestalt-free structure of the depth mind. Hence, the lack of a pregnant eye-catching pattern, the superimposition, overlapping and general ambiguity of forms which could never be achieved by conscious form control.[21]

This has always been the method adopted by artists, Ehrenzweig maintained. Modern art simply goes further in not restricting the vague and ambiguous forms of the artist's initial automatic form-creation to the background of their art. Instead modern art allows these vague forms to permeate the whole picture plane.

This is achieved by the artist contriving to retain fluid, gestalt-free, vague perception from start to finish by suppressing all definitive form ideas in keeping with modernist distaste for secondary revision reason and logic, argued Ehrenzweig. In their pursuit of vagueness modern artists are helped in starting each new work of art by projecting marks on their chosen medium in the form of scribbles and doodles. Stokes might well have deplored this as modelling. Not so Ehrenzweig. But he also commended what Stokes called carving, namely the artist's responsiveness to what they find in their material. He noted the painter's response, for instance, to the chance flow, bleeding and puddling of water-colour, to haphazard blobs of oil-paint, and to the fortuitous effects of the wear-and-tear of their brushes on their paper or canvas. Artists may also use whatever they happen to discover around them in creating assemblages and installations. Declaring, 'I do not seek, I find', Picasso instantiated this *objet trouvé* approach by 'picking up bicycle handlebars from a rubbish dump', said Ehrenzweig,[22] and using them as horns in his 1951 composition, *Goat Skull and Bottle*, a 1954 bronze cast of which is in the Picasso Museum in Paris.[23]

Generalizing from this and other examples, Ehrenzweig characterized art-making as a three-stage process. It begins in a paranoid-schizoid state of mind. At this stage the artist must be able to tolerate, 'without undue persecutory anxiety', given that this state of mind consists 'of projecting fragmented parts of the self into the work' in the form of marks which can, Ehrenzweig added, 'easily appear accidental, fragmented, unwanted and persecuting'. This is followed by a second stage of oceanic oneness of the artist with their emerging art-work, in which they bring together their initial scribbled marks and unconscious form perception and integrate it into consciously perceived gestalt shape and form. This is achieved through the artist's 'scanning that integrates art's substructure', said Ehrenzweig, through 'cross-ties [which] bind the single elements together [so that] an unbroken pictorial space emerges as the conscious signal of unconscious integration'. Third, and finally, he maintained, 'part of the work's hidden substructure [is re-introjected] into the artist's ego on a higher mental level'.[24]

Ehrenzweig illustrated this three-stage process of projection, oceanic scanning and re-introjection with the Abstract Expressionist art of Jackson Pollock, specifically Pollock's 1950 painting, *One: Number 31*,[25] referred to in Chapter 1. He drew attention to the fact that Pollock began the painting by projecting random blobs of paint onto his canvas, then scanned and unified the result, and third, presumably, took in the final picture with his eyes as we can in looking at it. Its dynamic effect is due to the 'weaving in and out of the picture plane', said Ehrenzweig, of what he elsewhere described as the dynamic and aesthetic oneness of unconscious and conscious chaos and order.[26]

To this example he added, as illustration of the oneness of inner and outer, unconscious and conscious, depth and surface perception, the fluctuating figure and ground of Braque's painting, *Glass and Pitcher* (Figure 9.5.1),[27] in which an area of the pitcher can also be seen as a profile of a head, and the pitcher's bulging shape can also be seen as a figure with palette and brushes. The oneness or unity of these different interpretations or meanings arguably add to the picture's dynamic effect. This effect is also conveyed, Ehrenzweig indicated, by the unstable coming together of two faces in a kiss in a line drawing (Figure 9.5.2),[28] also included in his 1967 book, *The Hidden Order of Art*.

It was in concluding this book that Ehrenzweig most likened the artist's oneness with their emerging art-work to the oneness of analysts with their analysands. First, like painting, analysis too begins with projection in the form of the analysand's free associations, he argued. Second, like the oceanic oneness of the artist with their emerging art-work in scanning it in bringing it to fruition, analysts scan and bring together what is unconscious and conscious in the analysand's free associations in formulating their inter- pretations. This leads to a third stage, as in art-making, as Ehrenzweig understood it. 'Through dedifferentiation (free-floating attention)', he main- tained, '[the analyst] is able to re-integrate the material and make it ready for re-introjection by the patient.'[29] And this can change the analysand, just as taking in with our eyes what we see in the artist's art can change us.

1

Figure 9.5.1 Braque: *Glass and Pitcher*

A. Ehrenzweig (1967) *The Hidden Order of Art.* St Albans: Paladin, 1970, Plate 19, copyright © ADAGP, Paris and DACS, London, 2006.

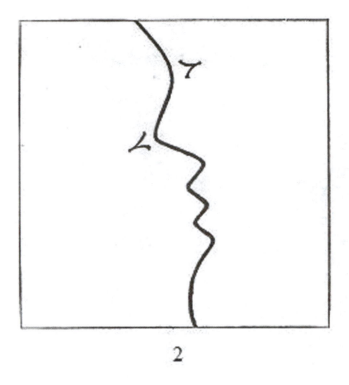

2

Figure 9.5.2 Double profile drawing

A. Ehrenzweig (1967) *The Hidden Order of Art.* St Albans: Paladin, 1970, p. 37.

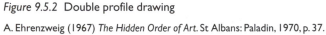

Creativity in the artist depends on their being able to cope with all three stages of art-making: projection, oceanic oneness and re-introjection. The same is true of analysis. 'The analyst must allow the patient's fragmented material to sink into the containing womb of his own (the analyst's) unconscious without premature wish to re-articulate it and put it back into the patient on a fully articulate level,' argued Ehrenzweig.[30] In this he equated what he called the artist's 'manic-oceanic' oneness with their art in scanning it with the stance of evenly-suspended attention which Freud urged analysts to adopt in doing analysis.[31]

In claiming that this second stage of art-making involves manic oceanic oneness of artists with their art, Ehrenzweig conflated Freud's account of oceanic oneness of inner and outer reality with Klein's account of the analysand's 'projective identification' oneness of their unconscious fantasies with the analyst.[32] He also conflated it with her account of defence against depressive position integration of paranoid-schizoid fragmentation of what is loved and hated by flight into manic omnipotence and control. Furthermore, in likening the analyst's free-floating attention to the artist's manic-oceanic scanning of their art in bringing together dynamically what they unconsciously and consciously see, Ehrenzweig overlooked, as many present-day analysts continue to overlook, ways in which psychoanalysis brings together the two different worlds of experience of the analysand and analyst. Winnicott, by contrast, drew attention to this. In doing so, he also distinguished, unlike Ehrenzweig, between the destructive chaos of paranoid-schizoid disintegration and the unintegration that Ehrenzweig equated with the undifferentiated vagueness of mystical experience as inspiration not only of religion but of art as well.

Chapter 10

Winnicott

Unintegration, not disintegration, is where we begin. This is what Winnicott conveys in describing our earliest experience of being mothered by those who first look after us as babies. He argued:

> There are long stretches of time in a normal infant's life in which a baby does not mind whether he is many bits or one whole being, or whether he lives in his mother's face or in his own body, provided that from time to time he comes together and feels something.[1]

It is the baby's earliest mothering, Winnicott suggested, that first determines whether this experience of unintegration is bearable, or becomes frightening disintegration. Klein similarly distinguished unintegration from disintegration, as well as from integration. Welcoming Winnicott's concept of unintegration, she added, 'I would also say that the early ego largely lacks cohesion, and a tendency towards integration alternates with a tendency towards disintegration, a falling into bits.'[2]

But how do the fantasies involved emerge and develop? Winnicott indicated that fantasy begins through the overlap of the infant's potential for imagination with the ideas its gestures prompt in the mother. The infant, he said, 'has instinctual urges and predatory ideas' and the mother has 'the power to produce milk, and the idea that she would like to be attacked by a hungry baby'.[3] The coming into relation of these two worlds of experience results in a situation in which, he continued, 'mother and child live an experience together'. This brings about 'a moment of illusion', which may be experienced as real or as a hallucination. 'In other language,' he added

> the infant comes to the breast when excited, and ready to hallucinate something fit to be attacked. At that moment the actual nipple appears and he is able to feel it was that nipple that he hallucinated. So his ideas are enriched by actual details of sight, feel, smell, and next time this material is used in the hallucination.[4]

It is the overlap or meeting of what the hungry baby is ready to imagine or hallucinate with the mother's readiness to feed it that gives its unintegrated experience objective form, in this instance in the shape of her breast.

Her facial response to what she sees in her baby's face also gives its subjective experience objective form. It is doubtless just such experiences that enable artists to rely on what Tolstoy called 'the capacity of man to receive another man's expression of feeling and to experience those feelings himself' without which there can be no art. It is art, he maintained, 'if a man having experienced either the fear of suffering or the attraction of enjoyment (whether in reality or in imagination), expresses these feelings on canvas or in marble so that others are infected by them'.[5]

We very early perceive and are 'infected', as Tolstoy put it, by perceiving what others feel. Describing this as it occurs in early infancy, Winnicott observed:

> What does the baby see when he or she looks at the mother's face? I am suggesting that, ordinarily, what the baby sees is himself or herself. In other words the mother is looking at the baby and what she looks like is related to what she sees there.[6]

The baby responds to what it sees her seeing as registered in her facial response.

This responsiveness begins very early. Within hours of birth the sight of the mother's face prompts the newborn baby to imitate what it sees in its mother's face by copying her mouth movements with its own.[7] Perhaps this is hard-wired in mirror neurons in the brain which, in the frontal cortex of monkeys, fire equally whether they see an action performed by another animal or they perform it themselves.[8] Whether this happens in newborn human babies is questionable given the very immature development of their frontal cortex at birth. Nevertheless it is clear that newborn babies are affected by, and imitate, the feelings they see and perceive in others.

Whatever the neuronal basis of this we learn what we feel through the overlap and meeting of our experience with that of others. The immediacy with which we perceive what others experience was long ago highlighted by the philosopher, Edith Stein, using the example of sadness 'read in another's face'.[9] She also emphasized that it is through perceiving others as conscious of us as conscious living beings that we too become conscious of ourselves as such. Winnicott wrote something similar. It is through the baby seeing the mother's feelings – her hatred, for instance – that it comes to know these feelings in itself. Analysands likewise need their analysts to know what they feel if they are to acquire or reacquire consciousness of what they feel. This is particularly true in depression, according to Winnicott. 'The depressed patient requires of his analyst the understanding that the analyst's work is to some extent his effort to cope with his own (the analyst's) depression,' he maintained.[10] Likewise, he argued, in psychosis the analysand needs the analyst's hatred and capacity to know their feelings of hate so as to know that they too hate.[11] We need to see others know about their feelings and experience to enable us to know what we feel.

We also need others to know about our fantasies and dreams so we can know them as such for ourselves. Winnicott was perhaps particularly aware of this because of his own difficulties in knowing and remembering his dreams. Indeed this was a major cause of his first becoming interested in psychoanalysis. Writing of the infant's initial unawareness that it has fantasies and dreams and that one fantasy might be related to another, he wrote:

> I think an infant cannot be said to be aware at the start that while feeling this and that in his cot or enjoying the skin stimulations of bathing he is the same as himself screaming for immediate satisfaction, possessed by an urge to get at and destroy something unless satisfied by milk.

Nor does the baby know, Winnicott added, 'that the mother he is building up through his quiet experiences is the same as the power behind the breasts that he has in his mind to destroy'. Toddlers similarly do not initially know their sleeping hallucinations as dreams. They need others to help them learn this. '[They] depend very much on adults for getting to know their dreams', he emphasized, particularly their anxiety dreams and terrors. 'At these times,' he stressed, 'children need someone to help them to remember what they dreamed.'[12]

It was with his account of transitional objects and transitional phenomena, however, that Winnicott most emphasized the overlap of the infant's and adult's subjective and objective worlds of experience as precursors of the images, symbols, and words without which there can be no talking cure psychoanalytic psychotherapy. Just as artists find in their chosen medium – in paint, for instance – material with which to make their invisible experience visible, so too the baby finds in its surroundings material with which its subjective, non-sensory and invisible experience becomes the elementary, objective, and visible stuff and signs of meaning.

Examples for Winnicott included the thumb-sucking baby taking, as he put it,

> an external object, say a part of a sheet or blanket, into the mouth along with the fingers; or somehow or other the bit of cloth is held and sucked, or not actually sucked . . . or the baby starts from early months to pluck wool and to collect it and to use it for the caressing part of the activity.[13]

These are examples of what Winnicott called 'transitional phenomena'. Other examples arising from the overlap and meeting of the infant's inner subjective world with outer reality include its 'mouthing', he said, 'accompanied by sounds of "mum-mum", babbling, and noises, the first musical notes and so on'.[14]

These phenomena, arising from the infant's interaction with what others say, do, and provide for it in its immediate environment, may result in the infant becoming attached to a transitional object, the presence of which becomes crucial to its well-being when it is upset. Such objects develop from what it finds in what others provide: 'perhaps a bundle of wool or the corner of a blanket or eiderdown', suggested Winnicott, 'or a word or tune, or a mannerism'. The importance to the baby of its transitional object can be seen from the comfort it derives from this object when it is tired or distressed. Winnicott called the baby's transitional object its first 'Not-Me possession'. It might call this possession, 'baa', he said, this being suggested by its parents saying, 'baby', 'bear', and so on.[15] With time these transitional object and transitional phenomena precursors of the infant's acquisition of symbols and words become diffused and absorbed in its shared 'cultural field' with others. They widen out into 'play . . . artistic creativity and appreciation . . . religious feeling . . . dreaming . . . obsessional rituals, etc'.[16]

Other examples of ways in which babies find objects provided by others through which their feelings become visible can be found in Winnicott's observations of babies playing with a shiny spatula he provided to catch their attention as he talked with their mothers. Often, he said, the following sequence occurred:

> The baby puts his hand to the spatula, but at this moment discovers unexpectedly that the situation must be given thought. He is in a fix. Either with his hand resting on the spatula and his body quite still he looks at me and his mother with big eyes, and watches and waits. . . . Before long he puts the spatula into his mouth and is chewing it with his gums, or seems to be copying father smoking a pipe . . . or else he holds it to my mouth and to his mother's mouth, very pleased if we pretend to be fed by it . . . [then] the baby first of all drops the spatula as if by mistake . . . its being restored again, he drops it on purpose . . . [and] when he is bored with it . . . reaches out to any other objects that lie at hand.[17]

These objects too become means by which what is otherwise invisible and unconscious in what babies experience and feel becomes visible and meaningful to others around them.

It is through what the baby finds and is given to find – in the first instance, the breast, according to Freud (see p. 15) – that it also comes to know what it feels by way of wishing and desiring. A charming example provided by Winnicott was a memory of himself, aged 4, waking up on Christmas Day to discover his parents had given him just what he might have wished for had he known of its existence, namely a cart made in Switzerland for carrying wood. 'How', he asked, 'did my parents know that this was exactly what I wanted?' He did not know such things existed. They knew, he said, 'because of their capacity to feel my feelings', and because, unlike him, he added, 'they knew about the carts because they had been to Switzerland'.

Similarly, Winnicott suggested, the psychoanalyst, Marguerite Sechehaye, enabled a schizophrenic girl to recover her ability to know about wishing and wanting by finding and giving her an apple just at the moment when she was ready to wish for something like that. 'It is the same as the mother's presenting a breast to the infant and, later on, introducing hard objects to the infant, and the fruits of the earth,' Winnicott commented. It is not a matter of 'creating the infant's needs,' he argued, 'but meeting these needs at the right moment'.[18]

As for our fantasies, he argued, we can discover them through using other people as figures in whom to discover their shape and form. This is not possible in states of oceanic oneness, projective identification, mirroring or blind thinking oneness with what is other than us as described by Freud, Klein, Lacan and Milner. Winnicott called these illusory states of oneness with otherness 'object-relating'. In so far as the baby misidentifies its fantasies with its mother it remains as fossilized as the mythical Narcissus adoring his reflected image in a pool of water without any means of knowing that this image was not someone else but an inverted image of himself.

To discover its fantasies, to discover what it imagines, the infant needs to experience its mother as separate from its fantasies and imaginings about her. Winnicott argued that achievement of this separateness develops in the infant through the mother surviving its fantasies of destroying her. This demonstrates that she is not one with these fantasies. She can thereby serve as someone separate in whom the infant can come to see and discover what its fantasies are as seemingly realized by her. Winnicott called this relation of the infant to the mother 'object-usage'.[19]

The analysand's use of the analyst as someone in and through whom to discover their unconscious fantasies operates similarly. It depends on their recognizing the analyst as separate from their fantasies about them. It depends on their recognizing differences between their world of experience and that of the analyst. Psychoanalytic therapy occurs in the overlap of these two worlds of experience. Winnicott called them 'two areas of playing'. This has the corollary, he added, 'that where playing is not possible then the work done by the therapist is directed towards bringing the patient from a state of not being able to play into a state of being able to play'.[20]

Winnicott arguably sometimes sought to achieve this by playing the squiggle game with children he saw in his paediatric work with them. Nonchalantly tearing sheets of paper in half, he explained the game to the child patient, saying:

This game that I like playing has no rules. I just take my pencil and go like that. . . . You show me if that looks like anything to you or if you can make it into anything, and afterwards you do the same for me and I will see if I can make something of yours.[21]

It is 'a kind of projection test',[22] he said. In playing it he took turns with his child patients in projecting or finding meaning in the squiggles or doodles they drew in completing them into drawings in which both saw meaning in terms of their different worlds of experience.

An example of his use of the squiggle game, which nicely illustrates his subsequently developed theory of object-relating and object-usage, involved a 9-year-old boy, Philip, referred to the paediatric department in which Winnicott worked because he had started bed-wetting after being expelled from boarding-school. Bed-wetting and its meaning are hardly easy to talk about with 9-year-old boys on first meeting them. Winnicott's wife, Clare, found it helpful for social workers like herself, in their initial work with children in their care, to 'participate in shared experiences, about which both we and the children feel something about something else,' she wrote, 'a third thing, which unites us but which at the same time keeps us safely apart because it does not involve direct exchange by us'.[23] Similarly Winnicott found it helpful to participate in the shared experience of playing the squiggle game with Philip at their first meeting.

Their game began with Winnicott making a squiggle which Philip made into a map of England (Figure 10.1.1). He then made a squiggle which Winnicott turned into what he saw as a face and Philip saw as a fish (Figure 10.1.2). Philip then turned a squiggle by Winnicott into a sea-lion and baby (Figure 10.1.3) and another squiggle by Winnicott into a figure he called Punch with tears in his clothes (Figure 10.1.4). 'There are tears in his clothes,' Philip explained, 'because he has been doing something with a crocodile, something dreadful, probably annoying it, and if you annoy crocodiles you are in danger of being eaten.'[24]

This enabled Winnicott to talk with Philip about dreams and about the frightening things they might mean. Their talk together led Philip to draw a wizard (Figure 10.1.5), who, he said, came at midnight when he was at boarding-school. Winnicott then talked with Philip about good and bad magic, and about sad moments in his life. The saddest time, said Philip, was when he was 5 and he was sent with his older brother to stay with their uncle and aunt while their mother was giving birth to their baby sister. Their uncle's sergeant-major voice filled the emptiness. Subsequently, on being sent to boarding-school, where he felt horribly home-sick, Philip again found his uncle's sergeant-major voice filling the emptiness. The wizard had his voice. He told him what to do. His ordering Philip to steal dangerous drugs from the matron's medicine cabinet, and Philip's obeying his order was the reason he had been expelled from school.

Figure 10.1 Philip: Squiggles and drawings

D.W. Winnicott (1953b) Symptom tolerance in paediatrics. *CP*: 109, 110, 113, 114.

'And there's father, all unconcerned,' he said,[25] referring to his father, who had been away from home during the war and had only recently returned home, and who featured in a boat in a drawing Philip now did in which he drew an eagle carrying a baby rabbit overhead (Figure 10.1.6). Evidently putting this together with what it evoked in him from his psychoanalytic training and experience, and from what he had learnt as a psychiatrist involved in supervising the evacuation of children away from their mothers during the war, Winnicott interpreted this drawing to Philip as symbolizing his jealousy of his mother having a baby with his father, and his jealousy of the baby because he wanted to have another chance of being a baby himself.

At their next meeting a few days later Philip announced – via a drawing of Winnicott, with a gun, driving the wizard out of his house (Figure 10.1.7) – that the wizard had gone, that he no longer heard his voice. He drew a picture of him. He called him 'funny' (Figure 10.1.8). This meant, said Winnicott, that, having previously expected others to laugh at him, Philip had got rid of this aspect of himself with the wizard. He had replaced the wizard, it seems, with Winnicott whom he saw as separate from himself, as embodiment of his fantasy of someone who would drive out and exorcise the wizard from the house of his mind, rather like the mediums consulted by his parents who, said Winnicott, were involved in spiritualism. 'I was simply a person who fits in and understands, and who verbalizes the material of the play', he wrote of the outcome of his second meeting with Philip.[26] Had psychoanalytic therapy been possible the conditions were now in place for it to begin according to Winnicott's subsequent claim that therapy entails the capacity of analysands for object-usage, their capacity, as he put it, 'to place the analyst outside the area of subjective phantasy', as both bearer of the analysand's fantasy and as also separate from them.[27]

But, although Winnicott emphasized that psychoanalytic therapy takes place in the space created by the overlap of the two different and separate worlds of the analysand and analyst, he said little about the world of the analyst separate from that of the analysand, just as he said little about the world of the mother separate from that of her baby. Despite seeking to allay anxieties in mothers about not being ideal by telling them it was sufficient for them to be 'good-enough',[28] the mothering he promoted involved the assumption that, as the analyst, Alice Balint, put it in describing the fantasy of the ideal mother, 'the interest of mother and child are identical'.[29] This brings me to Bion who was one of the first systematically to retell psychoanalysis as akin to art and, in doing so, also said more than Winnicott about the world of the analyst separate from that of the analysand, just as he also said more than Winnicott about the world of the mother separate from that of her baby.

Bion

Bion's attention to the separate worlds of experience of babies and their mothers, and of analysands and their analysts stemmed, at least in part, from his experience as a tank battalion officer during the First World War. Impressed by the high morale of soldiers working together in groups,[1] he sought to use this experience in developing group methods of officer selection during the Second World War,[2] and group methods of treating its hospitalized psychiatric casualties.[3] This doubtless contributed to his running therapy groups at London's Tavistock Clinic after the war was over.

Noting differences between his experience and that of the patients in the groups he ran at the Tavistock Clinic, he also noted a spurious feeling of oneness with the fantasies he felt they induced in him. At times, in group treatment, he said,

> The analyst feels he is being manipulated so as to be playing a part, no matter how difficult to recognize, in somebody else's phantasy – or he would do if it were not for what in recollection I can only call a temporary loss of insight, a sense of experiencing strong feelings and at the same time a belief that their existence is quite adequately justified by the objective situation without recourse to recondite explanation of their causation.[4]

Impelled by fantasies equating curiosity about what is going on in the group with destructive infantile curiosity about what goes on in the mother's body, he argued, members of groups often take refuge in fantasies equating the leader with a god-like figure on whom they depend. These fantasies might alternate with fantasies about the leader's dependence on them. He likened such alternating fantasies to the alternation between seeing now one edge, AB, now another, CD, in front in a line drawing of a cube (Figure 11.1.1).[5] He later called this phenomenon 'reversible perspective' in describing the illusion in which one might see a drawing as depicting a vase or two faces (Figure 11.1.2).[6] This illusion might be used defensively, he said, 'to make a dynamic situation static'.[7] Or it might 'be seen from both sides of

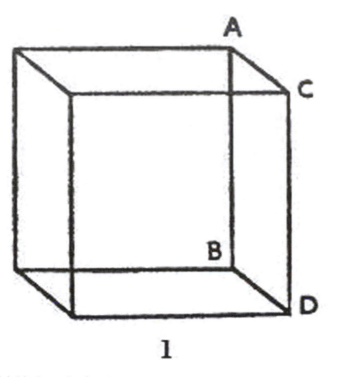

Figure 11.1.1 Necker cube drawing

W.R. Bion (1949) Experiences in groups IV. In W.R. Bion (1961) *Experiences in Groups*. London: Tavistock, p. 86. This and other Bion images are reproduced by kind permission of Francesca Bion.

the screen – both sides of the resistance,' he argued, illustrating the point with the example of Picasso painting on a piece of glass, 'so that it can be seen from both sides of the screen'.[8]

How does the analyst discover the fantasies involved in these different perspectives in patients in group therapy? Through the manifestations of these fantasies in signs or impressions made by the analysand on the analyst. It is the preconceptions that these impressions evoke, arguably, that constitute the source of the analyst's interpretations of the group patients' fantasies. Or, as Bion put it, 'many interpretations, and amongst them the most important, have to be made on the strength of the analyst's own emotional reactions'.[9]

The same is true of individual analysis. Bion's practice included patients who complained of having no fantasies or dreams. An example was a patient who, with four or five minutes gap between each sentence, grumbled:

'I have a problem I am trying to work out.'
'As a child I never had phantasies.'

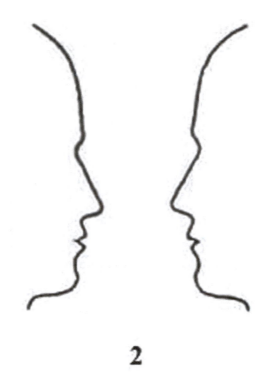

2

Figure 11.1.2 Vase/faces drawing

W.R. Bion (1963) *Elements of Psycho-Analysis.* London: Heinemann, p. 50.

> 'I knew they weren't facts so I stopped them.'
> 'I don't dream nowadays.'

After another pause, he said, bewildered, 'I don't know what to do now.' 'About a year ago you told me you were no good at thinking,' replied Bion, reacting to the impressions made on him by what the patient said and did. 'It must mean that without phantasies and without dreams,' he went on, 'you have not the means with which to think out your problems.'[10]

While this patient complained of not being able to dream and think, other patients manifested bodily reactions against thinking and dreaming. They replaced thinking with doing. They winced, twitched and agitatedly twisted on the couch. One patient convulsively jerked, cautiously scanned what seemed to be in the air around him and, when Bion commented that he seemed to feel surrounded by bad and smelly bits of himself, the patient complained he could not see.[11] Another patient got rid of what he could have dreamt or thought by expelling it as though it were something he could see. Conveying something of the impact on him of a session in which this occurred, Bion wrote:

As he passes into the room he glances rapidly at me . . . goes to the foot of the couch . . . stands, shoulders stooping, knees sagging, head inclined to the chair, motionless until I have passed him and am about to sit down. . . . As I lower myself into my seat he turns left about, slowly, evenly, as if something would be spilled, or perhaps fractured, were he to be betrayed into a precipitate movement. As I sit the . . . patient, now with his back to me, is arrested at a moment when his gaze is directed to the floor near that corner of the room which would be to his right and facing him if he lay on the couch . . . [after] a shudder of his head and shoulders . . . [he] seats himself on the couch . . . reclines slowly, keeping his eye on the same corner of the floor . . . is recumbent . . . a few more surreptitious glances and he is still. Then he speaks: 'I feel quite empty. Although I have eaten hardly anything, it can't be that. No, it's no use; I shan't be able to do any more today.'[12]

Affected by these impressions, Bion interpreted that, with his initial glance, the patient had taken in something from him with his eyes and then ejected it onto the floor so as to see and keep his eyes on it. In doing so he had emptied himself of what he had taken in from Bion and now experienced its presence on the floor as threatening. Hence his fear of not being able to do any more that day. Hence too his fear of what he had ejected returning as persecuting 'bizarre objects'.[13] After this he convulsively moved about and, when this stopped, he said, 'I have painted a picture'.[14] What was involved in the picture? Without Bion's interpretation it remained meaningless. Part of the picture he had painted was of the two of them, Bion interpreted, 'when he made himself and myself into two automata in a reciprocal but lifeless relationship'.[15]

Such patients, it seemed to Bion, get rid of their experience as one might rid oneself of a sleeping hallucination before doing the dream- or art-work needed to transform it into a form in which it can be seen or told as a meaningful dream picture or story. Bion attributed this to the patient not wanting to know what their experience might mean, perhaps because what it means threatens to be unbearably frustrating or depressing. Or it might turn out to mean that, hating those they love, they have harmed or driven them away. Freud arguably noted something similar in describing his patient, Sergei Pankieff, denying the castration meaning of sexual difference, as Freud understood it, so that it returned as a hallucination in which he saw his finger cut off, or castrated from his body (see p. 90). Examples from Bion's clinical practice included a widower who, seemingly unable to face whatever his wife's death meant to him, hallucinated seeing her alive and threatening him. Starting up suddenly, he pointed at Bion, saying 'My wife, it's my wife! She's coming for me! Stop her!'[16]

Writing of another patient, X, attacking the depressing meaning of hating and possibly destroying those he loved, Bion depicted this attacked meaning as a mass of projected fragments: 'the door slams; singing in his head; a pain in his ankle; "I don't know why; I'm sorry; the waitress brought some coffee; only half a cup"; and – despairingly, "I could not go on" '. X tried to bring the fragments together. But, because he could not bear to know the depressing meaning that might thereby emerge, he was left with what Bion called 'a series of pictorial images, ideograms, which will not coalesce'. They remained 'undigested . . . not proper pictorial images but facts sensually perceived yet remaining as bits of sensory awareness that have not been rendered fit for storage and are therefore not memories proper'.[17]

Bion called such undigested fragments of experience, 'β-elements'. They are the effect of transforming 'unsense-able mental phenomena', he said, into fragments evacuated to yield 'not a meaning, but pleasure or pain'.[18] Sometimes, evidently, his patients looked to him to digest and turn these fragments into meaning. An example, he said, was a patient who, cutting off one phrase from another, phrases such as 'going skating', complained that Bion could not bear it, as if he looked to Bion to bear taking in and being affected by his projected β-element fragments of experience so he could leave them long enough in Bion's mind 'to be modified,' as Bion put it, 'by their sojourn in my psyche'.[19]

Such experiences led Bion to hypothesize that initially, as babies, our sense-data acquire elementary 'α-element' meaning through the impressions we make on those who first mother us evoking already existing preconceptions in them. The mating of impressions from her baby with the separate world of experience they evoke in her presumably affects the way the mother holds, talks to, looks at and responds to her baby. She thereby converts its senseless seeming fragments of experience into sense, into the elementary stuff of meaning.

Bion somewhat over-complicated this with his 'α' and 'β' terminology, and by also calling the baby's projected sense-data, '♂', their maternal container, '♀', and their maternal transformation, '♂♀'. Experiencing the mother transforming its sense-data into meaning enables the baby to internalize this transforming function, '♂♀', so that gradually it learns to transform its sensory experience into meaning for itself. 'The relationship between mother and infant described by Melanie Klein as projective identification,' Bion said of this development, 'is internalized to form an apparatus for regulation of a pre-conception with the sense data of the appropriate realization.'[20]

Bion also described this apparatus as involving 'reverie', 'dream-work-α', 'α', or 'attention' on the model of Freud's account of hallucinatory primary mental process giving way to secondary process 'attention' to what our 'sense-organs' tell us about external reality.[21] Schizophrenic and psychotic states of mind, Bion argued, result from attacking this dream-work-α function, initially acquired through others mothering us as babies. As a result, he wrote:

in the psychotic we find no capacity for reverie, no α, or a very deficient α, and so none of the capacities – or extremely macilent capacities – which depend on α, namely attention, passing of judgement, memory, and dream-pictures, or pictorial imagery that is capable of yielding associations.[22]

It is their attacks on 'dream-work-α', argued Bion, that cause analysands in psychotic states of mind to suffer the ills of non-dreaming, and non-thinking, and to utter fragments – 'penis black with rage' or 'eye green with envy',[23] for instance – as though, he said, they were describing parts of a picture without giving the analyst any idea of its scale or the material with which it is made.

If the analysand's problems are due to attacking the dream- or art-work function by which, according to Freud, we transform our sleeping hallucinations (through condensation, displacement, visual presentation, secondary revision and symbolization) into what we remember as meaningful images and dreams, then the analyst's job, according to Bion, includes doing the necessary dream-work for their analysands so they can recover the ability to do this for themselves. Arguing along these lines, and thus in seeming complete contradiction with Freud's method of undoing the analysand's art- or dream-work constructions through encouraging them to free associate to bits and pieces of these constructions, Bion concluded that the analyst's work is not deconstruction but construction like the artist, of whom he wrote:

> He is someone who is able to digest facts, i.e. sense data, and then to present the digested facts, my α-elements, in a way that makes it possible for the weak assimilators to go on from there. Thus the artist helps the non-artist to digest, say, the Little Street in Delft[24] by doing α-work on his sense impressions and 'publishing' the result so that others who could not 'dream' the Little Street itself can now digest the published α-work of someone who could digest it. Vermeer was able to digest the facts in a particular way, or perhaps they were particular facts.[25]

Others have written similarly about painting.

A notable example is Heidegger. In the work of art, he said, 'the truth of beings has set itself to work'.[26] He famously illustrated this in musing, as follows, about Van Gogh's 1896 painting, *Old Shoes with Laces*:[27]

> From the dark opening of the worn insides of the shoes the toilsome tread of the worker stares forth. In the stiffly rugged heaviness of the shoes there is the accumulated tenacity of her slow trudge through the far-spreading and ever-uniform furrows of the field swept by a raw wind. On the leather lie the dampness and richness of the soil. Under the soles stretches the loneliness of the field-path as evening falls. In the shoes vibrates the silent call of the earth.[28]

Ironically, given Heidegger's emphasis on truth in art, as Derrida pointed out,[29] the boots depicted by Van Gogh in this painting are not those of a peasant. They are Van Gogh's city shoes. More relevant here, however, is Hannah Arendt's observation that the objects depicted in Van Gogh's paintings are 'thought-things'. They are the effect of 'the transformation they have undergone when thinking took possession of them,' she said.[30] Adopting Socrates' account of thinking as two-in-one silent talk with ourselves about whatever we are thinking about, she characterized painting, by implication, as resulting from the painter's two-in-one talk with themselves about what they are painting.

We could illustrate this with the work of Cézanne. He described his work as involving 'logical vision'.[31] We could describe Picasso's painting, *Les Demoiselles d'Avignon*,[32] similarly, as effect of Picasso, indirectly influenced by the mathematician, Henri Poincaré (see p. 112), reasoning with himself about bringing together different perspectives in one and the same picture. We could describe Picasso's painting, *Woman with a Mandolin*, as resulting from him reasoning with himself about bringing together different colours as described by Adrian Stokes in using it as an example of identity in difference in painting (see pp. 72–3).

Like Picasso, Bion too was influenced by Poincaré. He quoted approvingly his argument in his 1908 book, *Science and Method*, that if a fact is to have any value as means of generating new hypotheses in science, 'it must unite elements long since known, but till then scattered and seemingly foreign to each other, and suddenly introduce order where the appearance of disorder reigned'.[33] Incorporating this, together with his above-mentioned observation about Vermeer's painting, *The Little Street in Delft*, into his account of the work of the psychoanalyst, Bion also incorporated Freud's account of the approach to psychiatric diagnosis developed by his teacher, Martin Charcot. He 'had the nature of an artist – he was, as he himself said, a "*visuel*", a man who sees,' said Freud:

> He used to look again and again at the things he did not understand, to deepen his impression of them day by day, till suddenly an understanding of them dawned on him. In his mind's eye the apparent chaos presented by the continual repetition of the same symptoms then gave way to order: the new nosological pictures emerged.[34]

But, of course, this bringing together of impressions into meaningful images and pictures is not confined to the work of Vermeer, or to the work of the mathematician, scientist, or psychiatrist. It is also an everyday occurrence.

Examples include parents drawing pictures for their children, as Max Graf did in seeking to help his son become more conscious of his phobia of horses as rooted in fear of him as his father (see p. 20). Bion too drew pictures for his children. Examples include his drawing a picture (Figure 11.2.1) to show them something of his experience of being hospitalized for investigation of a suspected heart attack in 1959:

> [A] very nice fat lady comes and pushes a big thing that looks like an enormous iron cake. This whirls round and polishes the floor making a lovely noise as if you were being chased by a motor bus. You can see the lady likes doing it very much indeed. And it stops sick people thinking about their illness because they are thinking what that lovely noise can be.[35]

Another time he illustrated a letter to them about his experience as President of the British Psycho-Analytical Society at a dinner in London's Connaught Rooms to celebrate the publication in English in 1966 of Freud's collected psychological writings. He drew himself dwarfed between two women – Lady Hoare and Mrs Strachey (Figure 11.2.2) – adding

> Mrs Strachey didn't eat anything but she is extremely intelligent and only has one or two good ideas for dinner. She is very nice and only looks a bit sad because she had to bring her own good ideas. Lady Hoare as you can see is very intelligent AND brilliant.[36]

He also conveyed with a drawing (Figure 11.2.3) the difficulty of giving his after-dinner speech without 'tripping up over the microphone, falling flat on my face, bursting into tears, or shouting with laughter', because, he said, 'all their faces look so funny like plaice on a fish-mongers slab'.[37]

He also drew and painted pictures of their holiday home in Trimingham, near Cromer, the surrounding Norfolk countryside (Figures 11.3.1–2, Plate 13) and places in the Dordogne and Oxfordshire, where they also later lived (Figures 11.3.3–4, Plate 13). He also wrote about Trimingham and Cromer in seeking to work out for himself the difficulties faced by analysands unable to transform their experience into the material of knowing, remembering and thinking. He said:

> [S]uppose I am talking to a friend who asks me where I propose to spend my holiday: as he does so, I visualize the church of a small town not far from the village in which I propose to stay.

This might be uncontroversial. More surprising was his suggestion that, as he put it, 'the experience of this particular conversation with my friend, and this particular moment of the conversation . . . is being perceived sensorially by me and converted into an image of that particular village church'. Through this image-making, he argued, speakers transform their impressions of a conversation into a form in which it can be remembered and thought about. By contrast, he went on, patients in analysis might suffer from not being able

1

3

DIAMONDS SHINING BRILLIANTLY.

LADY H.

ME

MₘS

2

Figure 11.2 Bion: Drawings

W.R. Bion (1985) *All my Sins Remembered and The Other Side of Genius*. Abingdon: Fleetwood Press, pp. 169, 188, 189.

to do this image-making transformation of their experience into the material needed for knowing and thinking. As a result their experience may remain a meaningless 'thing', he said, 'lacking any of the quality we usually attribute to thought or its verbal expression'.[38]

This is reminiscent of the situation described by Freud in which thoughts become divorced from the perceptual reality of spoken words in which they originate. Thought may then proceed, he speculated in 'systems so far remote from the original perceptual residues that they have no longer retained anything of the qualities of those residues, and, in order to become conscious, need to be reinforced by new qualities' (see p. 24).[39] In analysis this calls for the analyst to provide the new qualities involved in transforming the analysand's experience into a form in which it can become knowable and thinkable through the analyst linking perceptible qualities of what goes on in the analytic setting with words. Impressed by the 'nameless dread',[40] often at the root of his analysands' ills, Bion argued, 'the analyst has to be a kind of poet, or artist, or scientist, or theologian to be able to give an interpretation or a construction . . . he must construct a language which he can talk and which the patient can understand'.[41]

He likened this task to that of the Impressionist painter, Monet, transforming his impressions of a landscape into a painting. 'Suppose a painter sees a path through a field sown with poppies and paints it,' he wrote, 'at one end of the chain of events is the field of poppies, at the other a canvas with pigment disposed on its surface.'[42] Monet transformed his impressions of a poppy field into a form we can see in his 1873 painting, *Poppies*.[43] So, too, analysts transform their impressions of the analysand's experience into interpretations which they can hear. The painter might use Impressionist techniques to transform their impressions into paintings. The analyst might use Freudian or Kleinian techniques to transform their impressions of the analysand's experience into an interpretation. The results may all be recognizably Impressionist in painting, or Freudian or Kleinian in psychoanalysis, despite varying with the impressions they transform.

Similarly Monet's paintings are all recognizably by him despite his paintings of haystacks,[44] and of Rouen Cathedral,[45] for instance, varying with the season or time of day when they were painted. Likewise, although Bion's paintings of the view from his and his wife Francesca's studies in their Croydon home, Redcourt, differ from 9 November and 10 December 1959 to 11 January 1960 when they were painted, they are all obviously by the same hand (Figure 11.4, Plate 14).

In the same way, the analyst's interpretations of their impressions of the analysand's experience vary with what their interpretations reflect. Paintings of water similarly vary with what it reflects as can be seen by comparing Bion's 1960s painting of the sea and cliffs near Swanage with his 1970s painting of the swimming pool in the garden of his and Francesca's home in California (Figure 11.5, Plate 15).

Psychoanalysis is also akin to painting in so far as painters empty their minds of what they have learnt so as to maximize their receptivity to the impressions made on them by what they see and paint. This receptivity is enhanced by their emptying their minds of, renouncing even, what has gone before, as suggested by Proust saying of his fictional character, Elstir, modelled on Monet and other painters, 'But – as Elstir found with Chardin – you can make a new version of what you love only by first renouncing it.'[46] The post-Impressionist painter, Paul Cézanne, did precisely this. Having learnt Impressionist techniques from Pissarro, he also studied the geology of his native Provence. But he started each new painting by renouncing what he had learnt, including what he had learnt from seeing paintings such as those of Chardin in the Louvre (see also p. 10). He emptied his mind of all this in contemplating what was before him. Then, when he had what he called his 'motif', he used what he had previously learnt from Pissarro, the Louvre, geology and so on. '[He] began to paint all parts of the painting at the same time,' said Merleau-Ponty, 'using patches of color to surround his original charcoal sketch of the geological skeleton it came to maturity all at once'.

This is vividly brought out in the examples of Cézanne's paintings of Mont Sainte Victoire from the late 1880s and 1905–6, now in the Courtauld, London,[47] and Tate, London,[48] reproduced in Michael Podro's account of painting and psychoanalysis.[49] Cézanne made sense out of non-sense, meaning out of non-meaning, out of what could have remained unconscious. 'The landscape thinks itself in me,' he reputedly said, 'and I am its consciousness.'[50] To this Merleau-Ponty added, 'The painter recaptures and converts into visible objects what would, without him, remain walled up in the separate life of each consciousness.'[51] They make conscious what, without them, might remain unconscious or subconscious.

Bion proceeded similarly. Freud emphasized the importance of analysts emptying their minds of their inclinations and expectations in doing analysis. Cézanne renounced what he had learnt in starting a new painting. So too Bion urged himself and his fellow-analysts to renounce and empty their minds of memory of the past, desire for the future, and the drive to understand what is going on in the present on starting each new analytic session. He described this as a means of approaching 'at-one-ment' with what Plato called the form of the good, Meister Eckhart called the Godhead, and Kant called the unknowable thing-in-itself. He could also have likened it to the oneness of the artist's public with their art as described by Berenson, as quoted by Milner (see p. 106), and to the oneness of the artist with their emerging art-work, as described by Ehrenzweig (see p. 120), or to the oneness of painting with the bodily experience it 'metaphorizes', as theorized by Wollheim.[52]

At-one-ment is akin to the objectless state of mind which, given its 'abandonment of sexual aims', Freud assimilated to sublimation.[53] It is also similar to what Winnicott called unintegration with its attendant experience, according to Klein, of paranoid-schizoid disintegration. Bion abbreviated this to 'Ps'. He likened the turbulence involved to Leonardo's drawings,[54] of 'writhing coils of hair' and 'swirling masses of water'.[55] He also likened it to what Milton called 'the void and formless infinite', and to the terror conveyed by Pascal's observation, '*Le silence éternel de ces espaces infinis m'effraie*'.[56] He also likened analysts emptying their minds to maximize their openness to the more or less meaningless impressions made on them of their analysands' experience to the state of mind Keats described as precondition of achievement in art. Keats called it 'Negative Capability'. It entails, he said, 'being in uncertainties, mysteries, doubts, without any irritable reaching after fact and reason'.[57]

From this state of uncertainty, provided the analyst does not repudiate it, as Bion recalled repudiating the horror of seeing the chest of a fellow-soldier blown off in the First World War, a motif may emerge. Bion likened the evolution of such motifs to the experience in which, he wrote, 'some idea or pictorial impression floats into the mind unbidden and as a whole'.[58] He wrote of impressions from the analysand evolving in the analyst's mind into 'a verbal picture gallery' through evoking images such as the myth of Oedipus, Bible stories of the Tree of Knowledge, the Tower of Babel, and so on.[59] The resulting emerging images are arguably an effect, in analysis, of impressions made by the analysand on the analyst mobilizing their sometimes conscious, sometimes unconscious preconceptions. These further come into play as the analyst transforms their emerging image or idea into an interpretation, just as Cézanne evidently drew on what he had learnt in turning his emerging motifs into paintings.

Paintings, however, can have no effect if they are not seen. Nor can psychoanalytic interpretations have any effect if they are not heard. Expressing this in terms of Leonardo's drawings of swirling water and hair, Bion wrote: 'He could see them and draw them for you. What he could not see or help was that you would not be made to look even if he did draw them for you.'[60] Or as Bion also put it, 'If you only looked you would "see-what-I-mean" ', and 'Look at your facts. Respect them even if you do not like them. The mists may clear and reveal a pattern.'[61]

The patient might reject the analyst's interpretation. They might treat it as a thing. Thus, for instance, when Bion interpreted to a patient that he 'felt he had been and still was witnessing an intercourse between two people,' said Bion, '[the patient] reacted as if he had received a violent blow'.[62] Or the patient might hear the analyst's words as words, but not be affected by them. This might be because the interpretation is too new and unfamiliar.

The innovative painter has a similar problem to the analyst in so far as he or she paints what has never been painted before. As Merleau-Ponty observed:

> What he expresses cannot, therefore, be the translation of a clearly defined thought, since such clear thoughts are those which have already been uttered by ourselves and others. . . . the artist launches his work just as a man once launched the first word, not knowing whether it will be anything more than a shout.

This is what is entailed in the artist trying, he said, 'to make visible how the world touches us'. We are not touched or affected unless the artist's art takes root in our consciousness. 'The painter can do no more than construct an image; he must wait for this image to come to life for other people,' Merleau-Ponty pointed out. That was the reason, he said, Cézanne questioned his paintings as they emerged, and 'hung on the glances other people directed towards his canvas'.[63]

Psychoanalysts are in a similar position. The effect of their interpretations depends on the analysand experiencing them. The effect of seeing a painting depends on whether we experience it directly, or only see it as a photograph, or only know what it is about. Bion distinguished in these terms knowing that Monet's 1873 *Poppies* painting is about poppies, and seeing and experiencing the painting itself. If the latter happens, one could add, we can experience 'a pulse in common' with what the painting shows us, to use Stokes' phrase in describing the impact of seeing Rembrandt's portrait paintings in London's National Gallery.[64]

Similarly there is a difference between knowing what the analyst's interpretation is about and experiencing it in a way that enables the analysand 'to "know" that part of himself to which attention has been drawn,' said Bion. According to his neo-Kantian aesthetics, 'the thing-in-itself can only be known in its realizations, it can never be fully known except through becoming one with it,' Mary Jacobus explains.[65] Hence the analysand experiencing and being affected by the analyst's interpretation entailed for Bion 'being' or 'becoming' that person.[66]

But this makes analysis akin to the suggestive seductions of advertising and political propaganda inviting us to become one with the object-directed desires they purvey. One way of forestalling this problem is to free each interpretation from 'saturation' with meaning, to use Bion's term, as soon as it is made, and to make it open to revision by whatever subsequent impressions and motifs emerge and evolve. We could understand this as a process in which, starting with the analysand's paranoid-schizoid fragments of experience, the analyst does the depressive position work of integrating these fragments into an interpretation. This then becomes open to revision in terms of what it suggests by way of fragmentary impressions, which, in evoking the analyst's preconceptions, result in the emergence of new integrating motifs and interpretations. Bion theorized this to-and-fro oscillation between disintegration and integration as oscillation between paranoid-schizoid and depressive position states of mind. He represented it as 'Ps↔D'.[67]

But this risked losing sight of Freud's Oedipus complex theory of neurosis and psychosis, as effect of socially transgressive sexual wishes and fantasies, in adopting instead Klein's paranoid-schizoid and depressive position terminology. It resulted in Bion portraying the art-work transformations achieved by analysts in formulating their interpretations as, in effect, a species of pattern-making.

'A successful outcome to the treatment, if it does lead eventually to a better adaptation to reality,' comment Laplanche and Pontalis in criticizing Kleinian psychoanalysis in these terms, 'is not expected from any corrective initiative, but from the dialectic "integration" of the fantasies as they emerge.'[68] Furthermore in shaping the analysand's fantasies by interpreting them in terms of preconceptions evoked by the impressions they make on the analyst, as made explicit by Bion in retelling psychoanalysis as art, the analyst repeats the process by which, according to Laplanche, the unconscious is first formed in each of us by others seducing us into taking on their preconceptions and fantasies in making sense of the impressions we evoke in them. How has this problem led to the further development of psychoanalysis nowadays?

Chapter 12

Laplanche

Laplanche's development of psychoanalysis is now becoming increasingly influential as a result of his concern with the origin of the unconscious fantasies which psychoanalytic psychotherapy seeks to make conscious, deconstruct and dispel. To this we could add the preconceptions signs of these fantasies evoke in the analyst. Where do these preconceptions come from? In part, as indicated by Bion in likening analysis to painting, they come from what analysts, like artists, learn from practising their trade. In this the analyst's preconceptions are akin to the knowledge of dream-symbolism acquired from their clinical experience which Freud recommended them to use to supplement their analysands' associations when these fail or become mute. Where, beyond this, do the analyst's and artist's preconceptions come from? Their preconceptions, as regards the meaning of symbols, are rooted, according to Freud, in an archaic language which, with accretions from later developments and inventions (zeppelins included: see p. 26) shape our understanding of the world we find ourselves in. Jung believed that knowledge of this language is inherited in each of us in the form of archetypes in the collective unconscious.

Laplanche adopts a different tack. In this he follows Lacan's rejection of Jung's account, in terms of individual inheritance, of the acquisition of the symbols of the culture in which we live. The analyst's interpretations are not based on inherited knowledge of the meaning of symbols and 'divine archetypes'. Our unconscious knowledge of these symbols is structured according to laws governing 'languages that are or were actually spoken,'[1] Lacan argued. This 'Other' of socially given language and symbolism is conveyed to us by 'others' in our immediate social world. It is this that brings the ego into being. 'We must distinguish two *others*, at least two – an other with a capital *O*, and an other with a small *o*, which is the ego,' he wrote. 'In the function of speech we are concerned with the *Other*.'[2]

Laplanche, together with Pontalis, argues that socially given language and symbolism are conveyed to us by others immediately involved with us from our earliest infancy onwards. In forwarding this argument they return to Freud's concept of deferred action; namely the reawakening of the past by the present thereby giving the past a new meaning which acts in deferred fashion to affect us here and now. The paintings of Chardin do this in so far as, according to Proust, they awaken to consciousness and make active in us what was previously subconscious. A well-honed psychoanalytic interpretation does the same. In making active otherwise unconscious meanings it repeats the process, ironically, by which experience first becomes traumatic and is repressed into unconsciousness on account of the new meanings it acquires in the course of the analysand's development. Freud initially attributed the traumatic effect of present experience to it giving new, sexually transgressive meaning to seduction to which the patient was subjected as a 3- or 4-year-old child. The defensive dream- or art-work disguise of this meaning constitutes their hysterical or obsessional neurosis, he argued.

Freud initially explained this effect biologically. 'Deferred revision is occasioned by events and situations, or by an organic maturation, which allow the subject to gain access to a new level of meaning and to rework his earlier experience,' write Laplanche and Pontalis in reporting Freud's early seduction theory of neurosis.[3] Soon after abandoning this theory, however, Freud argued that, irrespective of any seduction by others, 3- and 4-year-old children feel murderous rivalry with one parent because of their sexual desire for the other parent. It is not the biological maturation of puberty, as he had originally claimed, he soon after argued, that gives traumatic meaning, by deferred action, to early childhood experience. Rather, at least in the case of boys, it is the discovery that girls and women do not have a penis that gives new meaning to their previous experience.

Freud attributed the phobia of his 5-year-old patient, Little Hans, to his seeing that his baby sister, Hanna, did not have a penis. This gave new meaning, he indicated, to Hans' mother previously telling him that if he touched his penis she would send for the doctor to cut it off. 'And then what'll you widdle with?' she asked. To this Hans replied, dismissing the threat, 'With my bottom.'[4]

Freud similarly attributed the childhood neurosis of his Russian patient, Sergei Pankieff, to his seeing his sister's lack of a penis giving new meaning to his Nanya having told him, on seeing him playing with his penis, that children who did that got a 'wound' in that place.[5] But the more immediate cause of Pankieff's childhood neuroses, according to Freud, was the nightmare occurring on the Christmas Eve of his fourth birthday (see p. 17). This, it seems, reawakened and gave new meaning to a memory, dating from when he was an 18-month-old toddler, of seeing, or imagining seeing, perhaps on the basis of having seen animals copulating, his father in sexual intercourse with his mother, penetrating her from behind so he could see she had no penis. Thanks to what he had been told subsequently, he came to understand her lack of a penis as meaning she had been castrated. He discovered this meaning not through biological maturation, nor through seeing his sister's lack of a penis. For, when he saw her and her friend peeing, he dismissed their evident lack of a penis by telling himself they were peeing with their 'front bottom'.[6]

Crucial to the genesis of Pankieff's childhood neurosis were memories, recalled as free associations, of what others had told him when he was 2 or 3. These included recalling his Nanya threatening his masturbation by telling him boys who did that got a 'wound' in that place, and his English governess, who, said Freud, 'was inclined to disordered fancies', describing sugar-sticks as 'chopped-up snakes'.[7] This doubtless affected the meaning he gave to seeing or learning from others that his father had beaten a snake to pieces with his stick. He had also been told folk stories conveying images of castration. They included a story about a wolf who, going fishing in winter, and wanting to use his tail as bait, lost it when it was broken off in the ice. Another story, told him by his grandfather, and linked by Freud to Pankieff's memory that in his Christmas Eve nightmare 'the window opened of its own accord',[8] involved a wolf jumping through a tailor's window, whereupon the tailor pulled the wolf's tail off. This was followed by the tail-less wolf encouraging other wolves to climb onto its back to get up a tree where the tailor was trying to escape from them. It was these seemingly vengeful, castrating creatures staring threateningly at Pankieff in his nightmare, which he depicted in the drawing he showed Freud to convey the traumatic effect on him of the dream with which his case history begins (see p. 18 above).

It is the stories, anecdotes and so on which others tell us that, according to Laplanche (who, together with Pontalis, dwells on Pankieff's case in some detail), which shape the unconscious and conscious meanings we accord to what goes on around us. In Pankieff's case this included his sister telling him, 'Let's show our bottoms'. It also included her taking hold of his penis, saying that his Nanya did the same with the gardener. '[S]he used to stand him on his head, and take hold of his genitals,' she said.[9] Hearing what others say constitutes the prototype of the meanings constituting the unconscious: 'hearing is also', Laplanche and Pontalis add, 'the history or the legends of parents, grandparents, and the ancestors: the family sounds or sayings, this spoken or discrete discourse, going on prior to the subject's arrival, within which he must find his way'.[10]

Laplanche and Pontalis also remind their readers of Freud's observations bearing on their claim that the mother (as well as others) seduces the infant into taking on fantasies her care evokes in them. 'Freud constantly insisted on the seductive role of the mother (or of others), when she washes, dresses or caresses her child,' they write. To this they add:

> if we note also that the naturally erogenous zones (oral, anal, uro-genital, skin), are not only those which most attract the mother's attention, but also those which have an obvious exchange value (orifices or skin covering) we can understand how certain chosen parts of the body itself may not only serve to sustain a local pleasure, but also be a meeting

place with maternal desire and fantasy, and thus with one form of original fantasy.[11]

Laplanche has since described those who first look after us as infants seducing us into taking on the fantasies their care of us evokes in them.

He describes these fantasies as enigmatic, he says, 'by virtue of the simple fact that the infant does not know the code', not least because the adults involved do not have the code either.[12] They too are unconscious of the fantasies they seduce the infant into taking on as though they were their own. The infant is unconscious of what these fantasies signify. Laplanche illustrates this with another example, also described by Freud, this time the fantasies children imagine as they masturbate, specifically fantasies of another child being beaten.[13] Laplanche attributes the genesis of these fantasies to the child seeing or imagining seeing their father hitting one of their siblings. In recalling this as he or she masturbates the child acts on a message, 'steeped in fantasy', says Laplanche, introduced to it by others, 'which the child must in a second moment attempt to master, at once symbolise and repress'.[14]

We could illustrate ways in which others seduce us into taking on their conscious as well as unconscious fantasies with examples of ways advertisers and politicians use fantasy to persuade us to buy or adopt the commodities or propaganda they purvey. Or we could illustrate the seductions exercised on us by others with examples from the visual arts. The US art historians, Leo Bersani and Ulysse Dutoit, do this in their account of the paintings of Caravaggio. They illustrate Laplanche's development of psychoanalysis with the example of his painting, *St John the Baptist with a Ram* (Figure 12.1). 'Join me,' St John seems to say, 'although where I am is somewhere between two realms of being, between my physical, individuated existence and my being as a disseminated connectedness throughout the universe', they write. This 'between-ness', they point out, is 'concretely figured in the painting by a casual, poignant and haunting intimacy between two species' – human and animal, boy and ram.[15]

Does talking cure psychoanalysis similarly involve the analyst seducing the analysand into taking on their fantasies? Surely not? To avoid this Laplanche reiterates, in effect, Freud's warning against analysts indulging the counter-transference feelings evoked in them by their analysands. To forestall this indulgence, Freud advised analysts to model themselves on the surgeon who, he said, 'puts aside all feeling, even his human sympathy, and concentrates his mental forces on the single aim of performing the operation as skillfully as possible'. This 'emotional coldness', he continued, 'creates the most advantageous conditions for both parties: for the doctor a desirable protection for his own emotional life and for the patient the largest amount of help that we can give him to-day'.[16]

To this recommendation, and to Freud's advice to analysts to adopt a

Figure 12.1 Caravaggio: *St John the Baptist with a Ram*

The Capitoline Museum, Rome.

stance of evenly-suspended attention free from subjective inclination and expectation, and to his account of the analysand's transference identification of their unconscious fantasies with the analyst, Laplanche adds another observation. The analytic situation constitutes a 're-opening' of the internalization and 'enclosure' in the analysand's unconscious of fantasies induced in them by others from their earliest infancy onwards, he writes. He likens this enclosure to a 'tub'.[17] He thereby draws attention to its containing effect, as Bion might have called it, to its function as 'a space in which fantasy, the sexual drives and their derivatives can be brought into play through speech'.[18]

Laplanche also recommends psychoanalysts to adopt a method of deconstruction or 'decomposition' steered, he adds, 'according to the current, or the currents, of the primary process'. As counterbalance to the accompanying 'liberation of psychical energies', he argues, 'psychoanalysis offers itself as a guarantor of constancy; of containment . . . of a presence, of a solicitude, the flexible but attentive constancy of a frame'. It is this that enables the 'analytic unbinding' constituted by the analytic setting liberating analysands to say or do whatever comes into their minds by way of free association.[19]

Analysts direct Freud's psychoanalytic method of free association. They accompany the primary process of the analysand. They guard 'the enigma'. The analyst also 'provokes the transference', says Laplanche. Analysts offer 'a place for speech, for free speech', enhanced by their 'benevolent neutrality' in evoking, by their presence, the image of 'the blank screen or, rather, the mirror,' he argues. This gives scope for the analysand's projective identification, for their misidentifying their unconscious fantasies with the analyst so that, in being mirrored by the analyst, these fantasies can be put into words. The analyst's resulting interpretations imply, says Laplanche, 'You have projected, and I give you back your projection, I counter-project.'[20] We analysts, Laplanche continues, 'offer the analysand a "hollow", our own interior benevolent neutrality, a benevolent neutrality concerning our own enigma', in which the analysand can place something 'filled-in' or 'hollowed-out'.[21]

Lacan likened the resulting analyst–analysand dialogue to the art of conversation recommended by Socrates in the Meno. It teaches 'the slave to give his own speech its true meaning,' said Lacan.[22] It enables the analysand 'to become conscious of his relations . . . with all these Others [symbolism, language, the law, and so on] who are his true interlocutors, whom he hasn't recognized'. Lacan added (see p. 94):

(see p. 94)

> It is a matter of the subject progressively discovering which Other he is truly addressing, without knowing it, and of him progressively assuming the relations of transference at the place where he is, and where at first he didn't know he was.[23]

Whereas Jung believed symbols are inherited as archetypes in each of us individually in what he called the collective unconscious, Laplanche argues that what is unconscious in us originates as effect of others seducing us into taking on the enigmatic signifying fantasies whereby they mediate to us, through the happenstance of their personal biography, the legends, myths and symbols of the society in which we live. Examples include Pankieff's English governess mediating, through her disordered fantasies, socially given ideas about castration in describing sugar-sticks as chopped-up snakes. Through the analyst putting repressed fantasy versions of such images into words, as they emerge from unconsciousness in the analysand's transference identification of these fantasy images with the analyst, the analyst enables the analysand to see beyond the 'irreducible, traumatic, non-meaning' of the chaos to which, said Lacan, 'he [the analysand] is as a subject subjected'.[24]

What, though, is to be done when the analyst's interpretations are stymied by the analysand's free associations failing, proving insufficient, or becoming mute? Freud, as we have seen, argued that this warrants the analyst adding their knowledge of dream-symbolism to the analysand's free associations so as to arrive at an interpretation of the unconscious cause of their ills. How have psychoanalysts developed his observations, together with those of his successors about symbolization, painting and the visual arts in dealing with such eventualities?

Chapter 13

Kristeva

'If his lips are silent,' Freud famously wrote of the patient in analysis, 'he chatters with his finger-tips; betrayal oozes out of him at every pore. And thus the task of making conscious the most hidden recesses of the mind is one which it is quite possible to accomplish.'[1] Silence may well occur, with the analysand's free associations coming to a halt, or scarcely beginning, if they are melancholically depressed, phobic, or obsessive. Noting that when his patient, Little Hans, was 4 he explained his phobia of going out to his mother by telling her, 'I was afraid a horse would bite me', and noting that Hans told him he was frightened of what 'horses wear in front of their eyes and by the black round their mouths', Freud also noted the similarity between this and the appearance of Hans' father's spectacles and moustache.[2] The blackness served as a sign to Hans of his father's anger of which Hans was frightened, said Freud, because he was so fond of his mother.

Freud also attended to signs from his adult patients in arriving at interpretations of the unconscious meaning underlying their ills. He did this in the case of Dora (see p. 26). He also did this in the case of his obsessional lawyer patient, Ernst Lanzer. Faced with Lanzer 'showing every sign of horror and resistance', as Freud put it, as he recounted the rat punishment with which he was obsessed, Freud conveyed these signs to his readers by reporting, as follows, Lanzer's stammering account of the punishment: 'the criminal was tied up . . . a pot was turned upside down on his buttocks . . . some rats were put into it . . . and they bored their way in . . .'. Seeing, hearing and responding to these stammering hesitations as signs of Lanzer's distress, Freud provided the missing word – 'anus'.[3] He also noted that in recounting this anal rat punishment, which an army captain had told him, '[Lanzer's] face took on a very strange, composite expression. I could only interpret it as one of horror at pleasure of his own of which he himself was unaware', pleasure, it turned out, in horror at the idea of the rat punishment being inflicted on 'the lady whom he admired'.[4]

Bodily signs – black around a horse's mouth, in the case of Little Hans – may only be fortuitously related to what they signify – Hans' father's moustache was only fortuitously a sign for Hans of his father being angry with him because of his fondness for his mother, as Freud interpreted his fear of the black around horses' mouths. Signs may also be more directly related to what they signify – Lanzer's strange facial expression signifying pleasure in horror, for instance. Freud noted such signs. Interpreting them involves the analyst using their previously acquired knowledge and experience of what such signs might mean, just as weather forecasters use their experience of cloud formations, for instance, in using them as signs by which to predict the weather.

Freud did not write much about this. He did however write, as I have repeatedly said, about analysts using their knowledge of dream-symbolism in interpreting the unconscious cause of their analysands' ills. To this the psychoanalyst, Julia Kristeva, adds the importance of analysts also using knowledge gleaned from their personal and clinical experience in deciphering precursory marks or signs of what is unconscious in their analysands, just as mothers use the knowledge triggered by signs in their babies' gestures in transforming them into meaning. The artist does something similar. 'It is by lending his body to the world,' observed Merleau-Ponty, 'that the artist changes the world into paintings.'[5]

Perhaps Bion knew nothing of this observation of Merleau-Ponty. He nevertheless did something similar to the artist thus described by Merleau-Ponty in understanding his patients' twitching and jerking on the couch as signs of their getting rid of, and evacuating what they might otherwise think about. Particularly evocative were case notes, he observed, 'in which I came nearest to a representation of a sensory image; say an event visually recalled'.[6] He illustrated this with the following notes about his initial meeting with a patient:

> When he came to me I saw a man of 43, just under 6 ft. in height, of wiry build, sallow complexion and dull expressionless features. The discussion of his difficulties was perfunctory, carried on for his part in monosyllabic listlessness.[7]

Rereading this passage some years later, Bion reported, 'I am able to receive a visual impression which up to a point reminds me of something that cannot be sensuously grasped – depression.'[8]

In recounting this case Bion called the sensory image of depression 'a visual impression'. Kristeva calls such images 'semiotic', 'distinctive', 'precursory' marks, traces, imprints, indices or signs. They are impelled by bodily drives, she says. They orchestrate 'a *chora*'.[9] We interpret them in terms of the prevailing, socially given systems of symbolism and meaning into which we are born and in which we live. She also notes Freud's observation that, when ideas become too divorced from the perceptual qualities of words in talk with others in which the two-in-one silent talk with ourselves called thinking begins, ideas may then need to be reinforced with new perceptual qualities to become conscious (see p. 24), as occurs in the analysand talking with the analyst in psychoanalytic therapy about what is otherwise unconscious in them.

Kristeva highlights the importance to psychoanalytic treatment of perceptual qualities, signs and marks with the example of the use made by artists of colour in painting. Unlike other aspects of art – perspective for instance – colour is relatively free from socially given rules and conventions governing its creation. Colour therefore lends itself readily to revitalizing meaning repressed into unconsciousness by secondary revision conventions. Matisse observed:

> When the means of expression have become so refined, so attenuated that their power of expression wears thin, it is necessary to return to the essential principles which made human language. They are, after all, the principles which 'go back to the source,' which relive, which give us life. Pictures which have become refinements, subtle gradations, dissolutions without energy, call for beautiful blues, reds, yellows – matters to stir the sensual depths in men.[10]

Colour serves to bring back to consciousness what is repressed by the 'oversignifying logic', as Kristeva puts it, of secondary revision ruled by superego convention. Colour lends itself to this because, she says, 'it inscribes instinctual "residues" that the understanding subject has not symbolized'.[11]

She illustrates the inarticulate, semiotic or precursory material signs by which we become conscious of what is repressed in the name of prevailing systems of symbolization by drawing attention to a detail of Giotto's fresco, *The Last Judgement*,[12] on the end wall of the Arena Chapel in Padua. In this detail, she writes, 'contours of the characters are blurred, some colors disappear, others weaken, and still others darken: phosphorescent blue, black, dark red'.[13] By contrast Giotto's frescoes on the Chapel's side walls clearly delineate and convey the Bible stories familiar to his fellow Italians. He could have drearily repeated the language of art of their time in telling these stories. Instead he brought them to life with his innovative use of colour. Kristeva writes of Giotto's fresco, *The Annunciation to Anna*:[14]

> On the one hand, each mass of color is unfolded into its variants. For example the colours of cloth are opened out through the realistic effect of drapery folds into variants of pink absorbing gray, white, and green, thus molding a cape.

Kristeva adds:

> In addition and at the same time, these voluminous colors, as they come into being by intermixing and detaching themselves from the entire spectrum, become articulated with one another by close contrast

(at the same end of the spectrum) or by truly diverging contrast (complementary colors).[15]

She illustrates this with Giotto's fresco in Assisi, *The Massacre of the Innocents*.[16]

She also shows how the Venetian painter Giovanni Bellini's perhaps unconscious fantasies about mothering are evident from signs of these fantasies in his Byzantine and Roman Catholic influenced *Madonna and Child* paintings in Amsterdam (Figure 13.1.1),[17] and Bergamo (Figure 13.1.2),[18] in which he depicts the mother clutching at her baby son's chest and genitals. She contrasts this with signs of Bellini's changed fantasies about mothering after he became a father when, again using the language of art of his time, he pictured the baby Jesus clutching at the Virgin Mary's throat as if to throttle her in a *Madonna and Child* painting by him now in the Museo de Arte de São Paulo (Figure 13.1.3).[19]

Kristeva also depicts graphically the conjunction of signs and their elaboration in terms of socially given symbolic conventions by paralleling on the same page of her essay, 'Stabat mater', her account of signs of her becoming a mother with conflicts about the symbolization of mothering in Italian Renaissance painting. She writes:

> Mary's function as guardian of power, later checked when the Church became wary of it, nevertheless persisted in popular and pictorial representation, witness Piero della Francesca's impressive painting, *Madonna della Misericordia*,[20] which was disavowed by Catholic authorities at the time.[21]

She follows this by recounting as follows the signs of herself becoming a mother to her newborn son:

> I hover with feet firmly planted on the ground in order to carry him, sure, stable, ineradicable, while he dances in my neck, flutters with my hair, seeks a smooth shoulder on the right, on the left, slips on the breast, singles, silver vivid blossom of my belly, and finally flies away on my navel in his dream carried by my hands.

On the right-hand side of these lines Kristeva continues her account of conflicts about symbolizing mothering in Italian Renaissance painting:

> The famous nativity of Piero della Francesca in London,[22] in which Simone de Beauvoir too hastily saw a feminine defeat because the mother kneeled before her barely born son, in fact consolidates the new cult of humanistic sensitivity. It replaces the high spirituality that assimilated the Virgin to Christ with an earthly conception of a wholly human mother.[23]

1

Figure 13.1.1 Bellini: *Madonna and Child*

2

Figure 13.1.2 Bellini: *Madonna and Child*

Copyright © Accademia Carrara, Bergamo, Dip. no. 958.

3

Figure 13.1.3 Bellini: *Madonna and Child*

Museo de Arte de São Paulo.

As for analysts bringing to consciousness what is otherwise unconscious in their analysands through attending to its signs (as in Freud's above-cited account of his analysis of 5-year-old Hans and 27-year-old Lanzer), we could liken this to the art of Dostoevsky. We could liken it specifically to his account, as follows, of the encounter between Raskolnikov and Sonia in his novel, *Crime and Punishment*, after Raskolnikov has asked Sonia to guess the murderer of her friend, Lisaveta. 'Take a good look,' Raskolnikov tells Sonia. 'And as he said it another old and familiar sensation struck a chill in his heart: he looked at her, and suddenly he seemed to see Lisaveta's face in her face,' writes Dostoevsky:

> He had a vivid recollection of the expression of Lisaveta's face when he was coming towards her with the hatchet that evening and she was slowly drawing back from him to the wall, thrusting out her hand, with her face full of child-like terror, looking exactly as little children do when they are suddenly scared by something and gaze motionless and in dismay at the object that frightens them, and shrink back, thrusting out their little hands, about to burst into tears. Almost the same thing happened to Sonia just now: she looked at him helplessly for some time, and with the same expression of terror on her face and thrusting out her left hand all of a sudden, she touched his chest lightly with her fingers and slowly began to get up from the bed, moving farther and farther away from him and staring more and more fixedly at him. Her feeling of horror suddenly communicated itself to him: exactly the same expression of terror appeared on his face; he, too, stared at her in the same way, and almost with the same child-like smile.

Signs of horror on Sonia's face evoked previously unconscious horror at what he had done in Raskolnikov. Looking at her, seeing her love, Dostoevsky continues, 'he felt and knew that he was infinitely more unhappy than before'.[24]

Dostoevsky thus depicts Sonia as quasi-analyst who, responding to signs of what is unconscious in Raskolnikov, says, as it were, 'I recognise the unconscious motivations of your crime,' writes Kristeva.[25] Sonia, like the psychoanalyst, Kristeva claims, 'raises the unconscious from beneath the actions and has it meet a loving other'.[26] As well as depicting Raskolnikov's response to signs of horror and love in Sonia's face enabling him to become conscious of his unconscious horror of the murder he has committed, Dostoevsky also depicts Raskolnikov becoming conscious of his unconscious love of Sonia on being faced with her absence and possible death. Dostoevsky likens Sonia thus restoring Raskolnikov to consciousness of what was unconscious in him to Christ raising Lazarus from the dead. He thus situates this recovery from unconsciousness in terms of the Christian community of his time, just as Hannah Arendt argued that it is possible to forgive and be forgiven only through recognizing the meaning of what we have done in terms of the 'political and legal community' in which we live.[27]

What happens, though, when re-birth is obstructed by denial of death and loss? Freud depicted this as cause of melancholic depression. Rather than face love and hate of those who are lost, dead, or gone, the melancholic identifies with them, said Freud,[28] as though they were one with these loved and hated figures.

> Their sorrow doesn't conceal the guilt or the sin felt because of having secretly plotted revenge on the ambivalent object. Their sadness would be rather the most archaic expression of an unsymbolizable, unnameable narcissistic wound, so precocious that no outside agent (subject or agent) can be used as referent.[29]

The melancholic clings to their sadness. Kristeva calls it a 'Thing'. She likens it to what Lacan calls 'the Real' to signify whatever eludes the meanings conferred by mirroring what is given us by others to see and perceive. The nineteenth-century writer, Gérard de Nerval, pictured depression as the huge despondent angel of Dürer's engraving, *Melancholia*.[30] De Nerval called melancholia a black sun. So does Kristeva. The melancholic, she says, 'has the impression of having been deprived of an unnameable, supreme good, of something unrepresentable, that perhaps only devouring might represent, or an invocation might point out, but no word could signify'.[31]

If melancholia is due to evading loss, separation and death, and not doing 'the work of mourning', as Freud called it,[32] recovering from melancholia entails reversing this process. It entails doing the grief-work involved in facing loss and death. The Kleinian analyst, Hanna Segal, argues that art too entails grief-work. Art is aesthetic, she maintains, in so far as the artist faces death and loss and enables us to face it too.[33] This might well account for the powerful effect of Holbein's painting, *The Dead Christ in the Tomb* (Figure 13.2, Plate 16).[34] 'It is true, it is the face of a man who has only just been taken from the cross – that is, still retaining a great deal of warmth and life,' wrote Dostoevsky in recounting the effect on him of this painting via its effect on the dying Ippolit in his novel, *The Idiot*: 'rigor mortis had not yet set in, so that there is still a look of suffering on the face of the dead man,' says Ippolit, 'as though he were still feeling it'.[35]

Making us see the bodily signs of suffering and death, Holbein makes us see and feel them too. Holbein arguably succeeds in doing this by having faced death himself, specifically the dead body retrieved from the Rhine which he apparently used as model for this painting. It makes us see and feel the suffering and isolation of death by showing us the dead body 'stretched out alone', says Kristeva, without any mourners to offset death's loneliness, as in Mantegna's painting, *The Dead Christ* (see p. 115). Holbein also conveys the isolation of death by designing the painting to be placed in a recess above the viewer. And he also conveys the suffering of death by painting, Kristeva notes, 'the head bent backwards, the contortion of the right hand bearing the stigmata, the position of the feet, the whole being bonded by means of a dark palette of grays, greens, and browns'. We are also drawn into Christ's suffering by the body's hair and hand falling over the base holding it, she adds, 'as if they might slide over toward us'.[36]

Enabling analysands to recover from melancholic depression also arguably entails the analyst facing death and loss so as to enable the analysand to recover from eluding them by defensive oneness with what is gone. Women, Kristeva argues, have proved particularly adept at tracing the signs. 'From Sabina Spielrein to Marion Milner to Piera Aulagnier,' she writes, 'women psychoanalysts accompany states of being to their limit in giving themselves to them with an exceptionally fine and intense countertransference.' She attributes this to 'the familiarity of feminine genius with the trauma of death and mourning'.[37] Enabling the analysand to become conscious of what is unconscious in their melancholic oneness with those who are dead and gone as effect, according to Freud, of hating as well as loving them, entails the analyst grafting onto signs of the fantasies involved whatever preconceptions these signs evoke in them.

Kristeva gives the example of an analysand, Anne, who came into analysis complaining that she had lost her taste for life. Anne hated herself – her nothingness, uselessness, worthlessness. Sometimes she took refuge in spending days in bed, neither eating nor speaking. Or she crammed herself with food which disgusted her, just as she unconsciously seemed to incorporate others as both loved and hated inside her. Kristeva's words seemed to undergo a similar fate. Anne appreciated their logic. But she left them undigested. 'I talk as though I were on the edge of words and I have the feeling that I am on the edge of my skin,' Anne complained, 'but the depth of my unhappiness remains untouchable.' She had suffered a serious skin complaint which deprived her of being held by her mother as a baby. Grafting on to all this the images it evoked in her, Kristeva interpreted:

> Since you couldn't touch your mother you hid beneath your skin . . . and in that hiding place you enclosed your desire and hatred of her in the sound of your voice, since you heard hers from afar.[38]

This was followed by Anne telling Kristeva a dream involving a trial in which everyone was found guilty. It left Anne feeling liberated from someone torturing her. But she was not there. She was somewhere else. It all seemed empty. She preferred to sleep, never to wake up. By contrast her dream awakened in Kristeva a sense of manic excitement in Anne's tortured and tortuous relations with her lovers and with her mother before them. Her saying, 'I am somewhere else, dreaming of pain-softness without any image of it', also evoked in Kristeva an image of Anne's bulimic bingeing and vomiting as sterile. Grafting this onto Anne's signs of her unconscious love and hate of those who were important to her, Kristeva interpreted: 'On the surface there are torturers. But, further away, or elsewhere, where your punishment is, there is contortion between being and not being born.' With this Anne became more alive to what was otherwise unconscious. She said she was frightened of being sterile. She told Kristeva a dream:

> from my body came a little girl, who spat on the portrait of my mother, of which I have often told you, until I closed my eyes; I have never been able to recall my mother's face. It is as if she died before I could be born, and had dragged me into death with her. And, now there I am giving birth. And it is her who comes back.[39]

Melancholia involves defensive oneness with what is gone, with the mother from whom she was born in the case of Anne's dream. What is to be done though when the analysand, far from indulging any such oneness, abjects it?

> There looms, within abjection, one of those violent, dark revolts of being, directed against a threat that seems to emanate from an exorbitant outside or inside, ejected beyond the scope of the possible, the tolerable, the thinkable. It lies there, quite close, but it cannot be assimilated. It beseeches, worries, and fascinates desire, which, nevertheless, does not let itself be seduced. Apprehensive, desire turns aside; sickened, it rejects.[40]

Kristeva links abjection with horror of whatever evokes return to oneness with the mother's body in her womb, and in being breast- or bottle-fed by her.

> When the eyes see or the lips touch that skin on the surface of milk – harmless, thin as a sheet of cigarette paper, pitiful as a nail paring – I experience a gagging sensation and, still farther down, spasms in the stomach, the belly . . . nausea makes me balk at that milk cream . . . 'I' want nothing of that element . . . 'I' expel it.[41]

She also relates abjection to the defence which Freud called negation. He likened it to the baby's earliest judgement between good and bad in telling itself, as it were, 'I should like to eat this,' and 'I should like to spit it out'.[42] She also relates the horror involved in abjection to Freud's account of the horror of castration which he believed the mythical Medusa symbolizes. He traced 'the mythological symbol of horror – Medusa's head,' as the analyst, Sandor Ferenczi, did, 'to the impression of the female genitals devoid of a penis'.[43] For Kristeva, by contrast, Medusa's severed head and gaping mouth evoke dread of being engulfed and reabsorbed into oneness with the mother in her womb before birth into separate individuated existence and meaning. 'Medusa is the stuff of abjection as teeth-filled primitive mother of that archaic undifferentiated state in which there is neither subject nor object, nothing but the gluey and viscous stuff of abjection', she writes of a seventeenth-century drawing of her (Figure 13.3.1).[44]

Benvenuto Cellini's statue, *Perseus with the Head of Medusa* (Figure 13.3.2), makes us see our defensive reaction. Perseus stands, phallic sword in hand, holding Medusa's head aloft while treading down her decapitated, writhing corpse. One mirrors the other: 'lying-standing, severed-erect, man-woman,

1

Figure 13.3.1 Studio of Giacinto Calandrucci: *Head of Medusa*

The Louvre, Paris.

2

Figure 13.3.2 Cellini: *Perseus with the Head of Medusa*

young-old,' says Kristeva, 'more masterfully than other representations of the Medusa myth, Benvenuto Cellini's *Perseus* shows us that it is in the two-way mirror that the triumph over the mother lodges'.[45] To this she adds Poussin's picture, *Perseus and Andromeda, The Origin of Coral.*[46] It symbolizes the transformation of formlessness, made much of by Bataille, in this instance the formlessness of wet paint transformed into meaning on becoming dry on being exposed to the air in a painting. 'Medusa has to be beheaded for it [coral] to take form,' Kristeva comments, 'for menacing lack of form to become the visible coral, for what is slimy-soft-menacing-invisible to take shape.'[47]

Patriarchal societies such as our own may well abject Medusa and women as mothers in so far as they are equated with nature in contrast to men and culture, socially symbolized, according to Lacan, by the phallus. Freud understood social constructions, specifically religious rituals such as the Catholic Mass or Protestant Eucharist, as repeating and atoning for murder of the patriarchal leader of the primal horde in so far as they make eating and drinking bread and wine symbols of the body and blood of the son of God (see p. 24). Kristeva, by contrast, argues that it is not parricide but horror of woman as mother that motivates many religious rituals and taboos, specifically those instituted against the blood of menstruation and child-birth because of their connotation of return to oneness with the mother in the womb.

Many women, however, use the prevailing languages of symbolism and art of their time to celebrate rather than abject their bodies and sex. A notable example is Georgia O'Keeffe. Writing about the difficulty of conveying what is unsymbolized and therefore unconscious and unknown, as Freudian psychoanalysts might put it, she told the novelist, Sherwood Anderson, with scant regard for conventional grammar and punctuation,

> I feel that a real living form is the natural result of the individuals effort to create the living thing out of the adventure of his spirit into the unknown – where it has experienced something – felt something – it has not understood – and from that experience comes the desire to make the unknown – known – By unknown – I mean the thing that means so much to the person that he wants to put it down – clarify something he feels but does not clearly understand – sometimes he partially knows why – sometimes he doesn't – sometimes it is all working in the dark – but a working that must be done – Making the unknown – known – in terms of one's medium is all absorbing.[48]

O'Keeffe contrasted this with the art of her celebrated photographer lover, Alfred Stieglitz. She wrote to Anderson:

> My work this year is very much on the ground – There will be only two abstract things – or three at the most – all the rest is objective – as objective as I can make it – He [Stieglitz] has done with the sky something similar to what I had done with color before – as he says – proving my case – He has done consciously something that I did mostly unconsciously.[49]

O'Keeffe's resulting paintings can be understood as making known the unknown through the way she completed bodily signs of women's sexuality though using and going beyond the symbolic meanings developed by surrealist artists she knew in Paris. Salvador Dali symbolized dream-like, oneiric states of mind as deserts. O'Keeffe also used desert landscapes but not as background of phallic grandiosity, as Dali did, in his painting, *The Great Masturbator*,[50] for instance. Rather, she used these landscapes to make visible what is usually repressed or abjected regarding female sexuality in our still often woman-hating culture. Examples include her painting, *Small Purple Hills*.[51] Such paintings reveal, says Kristeva, 'an oneiric world: dream landscapes? volcanic craters? crust of earth tormented in canyons? or, more prosaically and intimately, burning membranes of feminine hollows, feminine sexuality, seen close up, enlarged, leaf-like sensitive folds on folds'.[52] O'Keeffe's earlier flower paintings have a similar effect. 'Let us then see *Black Iris III* [Figure 13.4],'[53] Kristeva invites her readers. Such paintings, she says,

> disclose 'the humid entrance to the obscure valley,' as the Chinese thinker puts it? Georgia O'Keeffe is the painter of feminine eroticism: present, blinding, but invisible under its natural and offered appearance; no transgression, no perversion – the pleasure is permanent, continual flourishing which dilutes itself in appeasement, neutrality, quietism. Not to be seen with coldness, but simply with neutral and interiorized distance which knows to wait its instant of flourishing. Passion filtered by ebbing.[54]

We could say that O'Keeffe made known the socially repressed unknown of female sexuality by grafting onto its signs means of representation developed by surrealist artists and others in the 1920s and 1930s when she created these paintings.

Freud's patient, Little Hans, by contrast, abjected signs of women's sex as mother. Horrified, aged 3½, on seeing his mother's blood when he visited her just after she had given birth to his sister, Hanna, he exclaimed, pointing at blood-filled bedpans in the room, 'But blood doesn't come out of my widdler'. Abjecting the horror, negating it, he focused on horses as symbols of his father. His horse phobia was also based on his hearing his friend's father tell her, 'Don't put your finger to the white horse or it'll bite you'.[55] Similarly Freud's lawyer patient, Lanzer, abjected horror of women's bodies. He expressed this horror in gross sexual fantasies about them. He also negated and displaced the emotional intensity of this horror (see p. 21), by becoming obsessed with the command of the army captain who, as I have said, detailed to him a horrific punishment involving rats penetrating into the offender's body, 'You must pay back the 3.80 kronen to Lieutenant A'.[56]

But abjecting horror of the body and of women's sexuality and displacing this onto obsessive repetition of men's words and commands can make

Figure 13.4 Georgia O'Keeffe: *Black Iris III*

The Metropolitan Museum of Art, New York, copyright © ARS, NY and DACS, London, 2006.

existence disembodied, lifeless abstraction. Hence the phobic or obsessive analysand's plea to the analyst, says Kristeva, 'I displace, therefore you must associate and condense for me'. Such a patient, she says, 'is asking the analyst to build up an imagination for him . . . for a rebirth that . . . will result from a speech that is recovered, rediscovered as belonging to him'.[57] This entails the analyst formulating constructions and interpretations which are 'true', she claims, in so far as they bring back to life, and evoke the analysand's free associations.[58] Perhaps it would be more correct to say that the analyst's interpretations are useful, rather than true, in so far as they enable their analysands to free associate and thus become more conscious of what is otherwise unconscious to them regarding the meaning of what they have done, or wished they had done.

How, though, is this to be brought about? Unlike Freud who argued that the analyst's attitude should be one of 'emotional coldness',[59] unlike Lacan who likened the analyst to a mirror, and unlike Laplanche who urges the analyst to adopt a stance of neutral benevolence, Kristeva urges her fellow analysts to shed this 'benevolent neutrality' and 'indifference'. For it is 'by implicating ourselves,' she explains, '[that] we bring to life, to meaning, the dead discourses of patients which summon us'.[60]

Winnicott, as I have said, wrote of psychoanalytic therapy taking place 'in the overlap of the two play areas, that of the patient and that of the therapist'.[61] Kristeva redescribes this in child analysis as 'interaction between the two imaginaries (the child's and the analyst's) as they focus on bodies and their acts'.[62] Its extension to adult analysis can be illustrated with the case of an anorexic patient, Agnes. 'A tall thin girl, translucent, taut as a piece of wire and crumbly as dry clay,' writes Kristeva. Her appearance evoked in Kristeva the following memory:

> I know I was weaned very early, Mama had a breast infection, and, as a child, I had little tolerance for milk – sheep's milk, cow's milk, goat's milk, concentrated, skim, whole, nothing did the trick. The slightest dash of cream made me vomit. Necessarily, because I had been taken off my mother's milk very early, too early, said my mother.[63]

Adding this re-evoked memory from her own infancy onto signs of Agnes' unconscious fantasies evident in her analysis led to their discovering a more or less unconscious command at the heart of Agnes' anorexia: 'Thou shalt not eat of that mother'.

This command collapsed the two-way daughter–mother dialogue, 'I swallow you / I spit you out. I love you / I kill you.' It collapsed this dialogue into illusory oneness of Agnes with her mother: 'I swallow myself / I spit myself out. I love myself / I kill myself.' Abjecting and negating this oneness, Agnes displaced its energy onto obedience and hyperdevotion, writes Kristeva, 'to the Law, to God, to the One'. This evoked another memory in Kristeva, of herself, as a child, similarly abjecting oneness with her mother and displacing its emotional intensity by instead overvaluing her father's command, 'Stand up straight!' He was, she adds, 'the foremost being of uprightness – of an exceptional uprightness – that I ever had occasion to meet'.[64]

Confronted with the analysand whose ills involve abjecting horror of oneness with the mother through flight into phobic, obsessional, fetishistic even, overvaluation of male-centred images, symbols and commands, the analyst's task involves grafting onto signs of what unconsciously horrifies the analysand the fantasies evoked in them by what the analysand says and does. Or so Kristeva claims.

This can be illustrated with her case history of an artist, Didier, obsessed with masturbating and with his art. Otherwise, it seems, he was utterly bored and boring. His talk in analysis was lifeless and mechanical. Kristeva conveys this by recounting one of his dreams in impersonal, third person terms:

> Didier is leaning out of a window in his family home. He feels ill, or someone pushes him. He falls into an open space. He experiences a moment of intense anxiety that makes him scream, though he is unsure about this. In any event, the dream is a silent one. He suddenly finds himself in front of [a] mirror and sees a reflection of his sister's face. This agitates him quite a bit and makes him wake up.[65]

As for his art, Didier described it in such technical detail Kristeva could not imagine it.

Questioning the wisdom of restricting his analysis to what he said, 'instead of also spending time on the means of expression by which I believe he had encoded his traumas and desires', Kristeva writes, she attended to the signs of unconscious fantasies motivating his obsessions in what he said about pictures of his art-work which he brought for her to see. From what he said about his art, it transpired that it combined collage and painting. His account of it was revealing. The signs of violence in what he said about it contrasted strikingly, says Kristeva, 'with the neutrality, extreme politeness, and abstract discourse that had characterized his previous dealings with me'. What he said revealed a split off artist-self who, reports Kristeva,

> worked with various entities – docile objects that were fractured, cracked, and broken up as if slaughtered ... not a single face espoused the fragments of these mutilated persons, who were primarily female, and who were shown to have a derisive nature and an unsuspected ugliness.[66]

He used to show his art to his mother when she was alive. She accepted it without showing any reaction to it. Not so Kristeva. She named the sadistic fantasies his description of it evoked in her. Consistent with her emphasis on the 'intertextuality' in art,[67] its interweaving of different socially given languages, discourses and conventions, she wove her discourse together with that of Didier. She performed a 'phantasmatic graft', she confesses, 'I offered Didier *my own* fantasies, which his paintings elicited in *me*.' He found what she said reductive and oversimplistic. But in variously accepting, adjusting, changing and rejecting her interpretations, based on grafting onto signs of what he unconsciously imagined the fantasies these signs evoked in her, he became more able to recover his fantasies to consciousness. They included recalling a dream in which he imagined he was both his parents making love with each other, and dreams of extreme violence towards his father for passively letting his mother dress him as a girl when he was a child. He worried Kristeva might be similarly passive, or reduce him to passivity. At the end of his analysis he made a picture of her from a photo in which she was holding a cigarette. But he had cut out the cigarette. 'Nothing between the hands, no penis, no fetish,' he said. 'I did well, didn't I.'[68]

Kristeva puts this in somewhat obscure terms. Put simply, her method of grafting or adding onto the precursory signs of the unconscious fantasies of Didier and Agnes the fantasies they evoked in her in completing these signs into interpretations makes psychoanalysis more than ever like painting. It makes analysis like painting understood as a one-person squiggle game in which the painter completes precursory squiggles, signs, or marks on their canvas by grafting onto them whatever these signs evoke in them, just as Freud recommended analysts, in effect, to graft onto their analysands' free associations the knowledge of dream-symbolism these associations evoke in the analyst when they otherwise prove an insufficient basis for an interpretation.

What, then, are we to make of installation art? Kristeva's account of examples of this art form suggests an image of the artist making precursory squiggles, signs or marks and leaving it to its beholders to complete these signs into whatever they might symbolize depending on what these signs evoke in them. Describing Hans Haacke's installation, *Germania* (Figure 13.5),[69] at the 1993 Venice Biennale, for instance, she writes that it required visitors to walk on shifting, crumbling ground. In such art, she continues,

> the entire body is called on to participate through its senses – sight, of course, but also hearing, touch, sometimes smell . . . communicating . . . what was once celebrated as incarnation . . . the desire to make one feel – through abstraction, form, color, volume, sensation – a real experience.

Installation art, Kristeva maintains, 'produces an unsettling complicity with our regressions, for when faced with these fragments, these flashes of sensations, these disseminated objects, you no longer know who you are'.[70] Does it mark the end of art as resource through which, and in analogy with which to retell the insights of Freud and their continuing relevance at the present time?

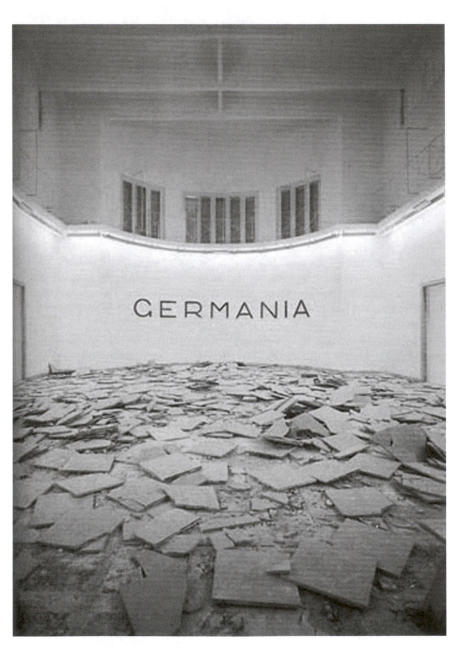

Figure 13.5 Hans Haacke: *Germania*

Venice Biennale, 1993, copyright © DACS, London, 2006.

Chapter 14

Conclusion

Installation art might not lend itself as readily to retelling Freud's insights in terms of, and as analogous to art as Picasso's painting, *Les Demoiselles d'Avignon*, with which this book began. Nor may installation art lend itself as readily as Picasso's drawings – his crayon drawing, *The Painter and his Model* (dated 4 July 1970), for example – to likening the relation of the artist to what they paint to the Freudian analyst's relation to what they analyse as I have pictured here (Figure 14.1).

Nevertheless many works of installation and twenty-first-century art are evidently very much inspired by psychoanalysis. A striking example is Louise Bourgeois's gigantic installations – *Maman*[1] and *I Do, I Undo, I Redo*[2] – filling

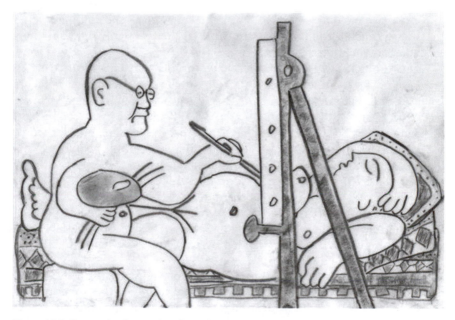

Figure 14.1 Sayers: Analyst and analysand

the turbine hall of London's Tate Modern gallery when it first opened in May 2000. Another example is her mixed-media work, *Sublimation*, exhibited in London's Hauser and Wirth gallery in Piccadilly in 2005.

Sublimation is a 'book'. It consists of fifteen vast 'pages' which were placed side by side along three walls of a large gallery when it was shown in Piccadilly. Its focus is trauma and the aftermath of trauma, both of which constitute the major subject matter of Freudian and post-Freudian therapy. Freud defined trauma as 'any excitations from outside which are powerful enough to break through the protective shield'. Trauma puts the pleasure principle out of action, he argued.

> There is no longer any possibility of preventing the mental apparatus from being flooded with large amounts of stimulus, and another problem arises instead – the problem of mastering the amounts of stimulus which have broken in and of binding them, in the psychical sense, so that they can then be disposed of.[3]

Trauma breaks into, and renders useless, what we have learnt from others as means of managing our experience by symbolizing and transforming it into meaning. Writing about visual imagery, Kristeva's teacher and friend, Roland Barthes, called trauma 'a suspension of language, a blocking of meaning'.[4] Meaning can also be conveyed, of course, by words. They are sown like seeds in us, says Kristeva. From earliest infancy they form 'mnemic traces' on which perceptions and bodily drives are grafted. '[It] is this unconscious conglomerate, ruled by the mnemic trace,' she continues, 'that I recover through the intermediary of words as they presently function in my adult preconscious psyche'.[5]

What, though, is to be done when words fail us? This returns me to *Sublimation*. Its pages tell a story, as I will explain using sketches I made on seeing it in London (see Figures 14.2 and 14.3). The story begins with a picture of a baby's teat (Figure 14.2.1). This is followed by a second page depicting two pink circular breasts (Figure 14.2.2), accompanied by words recalling Bourgeois's visit to a foundry, and the silence of the people working there, concentrating on what they were doing, when suddenly there is a clash of voices. She pictures this as two interweaving, red and black spirals (Figure 14.2.3),[6] followed by eyes surrounded by one circle intruding into another (Figure 14.2.4). The voices are those of a woman attacking her husband, she tells us. The pink breasts of *Sublimation*'s second page become staring pink pupils in eyes surrounded by panicky lines (Figure 14.2.5),[7] as the couple clash (Figure 14.2.6).[8]

They are the eyes of the fighting couple's son. Freud wrote of the trauma of children seeing their parents fighting. He wrote of their interpreting signs of what they see and hear of their parents' sexual intercourse together as signifying, he said, 'something that the stronger participant is forcibly

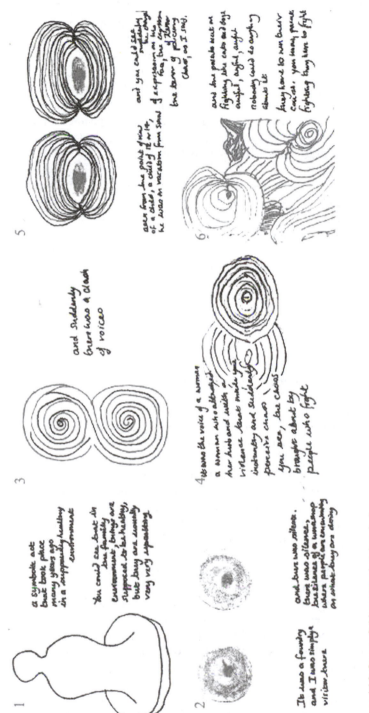

Figure 14.2 Sayers: Sublimation sketches 1–6

inflicting on the weaker'. He attributed this to children grafting, as Kristeva might have put it, onto the signs seen and heard of their parents together fantasies evoked by these signs by virtue of their already existing 'sadistic impulses' and 'accidental observations'. They may also interpret their parents' sexual coupling as aggressive fighting on the basis of sights and sounds of their mother 'defending herself against an act of violence', said Freud, or on the basis of their parents' marriage providing 'the spectacle of an unceasing quarrel, expressed in loud words and unfriendly gestures', which they assume is settled by the same means as they use to settle quarrels with their friends.[9]

Bourgeois shows us a child's reaction to just such quarrelling with a picture of the eyes of the son of the couple in her pictured story narrowing to dots in scribble (Figure 14.3.7: the figures' numbering follows the originals). He does not die, she says. He does not become incontinent. He does not piss or shit himself. He does not disintegrate. He gets a broom and starts cleaning up (Figure 14.3.8). Seeing this, Bourgeois adds, she starts crying at his thus controlling the chaos. She depicts it as tightly controlled scrawl (Figure 14.3.9). Even now, old as she is, she feels the chaos surging up within her, and the difficulty of controlling it (Figure 14.3.10). At that point, she says, one does something symbolic. One might, she adds, illustrating the options, become a perfectionist, work on the house, make a sculpture, make a pattern, paint a pretty flower (Figure 14.3.11–15).

Together all fifteen pages of *Sublimation* show the transformation of what traumatically breaks through the capacity both of Bourgeois and the son of the warring couple she depicts to symbolize signs of this breakthrough into the palpable stuff of manageable meaning. Religion does something similar, as Freud showed in his *Totem and Taboo* account of the rituals of the Catholic Mass and Protestant Eucharist transforming the horror of murderous impulses towards those who father and rule over us into the symbolism of eating and drinking the body and blood of the son of God. Religious purification rituals regarding the blood of menstruation and childbirth similarly symbolize and keep at bay, argues Kristeva, horror of return to oneness with the body of the mother before our birth into culture, symbolization and meaning.

Painting and the visual arts can likewise transform what is meaningless and potentially traumatic and, as such, liable to repression into unconsciousness through the artist making its signs into the palpable stuff of meaning in their art. Retelling Freud's insights in terms of, and as analogous to art highlights the continuing value of these insights for therapy. For it illuminates the art-making images, fantasies, nightmares and dreams involved in the genesis of, and recovery from the psychological ills still afflicting children and adults as they did in Freud's day.

Retelling the insights of Freud and his followers in terms of, and as analogous to painting and the visual arts also highlights the fact that, just as

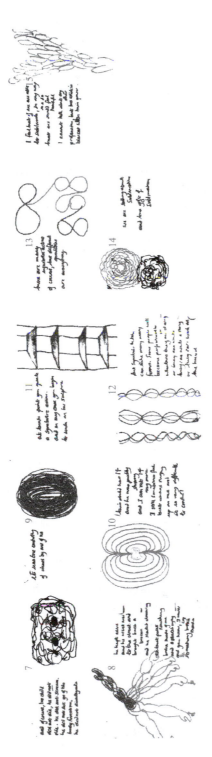

Figure 14.3 Sayers: Sublimation sketches 7–15

painters, for instance, make what is meaningless and potentially traumatic into what can become conscious, meaningful and manageable through being made into the palpable stuff of meaning which we can see, and deal with, so too analysts make what is silent and unconscious into the palpable stuff of meaning through transforming its signs into words that the analysand can hear. Attending to the embodied signs and impressions involved helps counter the tendency of psychoanalytic therapists to treat these signs as ethereal projection by the analysand of their fantasies into them as repositories of what, in the now discredited science of psychical research, was called thought-transference or telepathy.

In fact, though, just as artists lend their bodies to the world in creating paintings, so too psychoanalytic psychotherapists lend their eyes, ears and senses to what their analysands say and do in transforming signs of the unconscious into interpretations. Even if the painter's paintings are abstract they cannot come into being unless, as Merleau-Ponty pointed out, '[the] world has at least once emblazoned in [the painter] the ciphers of the visible'.[10] The same is true of analysis. However abstract the analyst's interpretations, they could not interpret the impressions made on them by their analysands unless they had a great deal of prior experience of taking in and making meaning of the impressions made on them by others in their life, personal and professional.

This brings me to another benefit of retelling Freud's insights in terms of, and as analogous to art. For, just as the innovative artist brings their personal experience together with what is given to them socially and professionally by way of prevailing norms and conventions in variously using and rebelling against them in creating their art, so too analysts are influenced by socially given conventions governing their personal and professional experience in completing signs of their analysands' unconscious fantasies into interpretable meaning. Freud made a virtue of this in recommending analysts to use their already acquired knowledge of symbolic meanings in completing their analysands' free associations into interpretations. Jung went further in advocating the translation of the analysand's dream- and fantasy-based imagery in terms of symbols and archetypes he found in ancient myth, religion, and philosophy.

Klein overlooked the socially given systems of meaning influencing her interpretations of her child and adult analysands' free associations. So have many of her followers. Not so Lacan, Laplanche and Kristeva. Drawing on their account of the socially and personally given patriarchal systems of symbolism and meaning shaping the unconscious fantasies with which psychoanalytic psychotherapy is concerned, I have proposed adding the perhaps preposterous-seeming suggestion that enabling these fantasies to become conscious is akin to the squiggle game. I have indicated more or less explicitly in the foregoing pages that psychoanalytic therapists complete signs of their analysands' unconscious fantasies into interpretative meaning just as the squiggle game player completes their fellow player's squiggles in terms of what these signs evoke in them from their previously acquired experience and ideas.

But what is to be done about the complaint, that unlike poetry, for instance, which 'stops us in mid-thought', visual images hurry the mind out of itself?[11] What is to prevent the therapist's interpretations, based on prior experience and ideas evoked by what the analysand says and does, similarly hurrying analysands out of themselves? What is to prevent the therapist's interpretation like the 'metaphorizing' of the body in painting, as described by Wollheim,[12] from seducing the analysand too readily into experiencing illusory oneness with what the analyst says, thus duping them, as we are all so often and so readily duped by advertisements and political propaganda into imagined oneness with their blandishments?

And what is to prevent the therapist's interpretations becoming akin to the ossifying dogmas and rituals of religion, or to the strait-jacketing signs and symbols which Freud argued constitute conversion hysteria, phobic and obsessional neurosis, and schizophrenia? The history of psychoanalysis is sadly replete with examples of just such dogmas: Freud's dogmas about women's and men's penis envy and castration complex construction of sexual difference as source of their ills; Jung's dogmas about archetypes of the collective unconscious; Klein's mother-centred dogmas about the death instinct, envy, and the good and bad breast; Lacan's dogmas about the phallus; Winnicott's dogmas about the good-enough mother.

One way of countering psychoanalysis and its interpretations becoming dogmatic is for analysts to regard their psychoanalytic interpretations as provisional and open to revision in the light of what they suggest to the analysand as evidenced by what he or she subsequently says and does. We could liken this to painters completing their painted marks, signs or squiggles into paintings which, by a process of deconstruction, suggest various fragmentary ideas which they then construct into further paintings. We could describe the psychoanalyst and painter as both adopting the dictum, 'I do, I undo, I redo', to use the name given by Louise Bourgeois to her above-mentioned installation celebrating the opening of London's Tate Modern gallery at the beginning of the twenty-first century.

If, though, psychoanalysis, like painting and the visual arts, is constituted by doing, undoing and redoing the signs and impressions and the symbols and interpretations they evoke in the analyst, how can its work ever end? Is this a recipe for despair? Not so, according to Merleau-Ponty:

> If no painting comes to be *the* painting, if no work is ever absolutely completed and done with, still each creation changes, alters, enlightens, deepens, confirms, exalts, re-creates, or creates in advance all the others. If creations are not a possession, it is not only that, like all things, they pass away; it is also that they have almost all their life still before them.[13]

The same is true of interpretations in psychoanalytic psychotherapy. They too are like creations in art, installation art included. Despite its much-bruited demise, the dream-, fantasy-, picture- and art-work doing, undoing and redoing method of free association and interpretation constituting talking cure psychoanalysis, introduced by Freud over a hundred years ago, still has a great deal to tell and retell us about transforming what is otherwise unconscious into what can be known, thought about, and learnt from nowadays.

Appendix

URLs for images discussed but not reproduced in this book.

I Introduction

Cézanne – *Les Grandes Baigneuses*
http://www.ibiblio.org/wm/paint/auth/cezanne/bath/cezanne.grandes-baigneuses.jpg
Matisse – *Le Bonheur de vivre*
http://www.ibiblio.org/wm/paint/auth/matisse/matisse.bonheur-vivre.jpg
Picasso – *Les Demoiselles d'Avignon*
http://cgfa.sunsite.dk/picasso/picasso2.jpg
Goya – *Maja and Celestina*
http://www.frick.org/assets/images/exhibitions/goya/
Goya_MajaAndCelestina.600.jpg
Goya – *Man Looking for Fleas in his Shirt*
http://www.frick.org/assets/images/exhibitions/goya/
Goya_ManLookingFleas.600.jpg
Jackson Pollock – *One: Number 31*
http://www.moma.org/visit_moma/images/audioThumbnails/pollock.jpg

2 Freud

Jean-Baptiste-Siméon Chardin – *La Table d'office*
http://catherine.briand.club.fr/chardin.jpg
Luca Signorelli – *The Last Judgement*
http://www.langgaard.dk/musik/musikfot/Anti-7.jpg
Michelangelo – *Moses*
http://cla.calpoly.edu/~smarx/courses/204/damoses/moses.jpg
Sergei Pankieff – *Wolf Dream*
http://www.freud.org.uk/wolfpic.jpg
Leonardo – *Madonna and Child with St Anne*
http://www.csulb.edu/~csnider/leonardo.st.anne2.jpg

3 Jung

Isaak Levitan – *The Quiet Abode*
http://www.tamsquare.net/pictures/L/Isaak-Levitan-The-Quiet-Abode-.jpg
Francis Bacon – *Study for Portrait of Van Gogh IV*
http://www.tate.org.uk/collection/T/T00/T00226_8.jpg
Van Gogh – *The Artist on the Road to Tarascon*
http://sorrel.humboldt.edu/~rwj1/van/e167.jpg
Lucian Freud – *Self-Portrait*
http://www.ibiblio.org/wm/paint/auth/freud/freud.reflection.jpg
Rembrandt – *Self-Portrait*
http://www.ibiblio.org/wm/paint/auth/rembrandt/self/rembrandt.1661.jpg

5 Klein

Goya – *Disasters of War*, number 39
http://www.eeweems.com/goya/great_deeds_700.jpg
Francis Picabia – *La Nuit espagnole*
http://www.doctorhugo.org/synaesthesia/art/index.html
Van Gogh – *Road with Cypress and Star*
http://www.ibiblio.org/wm/paint/auth/gogh/fields/gogh.cypress-star.jpg
Paul Klee – *Senecio*
http://www.thefineartcompany.co.uk/abstract/K17.jpg

6 Stokes

Michelangelo – *Pieta*
http://www.thais.it/scultura/image/media/sch00082.jpg
Michelangelo – *Slaves*
http://graphics.stanford.edu/projects/mich/poster/slave4.jpg
Leone Battista Alberti – Tempio Malatestiano
http://www.rimini-it.it/img/tempio_malatestiano.jpg
Agostino – *Diana*
http://www.wga.hu/art/d/duccio/agostino/diana.jpg
Luciano Laurana – courtyard at Palazzo Ducale, Urbino
http://www.usc.edu/dept/architecture/slide/ghirardo/CD1/060-CD1.jpg
Giorgione – *The Tempest*
http://www.artchive.com/artchive/g/giorgione/tempest.jpg
Bellini – *The Drunkenness of Noah*
http://www.tamsquare.net/pictures/B/Giovanni_Bellini_Drunken_Noah.jpg
Picasso – *Guernica*
http://www.terra.es/personal/asg00003/picasso/grguer2.jpg
Rembrandt – portraits
http://www.nationalgallery.org.uk/cgi-bin/WebObjects.exe/CollectionSearch.woa/wa/
newQuery?searchTerm=rembrandt

Turner – *Light and Colour*
http://www.tate.org.uk/collection/N/N00/N00532_8.jpg
Wilhelm de Kooning – *Untitled XIX, 1977*
http://www.canadianart.ca/travel/sw_dekooning.jpg
Wilhelm de Kooning – *Untitled III, 1979*
http://www.dallasnews.com/sharedcontent/dws/img/12–05/1201glkooning.jpg

7 Lacan

Salvador Dali – *Invisible Sleeping Woman*
http://www.topofart.com/images/artists/Salvador_Dali/paintings/dali029.jpg
Salvador Dali – *The Stinking Ass*
http://www.latifm.com/salvador_dali/small_image/the_stinking_ass.jpg
Holbein – *Portrait of Georg Gisze of Danzig*
http://www.tamsquare.net/thumbnail/H/Hans-Holbein-the-Younger-Portrait-of-Georg-Gisze-of-Danzig.jpg
Salvador Dali – *Retrospective Bust of a Woman*
http://www.moma.org/collection/provenance/items/images/301.92.jpg
Salvador Dali – *The Persistence of Memory*
http://www.moma.org/images/collection/FullSizes/00073100.jpg

8 Milner

William Blake – *The Ancient of Days*
http://www.users.muohio.edu/mandellc/eng339/ancient%20of%20days%20big.jpg

9 Ehrenzweig

Georges de la Tour – *The Nativity*
http://www.spiritsite.com/gallery/art/medmar/LaTourTheNativity.jpg
Picasso – *Goat Skull and Bottle*
http://www.museupicasso.bcn.es/guerraipau/imatges/a3.jpg
Jackson Pollock – *One: Number 31*
http://www.moma.org/visit_moma/images/audioThumbnails/pollock.jpg

11 Bion

Vermeer – *The Little Street in Delft*
http://www.ibiblio.org/wm/paint/auth/vermeer/little-street/little-street.jpg
Van Gogh – *Old Shoes with Laces*
http://homepage.newschool.edu/~quigleyt/vcs/jameson/vangogh_shoes.jpg
Picasso – *Les Demoiselles d'Avignon*
http://cgfa.sunsite.dk/picasso/picasso2.jpg
Monet – *Poppies*
http://claude-monet.org/artbase/Monet/1873-1873/w0274/apc.jpg

Monet – *Haystacks*
http://www.ibiblio.org/wm/paint/auth/monet/haystacks/
Monet – *Rouen Cathedral*
http://www.ibiblio.org/wm/paint/auth/monet/rouen/
Cézanne – Mont Sainte Victoire
http://www.ibiblio.org/wm/paint/auth/cezanne/st-victoire/1885/cezanne.st-victoire-1885.jpg
http://www.tate.org.uk/collection/N/N05/N05303_9.jpg
Leonardo – drawings of hair and water
http://www.royalcollection.org.uk/egallery/images/collection_small/912494.jpg
http://artscience.org/ni/nita/form/images/leonardo.jpeg

13 Kristeva

Giotto – *The Last Judgement* (detail)
http://www.wga.hu/art/g/giotto/padova/4lastjud/01_lastj.jpg
Giotto – *The Annunciation to Anna*
http://keptar.demasz.hu/arthp/html/g/giotto/padova/1joachim/joachi3.htm
Giotto – *The Massacre of the Innocents*
http://www.wga.hu/art/g/giotto/assisi/lower/ceiling/05christ.jpg
Piero della Francesca – *Madonna della Misericordia*
http://www.abcgallery.com/P/piero/francesca11.jpg
Piero della Francesca – *Nativity*
http://keptar.demasz.hu/arthp/art/p/piero/francesc/nativity.jpg
Dürer – *Melancholia*
http://i2.photobucket.com/albums/y26/siddhartha04/durer23.jpg
Poussin – *Perseus and Andromeda, The Origin of Coral*
http://www.mcah.columbia.edu/dbcourses/freedberg/thumb/poussin_drwg_ab1958_f114.jpg
Salvador Dali – *The Great Masturbator*
http://dali.urvas.lt/forviewing/pic24.jpg
Georgia O'Keeffe – *Small Purple Hills*
http://www.mystudios.com/women/klmno/okeeffe-small-purple-hills.jpg

14 Conclusion

Louise Bourgeois – *Maman*
http://www.stpauls.it/letture00/0008let/images/0008le21.jpg
Louise Bourgeois – *I Do, I Undo, I Redo*
http://image.guardian.co.uk/sys-images/Guardian/Pix/gallery/2005/10/10/smith_IDoIUndoIRedo3.jpg
Louise Bourgeois – *Sublimation* (details)
http://www.littlesongbox.co.uk/Files/Diary/sublimation.jpg
http://www.artnet.com/Magazine/reviews/laplaca/Images/laplaca3-30-8.jpg
http://www.arttra.co.uk/reviews/Louise_bourgeois/sublimination1.png

Notes

1 Introduction

1 C. Jung (1961) *Memories, Dreams, Reflections*. London: Fontana, 1993, p. 172.
2 S. Freud (1907) Obsessive actions and religious practices. *SE9*: 117–27.
3 http://www.ibiblio.org/wm/paint/auth/cezanne/bath/cezanne.grandes-baigneuses.jpg
4 http://www.ibiblio.org/wm/paint/auth/matisse/matisse.bonheur-vivre.jpg
5 http://cgfa.sunsite.dk/picasso/picasso2.jpg
6 S. Freud (1905) On psychotherapy. *SE7*: 257–68, 260–1.
7 C.G. Jung (1932) Picasso. *CW15*: 135–41, 137–8.
8 My thanks to Linda Schädler at the Zurich Kunsthaus for confirming inclusion of these paintings in the 1932 Picasso exhibition in Zurich.
9 Jung 1932: 138–9.
10 J. Jones (2003) Ghost world. *Guardian*, 26 September.
11 http://www.frick.org/assets/images/exhibitions/goya/Goya_MajaAndCelestina.600.jpg
12 http://www.frick.org/assets/images/exhibitions/goya/Goya_ManLookingFleas.600.jpg
13 http://www.frick.org/exhibitions/goya/exhibition.htm
14 In L. Aragon (1990) *Henri Matisse. Vol. 2*. New York: Harcourt, Brace, Jovanovich, 1971, p. 46; also in M. Thompson (1989) *On Art and Therapy*. London: Virago, p. 93.
15 S. Freud (1882) Letter to Martha Bernays. In E. Freud, L. Freud and I. Grubrich-Simitis (eds) (1978) *Sigmund Freud: His Life in Pictures and Words*. London: Deutsch, p. 95.
16 S. Freud (n.d.) in E. Freud et al. 1978, p. 181. My thanks to the late Paul Roazen for drawing my attention to these doodles, and to Michael Molnar, at London's Freud Museum, for suggesting their early 1920s date, contrary to the 1914 date given in E. Freud et al. 1978.
17 http://www.moma.org/visit_moma/images/audioThumbnails/pollock.jpg
18 S. Freud (1985) The aetiology of hysteria. *SE3*: 191–221, 198.
19 N. Lynton (1980) *The Story of Modern Art*. Oxford: Phaidon, p. 51.
20 S. Freud (1907) Obsessive actions and religious practices. *SE9*: 117–27.
21 M. Klein (1946) Notes on some schizoid mechanisms. *EG*: 1–24, 8, 22.
22 M. Klein (1935) A contribution to the psychogenesis of manic-depressive states. *LGR*: 262–89, 271, 284.
23 A. Stokes (1955a) Form in art. In M. Klein, P. Heimann and R.E. Money-Kyrle (eds) (1977) *New Directions in Psycho-Analysis*. London: Karnac, p. 407.

24 S. Freud (1930) *Civilization and its Discontents. SE21*: 64–145, 68.
25 S. Freud (1912) Recommendations to physicians practising psycho-analysis. *SE12*: 111–20, 111.
26 J. Laplanche (1992) The drive and its source-object: Its fate in the transference. *EO*: 117–32, 127.

2 Freud

1 J. Breuer and S. Freud (1895) *Studies on Hysteria. SE2*: 1–309, 30.
2 Breuer and Freud 1895: 38.
3 Breuer and Freud 1895: 294.
4 Breuer and Freud 1895: 295, 297.
5 J. Breuer and S. Freud (1893) On the psychical mechanisms of hysterical phenomena: Preliminary communication. *SE2*: 3–18, 12.
6 S. Freud (1895) Project for a scientific psychology. *SE1*: 295–387, 356.
7 See e.g. *La Table d'office* (c.1763) – http://catherine.briand.club.fr/chardin.jpg
8 M. Proust (1895) Chardin. *By Way of Saint-Beuve*. London: Chatto & Windus, 1958, p. 243.
9 M. Proust (1919) *Within a Budding Grove*. London: Penguin, 1983, p. 929.
10 M. Proust (1927) *Time Regained*. London: Penguin, 1983, p. 932.
11 S. Freud (1896) The aetiology of hysteria. *SE3*: 191–221.
12 S. Freud (1897) Letter to Fliess, 15 October. *SE1*: 263–6, 265.
13 http://www.langgaard.dk/musik/musikfot/Anti–7.jpg
14 S. Freud (1898) The psychical mechanism of forgetfulness. *SE3*: 289–97, 294 n.1.
15 Freud 1898: 294. Sigmund Freud, copyrights © The Institute of Psychoanalysis and The Hogarth Press, reprinted by permission of The Random House Group Ltd.
16 S. Freud (1907) Delusions and dreams in Jensen's *Gradiva. SE9*: 7–93, frontispiece.
17 http://cla.calpoly.edu/~smarx/courses/204/damoses/moses.jpg
18 S. Freud (1914) The Moses of Michelangelo. *SE13*: 211–36, 212, 222. Sigmund Freud, copyrights © The Institute of Psychoanalysis and The Hogarth Press, reprinted by permission of The Random House Group Ltd, and in the United States by permission of Basic Books, a member of Perseus Books, L.L.C.
19 Freud 1914: 226–7.
20 Freud 1914: 236.
21 M. Solms and O. Turnbull (2002) *The Brain and the Inner World*. London: Karnac, p. 211.
22 Solms and Turnbull 2002: 15.
23 S. Freud (1900) *The Interpretation of Dreams. SE4–5*: 1–621, 163.
24 Freud 1900: 130.
25 Freud 1900: 125.
26 Freud 1900: 269.
27 S. Freud (1905a) Fragment of an analysis of a case of hysteria. *SE7*: 7–122, 87.
28 Freud 1895: 326–7.
29 Freud 1900: *SE5*: 565, 566.
30 S. Freud (1915–17) *Introductory Lectures on Psycho-Analysis. SE15–16*: 1–463, 314.
31 S. Freud (1905b) *Three Essays on the Theory of Sexuality. SE7*: 135–243, 223.
32 S. Freud (1908) 'Civilized' sexual morality and modern nervousness. *SE9*: 181–204, 202.
33 S. Freud (1910a) *Five Lectures on Psycho-Analysis. SE11*: 9–55, 47.
34 S. Freud (1910b) A special type of choice of object made by men. *SE11*: 165–75, 171.
35 S. Freud (1901) *On Dreams. SE5*: 633–86, 666.

36 For detailed explanations of this aspect of the dream-work, see Freud 1900: 488–508; Freud 1901: 666–7.

37 S. Freud (1911a) Formulations on the two principles of mental functioning. *SE12*: 218–26, 220.

38 Freud 1900: 101.

39 S. Freud (1918) From the history of an infantile neurosis. *SE17*: 7–122, 29.

40 Freud 1918: 30. Sigmund Freud, copyrights © The Institute of Psychoanalysis and The Hogarth Press, reprinted by permission of The Random House Group Ltd, and in the United States by permission of Basic Books, a member of Perseus Books, L.L.C.

41 http://www.freud.org.uk/wolfpic.jpg

42 Freud 1918: 30.

43 Freud 1905a: 116.

44 S. Freud (1912a) The dynamics of transference. *SE12*: 99–108, 108.

45 S. Freud (1909a) Analysis of a phobia in a five-year-old boy. *SE10*: 5–147, 22–3.

46 Freud 1909a: 8.

47 Freud 1909a: 10, 11.

48 Freud 1909a: 13. Sigmund Freud, copyrights © The Institute of Psychoanalysis and The Hogarth Press, reprinted by permission of The Random House Group Ltd, and in the United States by permission of Basic Books, a member of Perseus Books, L.L.C.

49 Freud 1909a: 14.

50 Freud 1909a: 19.

51 Freud 1909a: 41.

52 Freud 1909a: 42.

53 Freud 1909a: 49. Sigmund Freud, copyrights © The Institute of Psychoanalysis and The Hogarth Press, reprinted by permission of The Random House Group Ltd and in the United States by permission of Basic Books, a member of Perseus Books, L.L.C.

54 Freud 1909a: 49.

55 Freud 1909a: 98.

56 S. Freud (1913) On beginning the treatment. *SE12*: 123–44, 134.

57 S. Freud (1910c) The future prospects of psycho-analytic therapy. *SE11*: 141–51, 144, 145.

58 S. Freud (1912b) Recommendations to physicians practising psycho-analysis. *SE12*: 111–20, 111.

59 S. Freud (1909b) Notes upon a case of obsessional neurosis. *SE10*: 155–318, 168.

60 Freud 1909b: 193.

61 Freud 1909b: 205.

62 J. Lear (2005) *Freud*. London: Routledge, p. 35.

63 Freud 1909b: 287, 296, 307.

64 Freud 1909b: 209.

65 Lear 2005: 36.

66 Lear 2005: 52.

67 See e.g. P. Fonagy and A. Bateman (2006) Mechanisms of change in mentalization-based treatment of BPD. *Journal of Clinical Psychology 62*: 411–30.

68 Lear 2005: 35.

69 http: //www.csulb.edu/~csnider/leonardo.st.anne2.jpg

70 'Vultures', as many have observed, is a mis-translation of the Italian word for kites used by Freud in his interpretation of Leonardo's painting.

71 S. Freud (1910d) Leonardo da Vinci and a memory of his childhood. *SE11*: 63–137, 82.

72 Freud 1910d: 116 n. Sigmund Freud, copyrights © The Institute of Psychoanalysis and The Hogarth Press, reprinted by permission of The Random House Group Ltd, and in the United States by permission of W.W. Norton & Company, Inc.
73 Freud 1911a: 224.
74 S. Freud (1913) *Totem and Taboo*. *SE13*: 1–161, 73.
75 S. Freud (1911b) Psycho-analytic notes on an autobiographical account of a case of paranoia. *SE12*: 9–79.
76 S. Freud (1912c) Postscript. *SE* 12: 80–2, 80.
77 S. Freud (1907) Obsessive actions and religious practices. *SE9*: 117–27.
78 Freud 1913: 73.
79 S. Freud (1915) The unconscious. *SE14*: 166–204, 202, 204.
80 Freud 1912b: 112.
81 S. Freud (1923) Psycho-analysis. *SE18*: 235–54, 239.
82 Freud 1901: 685.
83 S. Freud (1915–17) *Introductory Lectures on Psycho-Analysis*. *SE15–16*: 1–463, 150.
84 Freud 1901: 683.
85 Freud 1915–17: 154.
86 Freud 1915–17: 165.
87 Freud 1915–17: 66.
88 Freud 1901: 683–4.
89 Freud 1915–17: 154.
90 Freud 1915–17: 154–5.
91 Freud 1905a: 77.
92 Freud 1905a: 94.
93 Copyright © Gemäldegalerie Alte Meister, Staatliche Kunstsammlungen Dresden.
94 Freud 1905a: 96.
95 Freud 1905a: 104 n. 2.
96 J. Lacan (1954) The fluctuations of the libido. *The Seminar of Jacques Lacan, Book I*. New York: Norton, 1988, p. 184.
97 Lacan 1954: 186
98 S. Freud (1937) Analysis terminable and interminable. *SE23*: 216–53.
99 C. Jung (1961) *Memories, Dreams, Reflections*. London: Fontana, 1993, p. 173.

3 Jung

1 Letter from Freud to Pfister, 9 October 1918. In H. Meng and E.L. Freud (eds) (1963) *Psychoanalysis and Faith*. London: Hogarth Press, p. 63.
2 S. Freud (1939) *Moses and Monotheism*. *SE23*: 7–137, 117–18.
3 C.G. Jung (1905) The psychological diagnosis of evidence. *CW2*: 318–52, 321.
4 C.G. Jung (1906) Association, dream, and hysterical symptom. *CW2*: 353–407, 407.
5 F. Miller (1906) Quelques faits de l'imagination créatrice subconsciente. *Archives de psychologie 5*: 36–51.
6 C.G. Jung (1912) *Symbols of Transformation*. New York: Harper, 1956: 42, 454.
7 A. Samuels, B. Shorter and F. Plaut (1986) *A Critical Dictionary of Jungian Analysis*. London: Routledge, p. 16.
8 C.G. Jung (1913a) Psychoanalysis and neurosis. *CW4*: 243–51, 247, 248.
9 C.G. Jung (1913b) A contribution to the study of psychological types. *CW6*: 499–509, 502.
10 C.G. Jung (1961) *Memories, Dreams, Reflections*. London: Fontana, 1993, pp. 204, 205.

11 Jung 1961: 206, 207.
12 J. Hillman (1975) *Re-Visioning Psychology*. New York: Harper & Row, p. xi.
13 Samuels et al. 1986: 76.
14 C.G. Jung (1916) *Mandala of a Modern Man*. Frontispiece. *The Archetypes and the Collective Unconscious*. *CW9i*. Copyright © 1959 Routledge & Kegan Paul. Reproduced by permission of Taylor & Francis Books UK. Copyright © 1959 Bollingen. Reprinted in the USA by permission of Princeton University Press.
15 Jung 1961: 221.
16 C.G. Jung (1950) Concerning mandala symbolism. *CW9i*: 355–84, 364.
17 Jung 1950: Figure 6. *The Archetypes and the Collective Unconscious*. *CW9i*. Copyright © 1959 Routledge & Kegan Paul. Reproduced by permission of Taylor & Francis Books UK. Copyright © 1959 Bollingen. Reprinted in the USA by permission of Princeton University Press.
18 Jung 1950: 364, 365.
19 Jung 1961: 224.
20 C.G. Jung (1933) A study in the process of individuation. *CW9i*: 290–354, 291–2.
21 These and other images from Miss X's analysis can be found accompanying Jung's above-mentioned 1933 article in *The Archetypes and the Collective Unconscious*. *CW9i*. Copyright © 1959 Routledge & Kegan Paul. Reproduced by permission of Taylor & Francis Books UK.
22 Jung 1933: 292.
23 Jung 1933: 293.
24 Jung 1933: 307.
25 Jung 1933: 316.
26 Jung 1933: 317.
27 Jung 1933: 322.
28 Jung 1933: 346.
29 Jung 1933: 350.
30 Jung 1933: 352.
31 C.G. Jung (1916) The transcendent function. *CW8*: 69–91, 84–5.
32 C.G. Jung (1928) The technique of differentiation between the ego and the figures of the unconscious. *CW7*: 212–26, 213–14.
33 C.G. Jung (1935) The Tavistock Lectures. *CW18*: 170.
34 http://www.tamsquare.net/pictures/L/Isaak-Levitan-The-Quiet-Abode-.jpg
35 A. Chekhov (1895) *Seven Short Novels by Chekhov*. New York: Bantam, 1963, p. 254.
36 Jung 1935: 172.
37 C.G. Jung (1935) The Tavistock Lectures. *The Symbolic Life*. *CW18*: 177, copyright © 1977 Routledge & Kegan Paul. Reproduced by permission of Taylor & Francis Books UK.
38 Jung 1935: 178.
39 C.G. Jung (1935) The Tavistock Lectures. *The Symbolic Life*. *CW18*: 180, copyright © 1977 Routledge & Kegan Paul. Reproduced by permission of Taylor & Francis Books UK.
40 Jung 1935: 179–80.
41 Jung 1935: 181.
42 S. McNiff (1992) *Art as Medicine*. Boston, MA: Shambhala, p. 65.
43 McNiff 1992: 71.
44 McNiff 1992: 109.
45 McNiff 1992: 115.
46 D. Maclagan (2001) *Psychological Aesthetics*. London: Jessica Kingsley, p. 7.
47 Maclagan 2001: 133.

48 http://www.tate.org.uk/collection/T/T00/T00226_8.jpg
49 http://sorrel.humboldt.edu/~rwj1/van/e167.jpg
50 J. Leslie (2006) Exhibition note. *Van Gogh and Britain: Pioneer Collectors*. Compton Verney and National Galleries of Scotland.
51 http://www.ibiblio.org/wm/paint/auth/freud/freud.reflection.jpg
52 R. Hughes (2004) The master at work. *Guardian*, 6 April.
53 J. Elkins (1998) *What Painting Is*. New York: Routledge.
54 See e.g. http://www.ibiblio.org/wm/paint/auth/rembrandt/self/rembrandt.1661.jpg
55 In Jung 1961: 173.
56 D. Maclagan (2005) Re-imagining art therapy. *International Journal of Art Therapy 10*(1): 23–30, 24, 25.
57 McNiff 1992: 35, 48.
58 Jung 1961: 56.
59 D.W. Winnicott (1964) Review of Jung's book, *Memories, Dreams, Reflections. IJPA 45*: 450–5, 453, 454.
60 Winnicott 1964: 454, 455.

4 Spielrein

1 C. Covington and B. Wharton (eds) (2003) *Sabina Spielrein*. London: Routledge, p. 91.
2 Covington and Wharton 2003: 90.
3 C.G. Jung (1906) Letter dated 23 October. In W. McGuire (ed.) (1994) *The Freud/ Jung Letters*. London: Hogarth, p. 17.
4 S. Spielrein (c.1906–7) Unedited extracts from a diary. In Covington and Wharton 2003: 16–31, 23, 27.
5 C.G. Jung (1918) Letter dated 21 January. In Covington and Wharton 2003: 54.
6 S. Spielrein (1912) Destruction as the cause of coming into being. *Journal of Analytical Psychology* 1994, *39*: 155–86, 161–2.
7 Spielrein 1912: 162.
8 Spielrein 1912: 163.
9 Spielrein 1912: 163–4.
10 S. Freud (1915) The unconscious. *SE14*: 166–204, 203.
11 C.G. Jung (1917) Letter dated 13 September. In Covington and Wharton 2003: 50.
12 S. Spielrein (1917) Letter dated 20 December. In A. Carotenuto (ed.) (1984) *A Secret Symmetry: Sabina Spielrein between Jung and Freud*. New York: Pantheon, p. 62.
13 S. Spielrein (1917) Letter dated 21 December. In Carotenuto 1984: 77.
14 S. Spielrein (1918) Letter dated c.27–28 January. In Carotenuto 1984: 84.
15 S. Spielrein (1922) The origin of the child's words Papa and Mama. In Covington and Wharton 2003: 291.
16 Spielrein 1922: 292.
17 S. Freud (1920) Beyond the pleasure principle. *SE18*: 7–64, 55, 56.
18 B. Low (1920) *Psycho-Analysis*. New York: Harcourt, Brace & Howe, p. 75.
19 Freud 1920: 15.
20 Freud 1920: 14–15, 15 n. 1, 16.

5 Klein

1 M. Klein (1921) The development of a child. *LGR*: 1–53, 3.
2 Adapted from Klein 1921: 33–4.
3 Klein 1921: 35. Klein restricted the world 'phantasy' to unconscious fantasy. But

she also used the word 'phantasy' interchangeably with the word 'symbol', as I indicate later in this chapter. And she never clearly distinguished between what is conscious and unconscious. This makes her restriction of the term 'phantasy' to unconscious fantasy problematic. To avoid this I use the now more usual spelling, 'fantasy', in the sense suggested by its Greek origin, 'phantazo' meaning 'make visible', and to signify 'the mental corollary, the psychic representative of instinct'. S. Isaacs (1943) The nature and function of phantasy. In P. King and R. Steiner (eds) (1991) *The Freud-Klein Controversies 1941–45*. London: Routledge, p. 227.

4 Klein 1921: 40.

5 Klein 1921: 41.

6 E. Jones (1916) The theory of symbolism. *Papers on Psycho-Analysis*. Boston, MA: Beacon Press, 1961, pp. 98, 136.

7 Jones 1916: 87–8.

8 E. Gombrich (1953) Psycho-analysis and the history of art. *Meditations on a Hobby Horse*. London: Phaidon, 1963, pp. 30–1.

9 Jones 1916: 97.

10 Jones 1916: 93.

11 Jones 1916: 116.

12 S. Freud (1908) 'Civilized' sexual morality and modern nervous illness. *SE9*: 181–204, 187.

13 M. Klein (1923) Early analysis. *LGR*: 77–105, 87.

14 Klein 1923: 99 n.

15 M. Klein (1925) A contribution to the psychogenesis of tics. *LGR*: 106–127, 119, 120.

16 A. Freud (1926) *Introduction to the Technique of the Analysis of Children*. London: Imago, 1946, p. 29.

17 A. Freud 1926: 29–30.

18 A. Freud 1926: 35.

19 S. Freud (1923) *The Ego and the Id. SE19*: 12–66, 34.

20 A.Freud 1926: 48.

21 A. Freud 1926: 49.

22 M. Klein (1927) Symposium on child-analysis. *LGR*: 139–69.

23 M. Klein (1929) Infantile anxiety situations reflected in a work of art and in the creative impulse. *LGR*: 210–18.

24 O. Andkjæ Olsen (2004) Depression and reparation as themes in Melanie Klein's analysis of the painter Ruth Weber. *Scandinavian Psychoanalytic Review 27*: 34–42.

25 K. Michaëlis (1929) Der leere Fleck. *Berliner Tageblatt*, 24 March.

26 M. Klein (1930) The importance of symbol-formation in the development of the ego. *LGR*: 219–232, 221.

27 S. Freud (1926) *Inhibitions, Symptoms and Anxiety. SE20*: 87–174, 108.

28 Klein 1930: 221.

29 Klein 1930: 225.

30 J. Lacan (1954) Discourse analysis and ego analysis. *The Seminar of Jacques Lacan, Book I*. New York: Norton, 1988, p. 68.

31 J. Kristeva (2000) *Melanie Klein*. NewYork: Columbia University Press, 2001, p. 146.

32 Klein 1930: 225.

33 Klein 1930: 226.

34 Klein 1930: 227.

35 Klein 1930: 227.

36 M. Klein (1928) Early stages of the Oedipus conflict. *LGR*: 186–198, 191, 193.
37 S. Freud (1931) Female sexuality. *SE21*: 225–43, 235, 237.
38 S. Freud (1933) *New Introductory Lectures on Psycho-Analysis. SE22*: 1–182, 73, 80.
39 A. Freud (1936) *The Ego and the Mechanisms of Defence*. London: Hogarth, 1965, p. 120.
40 J. Strachey (1934) The nature of the therapeutic action of psycho-analysis. *IJPA 50*: 275–92.
41 K. Abraham (1924) A short study of the development of the libido. *Selected Papers*. London: Hogarth, 1927, pp. 418–501.
42 M. Klein (1935) A contribution to the psychogenesis of manic-depressive states. *LGR*: 262–89, 271.
43 J. Riviere (1936a) A contribution to the analysis of the negative therapeutic reaction. *IJPA 17*: 304–20, 313.
44 J. Riviere (1936b) On the genesis of psychical conflict in earliest infancy. *IJPA 17*: 395–422, 407.
45 M. Klein and J. Riviere (1937) *Love, Hate and Reparation*. London: Hogarth.
46 See e.g. http://www.eeweems.com/goya/great_deeds_700.jpg
47 Included under the subtitle, '2.7 Francis Picabia, a voyage into the unknown' in 'Art and synesthesia' by Hugo Heyrman, http://www.doctorhugo.org/synaesthesia/art/index.html
48 See e.g. http://www.ibiblio.org/wm/paint/auth/gogh/fields/gogh.cypress-star.jpg
49 W.R.D. Fairbairn (1938) Prolegomena to a psychology of art. *British Journal of Psychology 28*: 288–303, 297.
50 http://www.thefineartcompany.co.uk/abstract/K17.jpg
51 H. Read (1936) *Surrealism*. London: Faber & Faber, copyright © Succession Picasso/DACS, London, 2006.
52 Fairbairn 1938: 298.
53 From notes included in the exhibition, *Undercover Surrealism*, Hayward Gallery, London, 2006.
54 J. Rickman (1940) On the nature of ugliness and the creative impulse. *IJPA 21*: 294–313, 295.
55 Rickman 1940: 308.
56 See especially M. Klein (1945) The Oedipus complex in the light of early anxieties. *LGR*: 370–419.
57 M. Klein (1961) *Narrative of a Child Analysis*. London: Hogarth, 1975, p. 17.
58 Numbers for each drawing correspond to those used by Klein in numbering the plates reproducing Richard's drawings in her book about his analysis (Klein 1961).
59 Klein 1961: 199–200.
60 Klein 1961: 107–8.
61 Klein 1961: 111.
62 Klein 1961: 112.
63 Klein 1961: 316.
64 M. Jacobus (1995) *First Things*. London: Routledge, p. 194.
65 Klein 1961: 452.
66 Klein 1961: 15.
67 Klein 1961: 19.

6 Stokes

1 R. Read (2002) *Art and its Discontents: The Early Life of Adrian Stokes*. Aldershot: Ashgate.
2 M. Klein (1932) *The Psycho-Analysis of Children*. London: Hogarth, 1975, p. 266.

3 Klein 1932: 267.
4 A. Stokes (1947) *Inside Out. CWAS2*: 139–82, 148, 149.
5 Stokes 1947: 157.
6 Klein 1932: 273.
7 Klein 1932: 275.
8 Klein 1932: 276.
9 M. Klein (1935) A contribution to the psychogenesis of manic-depressive states. *LGR*: 262–89, 279.
10 Klein 1935: 280.
11 Klein 1935: 280, 282–3.
12 A. Stokes (1934) *Stones of Rimini. CWAS1*: 181–301, 235.
13 Stokes 1934: 236.
14 Stokes 1934: 235.
15 A. Stokes (1955a) Form in art. In M. Klein, P. Heimann and R.E. Money-Kyrle (eds) (1977) *New Directions in Psycho-Analysis*. London: Karnac, p. 408 n. 1.
16 http://www.thais.it/scultura/image/media/sch00082.jpg
17 See e.g. http://graphics.stanford.edu/projects/mich/poster/slave4.jpg
18 A. Stokes (1932) *The Quattro Cento. CWAS1*: 29–180, 34.
19 Stokes 1932: 40.
20 Stokes 1932: 40, 76.
21 Stokes 1934: 184.
22 Stokes 1934: 252.
23 *CWAS1*, Plate 2.
24 Stokes 1932: 145.
25 A. Stokes (1930a) Pisanello. *CWAS1*: 17–28, 20; for an image of the Tempio Malatestiano, see http://www.rimini-it.it/img/tempio_malatestiano.jpg
26 Stokes 1934: 265.
27 Stokes 1934: 300.
28 Stokes 1934: 299; for an image of this carving see http://www.wga.hu/art/d/duccio/agostino/diana.jpg
29 Stokes 1934: 231.
30 Stokes 1934: 230.
31 Copyright © V&A Images / Victoria and Albert Museum, London.
32 Stokes 1934: 243.
33 Stokes 1934: 248.
34 Stokes 1934: 251.
35 A. Stokes (1937a) *Colour and Form. CWAS2*: 1–83, 33.
36 http://www.usc.edu/dept/architecture/slide/ghirardo/CD1/060-CD1.jpg
37 Stokes 1932: 133–4.
38 Stokes 1932: 134.
39 http://www.artchive.com/artchive/g/giorgione/tempest.jpg
40 A. Stokes (1930b) Painting, Giorgione and Barbaro. *The Criterion 9* (36): 482–500, 482.
41 A. Stokes (1945) *Venice. CWAS2*: 85–138, 130.
42 R. Wollheim (1987) *Painting as an Art*. London: Thames & Hudson, p. 8.
43 http://www.tamsquare.net/pictures/B/Giovanni_Bellini_Drunken_Noah.jpg
44 Wollheim 1987: 336.
45 Copyright © Kunsthistorisches Museum, Wien oder KHM, Vienna.
46 Stokes 1937a: 68.
47 Stokes 1937a: 68–9.
48 Z. V.442 Copyright © Succession Picasso/DACS, London, 2006.
49 Stokes 1937a: 33–4.

50 Copyrights © Tate, London, 2006, © Succession Picasso/DACS, London, 2006.
51 A. Stokes (1967) *Reflections on the Nude*. *CWAS3*: 301–54, 334.
52 A. Stokes (1937b) Mr Ben Nicholson at the Lefèvre gallery. *CWAS1*: 315–16, 316.
53 Copyrights © Tate, London, 2006, © Angela Verren Taunt, 2006. All rights reserved, DACS, London, 2006.
54 Read 2002: 42.
55 Stokes 1937b: 316.
56 Copyrights © Tate, London, 2006, © Estate of the Artist, reproduced by kind permission of Ann Stokes.
57 http://www.terra.es/personal/asg00003/picasso/grguer2.jpg
58 H. Segal (1991) *Dream, Phantasy and Art*. London: Routledge, p. 80.
59 Segal 1991: 91, 92.
60 Segal 1991: 94.
61 A. Stokes (1951) *Smooth and Rough*. *CWAS2*: 211–56, 243.
62 Copyright © The Trustees of the British Museum.
63 Wollheim 1987: 345, 347.
64 Wollheim 1987: 347.
65 A. Stokes (1958) *Greek Culture and the Ego*. *CWAS3*: 77–141, 103.
66 Stokes 1955a: 407.
67 A. Stokes (1955b) *Michelangelo*. *CWAS2*: 1–76, 69.
68 S. Freud (1930) *Civilization and its Discontents*. *SE21*: 64–145, 66, 68.
69 Stokes 1955a: 407.
70 http://www.nationalgallery.org.uk/cgi-bin/WebObjects.exe/CollectionSearch.woa/wa/newQuery?searchTerm=rembrandt
71 Stokes 1955a: 409.
72 Stokes 1955a: 409.
73 A. Stokes (1965) *The Invitation in Art*. *CWAS3*: 261–99, 271, 272.
74 A. Stokes (1963) *Painting and the Inner World*. *CWAS3*: 207–59, 245.
75 http://www.tate.org.uk/collection/N/N00/N00532_8.jpg
76 Stokes 1963: 249.
77 Wollheim 1987: 307.
78 Wollheim 1987: 308.
79 http://www.canadianart.ca/travel/sw_dekooning.jpg
80 http://www.dallasnews.com/sharedcontent/dws/img/12–05/1201glkooning.jpg
81 Wollheim 1987: 348–9.
82 Wollheim 1987: 349.

7 Lacan

1 R. Greenson (1968) Dis-identifying from mother: Its special importance for the boy. *International Journal of Psycho-Analysis 49*: 370–4.
2 N. Chodorow (1978) *The Reproduction of Mothering*. Berkeley, CA: University of California Press.
3 A. Freud (1958) Adolescence. *Psychoanalytic Study of the Child 13*: 255–78.
4 E. Erikson (1950) *Childhood and Society*. New York: Norton. E. Erikson (1968) *Identity: Youth and Crisis*. New York: Norton.
5 P. Blos (1965) The second individuation process of adolescence. *Psychoanalytic Study of the Child 22*: 162–86.
6 See e.g. P. Tyson and R.L. Tyson (1990) *Psychoanalytic Theories of Development*. New Haven, CT: Yale University Press.
7 E. Kris (1952) *Psychoanalytic Explorations in Art*. New York: International Universities Press, pp. 177, 253–4.

8   H. Kohut (1971) *Analysis of the Self*. New York: International Universities Press.
9   M. Klein (1927, 1928) Symposium on child analysis; Early stages of the Oedipus conflict. *LGR*: 139–69, 186–197.
10 C. Lévi-Strauss (1949) *The Elementary Structures of Kinship*. Boston, MA: Beacon Press, 1969.
11 L.R. Lippard (1970) Introduction. *Surrealists on Art*. Englewood Cliffs, NJ: Prentice-Hall, pp. 1–8, 2.
12 A. Breton (1924) *The First Surrealist Manifesto*. In Lippard 1970: 10–21, 20.
13 Breton 1924: 21.
14 S. Dali (1932) The object as revealed in surrealist experiment. In Lippard 1970: 87–97, 87 n. 1.
15 J. Spector (1997) *Surrealist Art and Writing 1919/39*. Cambridge: Cambridge University Press, p. 17.
16 Breton 1924: 17.
17 Breton 1924: 17 n. 4.
18 P. Naville (1925) Beaux-Arts. *La Révolution surréaliste*, no. 3, p. 27. In Spector 1997: 102.
19 In Spector 1997: 105.
20 S. Freud (1901) *On Dreams*. *SE5*: 633–86, 666.
21 S. Dali (1930) The stinking ass. In Lippard 1970: 97–100, 97.
22 Dali 1930: 98.
23 http://www.topofart.com/images/artists/Salvador_Dali/paintings/dali029.jpg
24 Dali 1930: 98.
25 http://www.latifm.com/salvador_dali/small_image/the_stinking_ass.jpg
26 Dali 1930: 99, 100.
27 S. Freud (1922) Some neurotic mechanisms in jealousy, paranoia and homosexuality. *SE18*: 223–32.
28 J. Lacan (1948) Aggressiveness in psychoanalysis. *E*: 82–101, 85.
29 Copyright © Museo Nacional del Prado, Madrid.
30 Lacan 1948: 85–6.
31 Lacan 1948: 86.
32 Lacan 1948: 85.
33 M. Klein (1945) The Oedipus complex in the light of early anxieties. *LGR*: 370–419.
34 Lacan 1948: 93–4.
35 J. Lacan (1953) Some reflections on the ego. *IJPA 34*(1): 11–27, 13.
36 Lacan 1953: 14, 15.
37 Lacan 1948: 92.
38 Lacan 1948: 93.
39 J. Lacan (1949) The mirror stage as formative of the *I* function as revealed in psychoanalytic experience. *E*: 75–81, 76.
40 Lacan 1949: 78.
41 S. Freud (1933) *New Introductory Lectures on Psycho-Analysis*. *SE22*: 1–182, 73.
42 M. Klein (1946) Notes on some schizoid mechanisms. *EG*: 1–24, 14.
43 M. Klein (1935) A contribution to the psychogenesis of manic-depressive states. *LGR*: 262–89, 263.
44 Lacan 1953: 15.
45 Lacan 1953: 15.
46 S. Freud (1923) *The Ego and the Id*. *SE19*: 29.
47 *A Midsummer Night's Dream*, 5.1.14–17. I detail this further in my review of Mary Jacobus's book, *The Poetics of Psychoanalysis*, for the US journal, *Comparative Literature*, Winter 2007, *59*(1), in press.

48 Copyrights © Tate, London, 2006, © Salvador Dali, Gala-Salvador Dali Foundation, DACS, London, 2006.
49 In R. Descharnes (1962) *The World of Salvador Dali*. London: Macmillan, pp. 166, 222.
50 In E. Roudinesco (1993) *Jacques Lacan*. Cambridge: Polity, 1997, p. 34.
51 S. Freud (1914) On narcissism. *SE14*: 73–102: 77, 87.
52 H. Kohut (1968) The psychoanalytic treatment of narcissistic personality disorders. *The Psychoanalytic Study of the Child 23*: 86–113.
53 Lacan 1953: 12.
54 S. Freud (1923) The infantile genital organization. *SE19*: 141–5, 142, 145.
55 S. Freud (1918) From the history of an infantile neurosis. *SE17*: 7–122, 85.
56 In Lacan's system the real, says Sheridan, 'stands for what is neither symbolic nor imaginary'. In J. Lacan (1973) *Four Fundamental Concepts of Psycho-Analysis*. London: Penguin, 1979, p. 280.
57 J. Lacan (1955–6) On a question prior to any possible treatment of psychosis. *E*: 445–88, 462–3.
58 J. Lacan (1958) The signification of the phallus. *E*: 575–84, 582.
59 B. Benvenuto and R. Kennedy (1986) *The Works of Jacques Lacan*. London: Free Association Books, p. 134.
60 Lacan 1955–6: 463.
61 S. Freud (1925) Some psychical consequences of the anatomical distinction between the sexes. *SE19*: 248–58, 252, 257.
62 See e.g. S. Sayers (2003) Creative activity and alienation in Hegel and Marx. *Historical Materialism 11*(1): 107–28.
63 J. Lacan (1954) The object relation and the intersubjective relation. *The Seminar of Jacques Lacan, Book I*. Cambridge: Cambridge University Press, 1988, p. 215.
64 Lacan 1973: 95.
65 Lacan 1973: 96.
66 Photo copyright © The National Gallery, London.
67 http://www.tamsquare.net/thumbnail/H/Hans-Holbein-the-Younger-Portrait-of-Georg-Gisze-of-Danzig.jpg
68 J. Berger (1972) *Ways of Seeing*. Harmondsworth: Penguin, pp. 90, 91.
69 J. Wisdom (1950) The concept of mind. *Other Minds*. Oxford: Blackwell, 1952, p. 240.
70 Lacan 1973: 88.
71 http://www.moma.org/collection/provenance/items/images/301.92.jpg
72 http://www.moma.org/images/collection/FullSizes/00073100.jpg
73 Lacan 1973: 88.
74 Lacan 1973: 88–9.
75 Lacan 1973: 89.
76 Lacan 1973: 92.
77 J. Lacan (1960) Remarks on Daniel Lagache's presentation: 'Psychoanalysis and personality structure'. *E*: 543–74, 565, copyright © 2006, 2002 by W.W. Norton and Company, Inc. Used by permission of W.W. Norton and Company, Inc.
78 Lacan 1948: 87, 89.
79 J. Lacan (1955) *The Seminar of Jacques Lacan, Book II*. Cambridge: Cambridge University Press, 1988, p. 246.
80 G. Bataille (1928) *The Story of the Eye*. Harmondsworth: Penguin, 1982.
81 J. Lacan (1956) Seminar on 'The Purloined Letter'. *E*: 6–48.

8 Milner

1   J. Field (1934) *A Life of One's Own*. London: Virago, 1986, pp. 48, 49.
2   Field 1934: 70.
3   Field 1934: 76.
4   Field 1934: 108.
5   Field 1934: 70.
6   Field 1934: 175.
7   Field 1934: 119.
8   S. Freud (1900) *The Interpretation of Dreams. SE4–5*: 1–621, 566.
9   Field 1934: 61, 62.
10 J. Field (1937) *An Experiment in Leisure*. London: Virago, 1986, p. 171.
11 Reproduced from the first edition of *A Life of One's Own*, London: Chatto & Windus, p. 155; all other references to this book are to the 1986 Virago edition.
12 Field 1934: 147–8.
13 Field 1934: 150.
14 http://www.users.muohio.edu/mandellc/eng339/ancient%20of%20days%20big.jpg
15 Field 1934: 152, 153.
16 E.M. Forster (1927) *Aspects of the Novel*. San Diego, CA: Harcourt Brace Jovanovich, 1955, p. 101, in Field 1934: 151.
17 Field 1934: 159, 161.
18 Field 1937: 58.
19 Field 1937: 185.
20 Field 1934: 21.
21 Field 1934: 163.
22 Field 1934: 163–4.
23 Field 1934: 165.
24 Field 1934: 165.
25 Field 1934: 106.
26 Field 1934: 89.
27 Field 1937: 210, 212.
28 S. Spielrein (1912) Destruction as the cause of coming into being. *Journal of Analytical Psychology* 1994, *39*: 155–86.
29 Field 1937: 40.
30 W. James (1902) *The Varieties of Religious Experience*. London: Fontana, 1960, p. 403.
31 See e.g. S. Freud (1924) The economic problem of masochism. *SE19*: 159–70.
32 I discuss this further in J. Sayers (1991) *Mothering Psychoanalysis*. London: Hamish Hamilton.
33 Field 1937: 31, 32.
34 Field 1937: 197–8.
35 Field 1937: 180.
36 Field 1937: 180–1.
37 M. Milner (1950) *On Not Being Able to Paint*. London: Heinemann, 1957, p. 6.
38 Milner 1950: 6–7.
39 Reproduced from the front cover of the 1971, Oxford: Heinemann Educational edition of *On Not Being Able to Paint*.
40 Milner 1950: 48.
41 M. Podro (1990) The landscape thinks itself in me. *International Review of Psycho-Analysis 17*: 401–12, Figure 2.
42 Milner 1950: 50.
43 Milner 1950: 62.
44 S. Freud (1933) *New Introductory Lectures on Psycho-Analysis. SE22*: 1–182, 73.

45 Milner 1950: 74.
46 Milner 1950: 75.
47 Milner 1950: 75.
48 M. Klein (1946) Notes on some schizoid mechanisms. *EG*: 1–24, 22, 23.
49 Milner 1950: 75.
50 Milner 1950: 25.
51 Milner 1950: 25.
52 Milner 1950: 131.
53 W. James (1902) *The Varieties of Religious Experience*. London: Collins, 1960, p. 404. I discuss this further in J. Sayers (2003) *Divine Therapy*. Oxford: Oxford University Press.
54 R. Rolland (1927) Letter to Freud, dated 5 December. In W.B. Parsons (1999) *The Enigma of the Oceanic Feeling*. Oxford: Oxford University Press, p. 36.
55 M. Milner (1952) The role of illusion in symbol formation. *SM*: 83–113, 97.
56 Milner 1950: 117.
57 Milner 1950: 118.
58 Milner 1950: 119.
59 Milner 1950: 71–2.
60 Milner 1950: 115–16.
61 My thanks to the late Paul Roazen for drawing my attention to the following very helpful article on this point by J. Turner (2002) A brief history of illusion: Milner, Winnicott and Rycroft. *IJPA 83*: 1063–82.
62 D. Winnicott (1971) *Playing and Reality*. Harmondsworth: Penguin, 1974, p. 115.
63 Milner 1950: 16.
64 S. Freud (1930) *Civilization and its Discontents*. *SE21*: 64–145, 68.
65 E. Jones (1916) The theory of symbolism. *Papers on Psycho-Analysis*. Boston, MA: Beacon Press, 1961.
66 Milner 1952: 86.
67 R. Wollheim (1987) *Painting as an Art*. London: Thames & Hudson, p. 305.
68 Field 1934: 119.
69 M. Milner (1956) Psychoanalysis and art. *SM*: 192–215, 211.
70 Milner 1952: 93.
71 Milner 1952: 95.
72 Milner 1952: 97, 100.
73 M. Milner (1969) *The Hands of the Living God*. London: Virago, 1988, p. 14.
74 Milner 1969: 40.
75 Milner 1969: 154.
76 Milner 1969: 155.
77 Milner 1969: 164.
78 Milner 1969: 163–4.
79 D.W. Winnicott (1954) Metapsychological and clinical aspects of regression within the psycho-analytical set-up. *Collected Papers*. London: Tavistock, 1958, p. 280.
80 M. Milner (1977) Winnicott and overlapping circles. *SM*: 279–86, 280.
81 N. Coltart (1985) Freud and Buddhism. *Slouching Toward Bethlehem*. London: Free Association Books, 1992, p. 174.
82 J. Sandler (1993) On communication from patient to analyst. *IJPA 74*: 1097–107, 1101.
83 Sandler 1993: 1101.
84 S. Freud (1923) *The Ego and the Id. SE19*: 12–66, 31.
85 Sandler 1993: 1101.
86 Sandler 1993: 1103 – italics in original.

9 Ehrenzweig

1 M. Klein (1935) A contribution to the psychogenesis of manic-depressive states. *LGR*: 262–89, 271.
2 M. Klein (1946) Notes on some schizoid mechanisms. *EG*: 1–24, 14.
3 A.J. Miller (2001) *Space, Time, and the Beauty that Causes Havoc*. New York: Basic Books, p. 105.
4 A. Ehrenzweig (1953) *The Psycho-Analysis of Artistic Vision and Hearing*. London: Routledge, p. 24.
5 A. Ehrenzweig (1948) Unconscious form-creation in art: Parts I and II. *British Journal of Medical Psychology 21*: 185–214, 186.
6 Ehrenzweig 1953: 188.
7 H. Read (1934) *Art and Industry*. London: Faber & Faber, p. 113.
8 A. Ehrenzweig (1949) Unconscious form-creation in art: Part III. *British Journal of Medical Psychology 22*: 88–109, 103.
9 E. Gombrich (1972) *The Story of Art*. London: Phaidon, p. 35.
10 Copyright © Soprintendenza per il Patrimonio Storico Artistico di Milano.
11 Ehrenzweig 1953: 181.
12 Ehrenzweig 1953: 181.
13 Ehrenzweig 1953: 201.
14 Ehrenzweig 1953: 194.
15 Ehrenzweig 1953: 199.
16 Ehrenzweig 1953: 199.
17 http://www.spiritsite.com/gallery/art/medmar/LaTourTheNativity.jpg
18 W. James (1892) *Psychology*. New York: Fawcett, 1963, pp. 156, 157.
19 See, in particular, W. James (1902) *The Varieties of Religious Experience*. London: Fontana, 1960.
20 S. Freud (1900) *The Interpretation of Dreams*. *SE4–5*: 1–621, 103.
21 Ehrenzweig 1948: 191.
22 A. Ehrenzweig (1956) The modern artist and the creative accident. *The Listener*, 12 January, pp. 53.4, 54.
23 http://www.museupicasso.bcn.es/guerraipau/imatges/a3.jpg
24 A. Ehrenzweig (1967) *The Hidden Order of Art*. St Albans: Paladin, 1970, pp. 117, 118.
25 http://www.moma.org/visit_moma/images/audioThumbnails/pollock.jpg
26 Ehrenzweig 1967: 82.
27 Ehrenzweig 1967, Plate 19, copyright © ADAGP, Paris and DACS, London, 2006.
28 Ehrenzweig 1967: 37.
29 Ehrenzweig 1967: 288.
30 Ehrenzweig 1967: 289.
31 Ehrenzweig 1967: 304–5.
32 Klein 1946: 8.

10 Winnicott

1 D.W. Winnicott (1945) Primitive emotional development. *CP*: 145–56, 150.
2 M. Klein (1946) Notes on some schizoid mechanisms. *EG*: 1–24, 4.
3 Winnicott 1945: 152.
4 Winnicott 1945: 152–3.
5 L. Tolstoy (1898) *What is Art?* London: Oxford University Press, 1930, pp. 121, 122.
6 D.W. Winnicott (1967) Mirror-role of mother and family in child development. In D.W. Winnicott (1971) *Playing and Reality*. London: Penguin, 1974, p. 131.

7 See e.g. A.N. Meltzoff (2005) Imitation and other minds. In S. Hurley and N. Chater (eds) *Perspectives on Imitation*. Cambridge, MA: MIT Press.

8 See e.g. V. Gallese (2006) Mirror neurons and intentional attunement. *Journal of the American Psychoanalytic Association 54*: 46–57.

9 E. Stein (1917) *On the Problem of Empathy*. The Hague: Nijhoff, 1964, p. 17.

10 Winnicott 1945: 146–7.

11 D.W. Winnicott (1947) Hate in the countertransference. *CP*: 194–203.

12 Winnicott 1945: 151.

13 D.W. Winnicott (1953a) Transitional objects and transitional phenomena. *CP*: 229–42, 231.

14 Winnicott 1953a: 232.

15 Winnicott 1953a: 232.

16 Winnicott 1953a: 233.

17 D.W. Winnicott (1941) The observation of infants in a set situation. *CP*: 52–69, 53, 54.

18 D.W. Winnicott (1962a) Providing for the child in health and in crisis. In D.W. Winnicott, *The Maturational Processes and the Facilitating Environment*. London: Hogarth, 1965, p. 70.

19 D.W. Winnicott (1969) The use of an object and relating through identifications. In Winnicott 1971: 101–111, 103.

20 D.W. Winnicott (1971) Playing: A theoretical statement. In Winnicott 1971: 44–61, 44.

21 D.W. Winnicott (1968) The squiggle game. *Psycho-Analytic Explorations*. Cambridge, MA: Harvard University Press, 1989, pp. 301–2.

22 D.W. Winnicott (1953b) Symptom tolerance in paediatrics. *CP*: 101–17, 108.

23 C. Winnicott (1964) Communicating with children. *Face to Face with Children*. London: Karnac, 2004, p. 189.

24 Winnicott 1953b: 108.

25 Winnicott 1953b: 113.

26 Winnicott 1953b: 114–15.

27 Winnicott 1969: 102.

28 See e.g. D.W. Winnicott (1962b) Ego integration in child development. In Winnicott 1965: 57.

29 A. Balint (1939) Love for the mother and mother-love. *IJPA* 1949, *30*: 251–9, quoted by N. Chodorow (1978) *The Reproduction of Mothering*. Berkeley, CA: University of California Press, p. 77.

11 Bion

1 This is referred to obliquely in W.R. Bion (1940) The war of nerves. In E. Miller and H. Crichton-Miller (eds) *The Neuroses of War*. London: Macmillan, pp. 180–200.

2 W.R. Bion (1946) The leaderless group project. *Bulletin of the Menninger Clinic 10* (3 May): 77–81.

3 W.R. Bion and J. Rickman (1943) Intra-group tensions in therapy. *Lancet 2*: 218–21. In W.R. Bion (1961) *Experiences in Groups*. London: Tavistock, pp. 11–26.

4 W.R. Bion (1952) Group dynamics: A review. In Bion 1961: 139–91, 149.

5 W.R. Bion (1949) Experiences in groups IV. In Bion 1961: 77–91, 86.

6 W.R. Bion (1963) *Elements of Psycho-Analysis*. London: Heinemann, p. 50.

7 Bion 1963: 60.

8 W.R. Bion (1991) *A Memoir of the Future*. London: Karnac, p. 465.

9   Bion 1952: 149.
10 W.R. Bion (1954) Notes on the theory of schizophrenia. *ST*: 23–35, 25.
11 W.R. Bion (1957) Differentiation of the psychotic from the non-psychotic person-
    alities. *ST*: 43–64.
12 W.R. Bion (1958a) On hallucination. *ST*: 65–85, 65, 66.
13 Bion 1958a: 84.
14 Bion 1958a: 71.
15 Bion 1958a: 72.
16 W.R. Bion (1959a) Various forms of dream manifestation. 16 October. *C*: 93–4, 94.
17 W.R. Bion (1959b) X. 30 October. *C*: 102.
18 W.R. Bion (1970) *Attention and Interpretation*. London: Heinemann, p. 37.
19 W.R. Bion (1958b) On arrogance. *ST*: 86–92, 90, 92.
20 W.R. Bion (1962a) *Learning from Experience*. London: Heinemann, p. 91.
21 S. Freud (1911) Formulations on the two principles of mental functioning. *SE12*:
    218–26, 220.
22 W.R. Bion (1959c) α. 5 August. *C*: 53.
23 W.R. Bion (1965) *Transformations*. London: Heinemann, p. 115.
24 http://www.ibiblio.org/wm/paint/auth/vermeer/little-street/little-street.jpg
25 W.R. Bion (1960) α. 24 February. *C*: 141–4, 143–4.
26 M. Heidegger (1934–5) The origin of the work of art. *Basic Writings*. London:
    Routledge, 1978, p. 162.
27 http://homepage.newschool.edu/~quigleyt/vcs/jameson/vangogh_shoes.jpg
28 Heidegger 1934–5: 159.
29 J. Derrida (1978) *The Truth in Painting*. Chicago, IL: University of Chicago Press,
    1987.
30 H. Arendt (1971) *The Life of the Mind. I. Thinking*. London: Secker & Warburg,
    1978, pp. 184–5.
31 In R. Kendall (ed.) (2004) *Cézanne by Himself*. London: Time Warner, p. 193.
32 http://cgfa.sunsite.dk/picasso/picasso2.jpg
33 W.R. Bion (1959d) Scientific method. 10 January. *C*: 2–22, 2.
34 S. Freud (1893) Charcot. *SE3*: 11–23, 12.
35 W.R. Bion (1985) *All my Sins Remembered and The Other Side of Genius*.
    Abingdon: Fleetwood Press, p. 169.
36 Bion 1985: 188 – underlined capital letters in original.
37 Bion 1985: 189.
38 W.R. Bion (n.d.) Communication. *C*: 172–83, 180.
39 S. Freud (1915) The unconscious. *SE14*: 166–204, 202.
40 W.R. Bion (1962b) A theory of thinking. *ST*: 110–19, 116.
41 W.R. Bion (1973) São Paulo. *Brazilian Lectures*. London: Karnac, 1990, p. 17.
42 Bion 1965: 1.
43 http://claude-monet.org/artbase/Monet/1873-1873/w0274/apc.jpg
44 http://www.ibiblio.org/wm/paint/auth/monet/haystacks/
45 http://www.ibiblio.org/wm/paint/auth/monet/rouen/
46 M. Proust (1927) *Remembrance of Things Past: 3*. London: Penguin, 1983, p. 1102.
    See also M. Podro (1998) *Depiction*. New Haven, CT: Yale University Press.
47 http://www.ibiblio.org/wm/paint/auth/cezanne/st-victoire/1885/cezanne.st-
    victoire-1885.jpg
48 http://www.tate.org.uk/collection/N/N05/N05303_9.jpg
49 M. Podro (1990) 'The landscape thinks itself in me.' The comments and procedures
    of Cézanne. *International Review of Psycho-Analysis 17*: 401–8.
50 M. Merleau-Ponty (1945) Cézanne's doubt. In H.L. Dreyfus and P.A. Dreyfus (eds)
    (1964) *Sense and Non-Sense*. Chicago, IL: Northwestern University Press, p. 17.

51 Merleau-Ponty 1945: 17–18.
52 R. Wollheim (1987) *Painting as an Art*. London: Thames & Hudson, p. 305.
53 S. Freud (1923) *The Ego and the Id. SE19*: 12–66, 30.
54 See e.g. http://www.royalcollection.org.uk/egallery/images/collection_small/ 912494.jpg; http://artscience.org/ni/nita/form/images/leonardo.jpeg
55 Bion 1991: 156.
56 Bion 1965: 171.
57 Bion 1970: 125.
58 W.R. Bion (1967) Notes on memory and desire. In E. Bott Spillius (ed.) (1988) *Melanie Klein Today, Vol. 2*. London: Routledge, p. 19.
59 W.R. Bion (1971) The Grid. *Two Papers*. London: Karnac, 1989, p. 11.
60 Bion 1991: 156.
61 Bion 1991: 430, 472.
62 W.R. Bion (1959e) Attacks on linking. *ST*: 93–109, 95.
63 Merleau-Ponty 1945: 19, 20, 25.
64 A. Stokes (1955) Form in art. In M. Klein, P. Heimann and R.E. Money-Kyrle (eds) (1977) *New Directions in Psycho-Analysis*. London: Karnac, p. 407.
65 M. Jacobus (2005) *The Poetics of Psychoanalysis*. Oxford: Oxford University Press, p. 251.
66 Bion 1965: 164.
67 Bion 1965: 96.
68 J. Laplanche and J.-B. Pontalis (1968) Fantasy and the origins of sexuality. *IJPA* *49*(1): 1–18, 1.

12 Laplanche

1 J. Lacan (1958) The direction of the treatment and the principles of its power. *E*: 489–542, 496.
2 J. Lacan (1955) Introduction of the big Other. *The Seminar of Jacques Lacan, Book II*. Cambridge: Cambridge University Press, 1988, p. 236 – italics in original.
3 J. Laplanche and J.-B. Pontalis (1967) *The Language of Psycho-Analysis*. London: Hogarth, 1980, p. 112.
4 S. Freud (1909) Analysis of a phobia in a five-year-old boy. *SE10*: 5–147, 8.
5 S. Freud (1918) From the history of an infantile neurosis. *SE17*: 17–122, 24.
6 Freud 1918: 25.
7 Freud 1918: 25.
8 Freud 1918: 42.
9 Freud 1918: 20.
10 J. Laplanche and J.-B. Pontalis (1968) Fantasy and the origins of sexuality. *IJPA* *49*: 1–18, 11.
11 Laplanche and Pontalis 1968: 16–17.
12 J. Laplanche (1984) The drive and its source-object: Its fate in the transference. In J. Laplanche (1999) *Essays on Otherness*. London: Routledge, p. 127.
13 S. Freud (1919) 'A child is being beaten': A contribution to the study of the origin of sexual perversions. *SE17*: 179–204.
14 J. Laplanche (1992a) Masochism and the general theory of seduction. In Laplanche 1999: 197–213, 212.
15 L. Bersani and U. Dutoit (1998) *Caravaggio's Secrets*. Cambridge, MA: MIT Press, p. 82.
16 S. Freud (1912) Recommendations to physicians practising psycho-analysis. *SE12*: 11–120, 115.

17 J. Laplanche (1992b) Transference: Its provocation by the analyst. In Laplanche 1999: 214–33, 226.
18 J. Fletcher (ed.) *Essays on Otherness*. London: Routledge, 1999, p. 226 n. 16.
19 Laplanche 1992b: 227.
20 Laplanche 1992b: 227, 228.
21 Laplanche 1992b: 229.
22 J. Lacan (1954) *The Seminar of Jacques Lacan, Book I*. Cambridge: Cambridge University Press, 1988, p. 278.
23 Lacan 1955: 246.
24 J. Lacan (1964) *The Four Fundamental Concepts of Psycho-Analysis*. London: Penguin, 1979, p. 251.

13 Kristeva

 1 S. Freud (1905) Fragment of an analysis of a case of hysteria. *SE7*: 7–122, 78.
 2 S. Freud (1909a) Analysis of a phobia in a five-year-old boy. *SE10*: 5–147, 34, 41.
 3 S. Freud (1909b) Notes upon a case of obsessional neurosis. *SE10*: 155–318, 166.
 4 Freud 1909b: 166–7.
 5 M. Merleau-Ponty (1961) Eye and mind. *The Primacy of Perception*. Chicago, IL: Northwestern University Press, p. 162.
 6 W.R. Bion (1967) *Second Thoughts*. London: Karnac, 1984, p. 124.
 7 Bion 1967: 3–4.
 8 Bion 1967: 121.
 9 J. Kristeva (1987) *Black Sun*. New York: Columbia University Press, 1989, p. 264 n. 24 – italics in original.
10 J. Kristeva (1972) Giotto's joy. In L.S. Roudiez (ed.) (1980) *Desire in Language*. New York: Columbia University Press, p. 221.
11 Kristeva 1972: 221.
12 http://www.wga.hu/art/g/giotto/padova/4lastjud/01_lastj.jpg
13 Kristeva 1972: 213.
14 http://keptar.demasz.hu/arthp/html/g/giotto/padova/1joachim/joachi3.htm
15 Kristeva 1972: 229, 230.
16 http://www.wga.hu/art/g/giotto/assisi/lower/ceiling/05christ.jpg
17 Copyright © Rijksmuseum Amsterdam.
18 Copyright © Accademia Carrara, Bergamo, Dip. no. 958.
19 J. Kristeva (1975) Motherhood according to Bellini. In Roudiez 1980: 237–70.
20 http://www.abcgallery.com/P/piero/francesca11.jpg
21 J. Kristeva (1976) Stabat mater. *Tales of Love*. New York: Columbia University Press, 1987, p. 244.
22 http://keptar.demasz.hu/arthp/art/p/piero/francesc/nativity.jpg
23 Kristeva 1976: 246.
24 F. Dostoevsky (1866) *Crime and Punishment*. London: Penguin, 1951, pp. 424, 435.
25 Kristeva 1987: 204.
26 Kristeva 1987: 204–5.
27 M. Jacobus (2005) *The Politics of Psychoanalysis*. Oxford: Oxford University Press, p. 64.
28 S. Freud (1917) Mourning and melancholia. *SE14*: 243–58.
29 Kristeva 1987: 12.
30 http://i2.photobucket.com/albums/y26/siddhartha04/durer23.jpg
31 Kristeva 1987: 13.
32 Freud 1917: 245.

33 H. Segal (1952) A psychoanalytic approach to aesthetics. *The Work of Hanna Segal*. New York: Jason Aronson, 1981.
34 Copyright © photo: Martin Bühler, Kunstmuseum, Basel.
35 F. Dostoevsky (1868–9) *The Idiot*. Hardmondsworth: Penguin, 1955, p. 446.
36 Kristeva 1987: 113, 114.
37 J. Kristeva (1998) *Visions capitales*. Paris: Editions de la Réunion des musées nationaux, p. 137 – my translation of this and other subsequent quotations from *Visions capitales*.
38 Kristeva 1987: 56.
39 Adapted and translated from J. Kristeva (1996) Le pardon peut-il guérir? *La Révolte intime*. Paris: Fayard, 1997, p. 39.
40 J. Kristeva (1980) *Powers of Horror*. New York: University of Columbia Press, 1982, p. 1.
41 Kristeva 1980: 2–3.
42 S. Freud (1925) Negation. *SE19*: 235–9, 237.
43 S. Freud (1923) The infantile genital organization. *SE19*: 141–5, 144.
44 Kristeva 1998: 37.
45 Kristeva 1998: 41.
46 http://www.mcah.columbia.edu/dbcourses/freedberg/thumb/poussin_drwg_ab1958_f114.jpg
47 Kristeva 1998: 40.
48 G. O'Keeffe (c.1923) in S. Greenough (ed.) (1987) *Georgia O'Keeffe: Life and Letters*. New York: Little, Brown, p. 174.
49 O'Keeffe (1924) in Greenough 1987: 176.
50 http://dali.urvas.lt/forviewing/pic24.jpg
51 http://www.mystudios.com/women/klmno/okeeffe-small-purple-hills.jpg
52 J. Kristeva (1989) Georgia O'Keeffe: la forme inévitable. In S. Greenough (ed.) (1989) *Georgia O'Keeffe*. Paris: Adam Biro, p. 12 – my translation.
53 The Metropolitan Museum of Art, New York, copyright © ARS, NY and DACS, London, 2006.
54 Kristeva 1989: 13 – my translation.
55 Freud 1909a: 10, 29.
56 Freud 1909b: 168.
57 Kristeva 1980: 50.
58 J. Kristeva (1982) Psychoanalysis and the polis. In T. Moi (ed.) (1986) *The Kristeva Reader*. Oxford: Blackwell, p. 309.
59 S. Freud (1912) Recommendations to physicians practising psycho-analysis. *SE12*: 109–20, 115.
60 Kristeva 1982: 319.
61 D.W. Winnicott (1971) *Playing and Reality*. London: Penguin, 1974, p. 63.
62 Kristeva 2000: 148.
63 J. Kristeva (1997b) in C. Clément and J. Kristeva (2001) *The Feminine and the Sacred*. New York: Columbia University Press, p. 115.
64 Kristeva 1997b: 116, 140.
65 J. Kristeva (1993) *New Maladies of the Soul*. New York: Columbia University Press, 1995, p. 15.
66 Kristeva 1993: 18, 19.
67 J. Sutherland (2006) The ideas interview: Julia Kristeva. *Guardian*, 14 March.
68 Kristeva 1993: 25.
69 Venice Biennale, 1993, copyright © DACS, London, 2006.
70 Kristeva 1996: 10, 11.

14 Conclusion

1 http://www.stpauls.it/letture00/0008let/images/0008le21.jpg
2 http://image.guardian.co.uk/sys-images/Guardian/Pix/gallery/2005/10/10/smith_IDoIUndoIRedo3.jpg
3 S. Freud (1920) *Beyond the Pleasure Principle. SE18*: 7–64, 29–30.
4 R. Barthes (1961) The photographic message. *Barthes: Selected Writings*. London: Fontana, 1983, p. 209.
5 J. Kristeva (1996) *The Sense and Non-Sense of Revolt*. New York: Columbia University Press, 2000, p. 48.
6 http://www.littlesongbox.co.uk/Files/Diary/sublimation.jpg
7 http://www.artnet.com/Magazine/reviews/laplaca/Images/laplaca3-30-8.jpg
8 http://www.arttra.co.uk/reviews/Louise_bourgeois/sublimination1.png
9 S. Freud (1908) The sexual theories of children. *SE9*: 209–26, 220, 221–2.
10 M. Merleau-Ponty (1961) Eye and mind. *The Primacy of Perception*. Chicago, IL: Northwestern University Press, p. 166.
11 M. Jacobus (2005) *The Poetics of Psychoanalysis*. Oxford: Oxford University Press, p. 215.
12 R. Wollheim (1987) *Painting as an Art*. London: Thames & Hudson, p. 305.
13 Merleau-Ponty 1961: 190 – italics in original.

Index